Telemental Health Care for Children and Families

Larissa N. Niec • Ciera E. Schoonover
Editors

Telemental Health Care for Children and Families

Springer

Editors
Larissa N. Niec
Central Michigan University
Mount Pleasant, MI, USA

Ciera E. Schoonover
Middle Tennessee State University
Murfreesboro, TN, USA

ISBN 978-3-031-69263-5 ISBN 978-3-031-69264-2 (eBook)
https://doi.org/10.1007/978-3-031-69264-2

This Springer imprint is published by the registered company Springer Nature Switzerland AG
The registered company address is: Gewerbestrasse 11, 6330 Cham, Switzerland

To the visionaries who imagined a way for mental health care to reach the children so often left out;
To Todd for having the answers to all the worst technology questions;
And to Mom and Dad for instilling in me the desire to make a difference.
—Larissa N. Niec, PhD
To my family, who gave up time with me so I could write. And to the children still waiting for mental health care. Let this book move us toward making evidence-based interventions accessible to all.
—Ciera E. Schoonover, PhD MSW

Contents

Part I Introduction

1 **Telemental Health Care for Children and Adolescents: Fulfilling a Promise** 3
Larissa N. Niec and Ciera E. Schoonover

Part II Assessment

2 **Remote Assessment of Child Cognitive Functioning: Virtually Standard?** 19
Shalena Heard, Rebecca Warwick, and Alison Pritchard

Part III Child-Focused Interventions

3 **Guidance for the Telehealth Delivery of Cognitive-Behavioral Therapy for Anxiety Disorders in Youth** 51
Ovsanna Leyfer, Alyssa M. Farley, Rachel A. Merson, and Donna B. Pincus

4 **Telehealth Delivery of Trauma-Focused Cognitive-Behavioral Therapy** 69
Regan Stewart, Rosaura Orengo-Aguayo, and Caroline Shanholtz

5 **Telemental Health Delivery of ABA Services** 91
Matthew J. O'Brien

Part IV Parenting Interventions

6 **Telemental Health Parent Training and Support for Children with Autism Spectrum Disorder: COMPASS for Hope (C-HOPE)** 113
Robert J. Reese, Lisa A. Ruble, and Alyssa L. Clements-Hickman

7 **Mom Power via Telemental Health** ... 135
Diana Morelen, Sarah Gray, Jamie Lawler, Kelly Daniel, Hilary Skov, Sanshawanna Jones, Renee Lamoreau, Sarah Freeman, and Katherine Rosenblum

8 **Byte-Sized Bonding: The Tech-Savvy Route to Internet-Based Parent-Child Interaction Therapy** ... 159
Abigail Peskin and Jason F. Jent

Part V Telehealth Through An Equity Lens

9 **Affirmative Telemental Healthcare with LGBTQ+ Youth** ... 179
Melissa A. Cyperski

Part VI Future Directions

10 **Future Directions in Telemental Health Care: Science Fiction or Grand Solution?** ... 201
Larissa N. Niec

Index ... 205

Part I
Introduction

Chapter 1
Telemental Health Care for Children and Adolescents: Fulfilling a Promise

Larissa N. Niec and Ciera E. Schoonover

Telemental Health Care for Children and Adolescents: Fulfilling a Promise

The capacity to communicate healthcare information to others remotely is nearly 120 years old. As early as 1906, Dutch scientist Willem Einthoven transmitted electrocardiogram data over telephone lines to reach a distance approximately 1 mile away (Einthoven 1906/1957). Einthoven suggested that ultimately such technology might be used in areas with health provider shortages to address unmet health needs (Bashshur & Bashshur, 2023). By the 1920s, Norway had developed the ability to transmit health data from ship to shore in order to provide medical consultation to sailors; other countries soon followed with similar facilities (Bashshur & Shannon, 2010). Around the same time, the idea that patients and healthcare providers could communicate remotely through both audio and visual means arose, well before the technology that allowed it. In 1924, the cover of the magazine *Radio News* portrayed a patient interacting with a doctor through a monitor and speakers (IOM [US] Committee on Evaluating Clinical Applications of Telemedicine & Field, 1996). It was envisioned that the so-called radio doctor would be able to provide care to patients from great distances.

Thus, for more than a century, technology for distance communication has been imagined as a means to reduce barriers to accessing healthcare services, particularly for families in geographically isolated communities. The idea that mental health

L. N. Niec (✉)
Center for Children, Families, and Communities, Central Michigan University, Mount Pleasant, MI, USA
e-mail: niec1l@cmich.edu

C. E. Schoonover
Middle Tennessee State University, Murfreesboro, TN, USA
e-mail: ciera.schoonover@mtsu.edu

L. N. Niec, C. E. Schoonover (eds.), *Telemental Health Care for Children and Families*,
https://doi.org/10.1007/978-3-031-69264-2_1

services could also be provided via distance technology—telemental health care—arose nearly simultaneously, and in fact, the first telemedicine program of any kind to be published was a psychiatric program developed at the University of Nebraska in 1959 (Baer et al., 1997a).

Despite the early enthusiasm for telemedicine, interest in developing the concept has waxed and waned through the decades, influenced by changes in the technology as well as the attitudes of providers and the public toward those changes. During the twentieth century, programs came and went, and telehealth did not fulfill its promise to conquer the barriers that limit access to care for underserved communities. In fact, only very recently has telemental health begun to show a glimmer of a possibility that it might meet, on a grander scale, mental health needs that have not been met by in-person services.

In this chapter we briefly review the history of telemental health care, discuss initial research findings, and consider the early hopes for and challenges of providing telehealth services. We then consider recent changes in the utilization of telemental health and discuss ethical issues particular to providing psychological services at a distance, setting the stage for the following chapters, which review child and family interventions that have been successfully implemented through remote technological means.

History of Telemental Health Care

Before we continue the discussion, it is important to define the terms "telemedicine," "telehealth," and "telemental health" as used throughout this book. "Tele" comes from the Greek "telē" meaning "distance" or "far off" (*Oxford English dictionary (OED),* 1989). One of the earliest known uses of the term "telemedicine" occurred in 1968 in a news article on an early program operated through Massachusetts General Hospital (MGH, McLaughlin, 1968). Broadly defined, telemedicine is the remote provision of health care through the use of communication technology. Telemedicine thus encompasses services such as the delivery of test results to a patient via telephone, the use of online assessment tools to screen for health conditions, the provision of asynchronous healthcare education materials, and the delivery of healthcare appointments using audio and visual communication devices. The goal of this book is to discuss the state of the science in remote mental health interventions for children and families, with an emphasis on interventions that can be delivered fully remotely. We use the terms "telehealth" and "telemedicine" interchangeably to refer to any type of health care delivered through remote technology but reserve the term "telemental health" to refer to psychological and psychiatric interventions.

Calls for the use of telemedicine to reduce barriers to psychiatric care were a key motivation that led to the creation of early demonstration projects, such as the pioneering work at the Nebraska Psychiatric Institute in 1959 (Baer et al., 1997a, b). From the University of Nebraska, physicians used interactive television (IATV) to provide consultation services to medical students and later clinical services such as group therapy to patients at the Norfolk State Hospital more than 100 miles away (IOM [US] Committee on Evaluating Clinical Applications of Telemedicine & Field, 1996). Like the Nebraska program, the telemental health program at Massachusetts General Hospital in Boston also linked psychiatrists to staff at a remote location, a medical station at Logan Airport (Dwyer, 1973). Although the distance between the two Boston sites was less than 3 miles, traffic congestion could make the travel time significant, and the Logan location was easier to access for patients living outside of the city. Patients who came to the medical station were escorted to the room with the interactive television and introduced to the psychiatrist at MGH. The services provided included diagnostic interviews, medication monitoring, brief or extended individual psychotherapy, and group therapy. Success with the program led to its expansion to additional locations. It became possible to provide psychiatric consultations within schools, court systems, and detention centers.

The initial research on telemental health programs such as those in Nebraska and Massachusetts was descriptive, with a focus on the feasibility and acceptability of conducting mental health services remotely. An observation study of the MGH program found it to be not only feasible, but as having the potential to provide prevention and early treatment services in a cost-effective manner (Dwyer, 1973). Nearly another decade passed, however, before the research moved from uncontrolled descriptive studies to some more rigorous designs. One of the first controlled designs of telemental health care was a clever analogue study conducted in Canada (Dongier et al., 1986). The study site was a small, rural psychiatric hospital that had no full-time psychiatrist. To simulate a telemental health program, visiting psychiatrists used closed circuit television (CCTV) and provided services to patients on a different floor of the hospital. Fifty patients were provided with telemental health services, while a control sample of 35 patients matched to the treatment group on diagnosis, sex, and age were provided with in-person services. The psychiatrists, the patients, and the support staff completed evaluations of the services subsequent to each meeting. Patients who received telemental health and those who received in-person services rated their comfort with the process and the quality of services similarly. However, psychiatrists and support staff rated the telemental health condition as inferior to the in-person condition (Dongier et al., 1986). The study was one of the first to quantify the negative perceptions of healthcare professionals toward telemental health using a control group. It drew attention to one of the significant barriers to the expansion of telemental health services, provider attitudes.

Entering the 1990s, as the concept of evidence-based treatment began to gain importance, the focus of telemental health studies began to shift from feasibility to efficacy. However, the empirical base grew slowly. Calls for better evaluation of telemental health care echoed throughout the decade (Baer et al., 1997a, b; Brown, 1998; Graham, 1996). Many descriptive studies continued to refer to the "promise" of telemental health care, but few studies provided the evidence to support it. At the close of the twentieth century, some researchers recommended that the dissemination of telemental health programs should cease until clearer evidence existed for its effectiveness (Baer et al., 1997b). Others concluded that telemental health services were not tenable at all (Werner & Anderson, 1998).

Hoped-For Advantages

The primary advantage of telemedicine imagined as early as 1906 was the ability to increase access to quality care. Although the initial conceptualization of the problem focused on the needs of rural, isolated communities, by the 1960s, urban programs—such as the program at MGH—were seen as valuable in low-resourced neighborhoods (IOM [US] Committee on Evaluating Clinical Applications of Telemedicine & Field, 1996). It was believed that telemental health services would reduce barriers such as insufficient transportation for patients, small facilities' lack of diagnostic tools, and mental health provider shortages. In 1994 the US Congressional Ad Hoc Steering Committee on Telehealth was formed to consider how rapid developments in technology could be leveraged to increase access to care in rural areas (Chavez, 1997). Yet by 1997, only 30% of rural hospitals had any form of telemedicine services for patient care (Chavez, 1997). The Steering Committee declared that the barriers limiting the use of telemental health nationally must be addressed, but the plea went largely unanswered (Conrad, 1998).

Early Barriers

Multiple barriers prevented the early telemental health services from reaching a national scale. Most of those barriers were related to the economics of telemedicine or the attitudes toward it. Early telemental health programs were particularly costly to implement. The equipment—with its relatively new technology—was expensive (Strehle & Shabde, 2006). The cost of maintaining connections between sites, either via telephone lines (which were slow) or via communication satellites, was also significant (Dongier et al., 1986). In addition, from the earliest programs in the 1950s through the early 2000s, most telemental health services involved two medical sites—with the provider at one office and the patient and supporting staff at another. This set-up required nearly double the space and staff that in-person services required (Werner & Anderson, 1998), yet it did not avoid the need for patients to travel to receive care, only reducing the distance. Finally, the reluctance of insurance programs to pay for remote care made telemental health services difficult to fund (Chavez, 1997). Early programs were most often grant funded and thus were not sustainable in the long term (IOM [US] Committee on Evaluating Clinical Applications of Telemedicine & Field, 1996). The conclusions drawn by some investigators were dire: "After considering economic and other variables involved in a simple case of telepsychiatry, we conclude that telepsychiatric services are technologically feasible, pragmatically difficult, and not economically supportable at this time" (Werner & Anderson, 1998, p. 1290).

The negative attitudes of providers toward telemental health services extended well beyond concerns about cost. Commonly reported concerns included perceptions that telemental health services were impersonal and would impede the development of the therapeutic relationship, that confidentiality could not be maintained within the telemental health process, that difficulties using the telehealth equipment would disrupt sessions, and that telemental health was more hassle than in-person services (Connolly et al., 2020; Dongier et al., 1986; Pignatiello et al., 2019; Swinton et al., 2009; Werner & Anderson, 1998). It is the case that the practice of telemental health within a system of care sometimes requires changes in providers' roles and/or the expansion of responsibilities (Campbell et al., 2021). Lack of training to manage those new roles may have played a part in maintaining negative attitudes toward early telemental health programs. As of 1997, only 26 medical school programs provided students training in the delivery of telemedicine, and no psychology graduate programs offered training in telemental health care (Chavez, 1997).

A Tipping Point: The 2020 COVID-19 Pandemic

Despite the early barriers, advances in technology at the start of the twenty-first century caused a new wave of interest in telemedicine (Flaum, 2013; Pignatiello et al., 2011). Emerging evidence suggested that some telemental healthcare services, including pediatric services, could be as effective as in-person services and have similar rates of attrition and comparable patient satisfaction (Barak et al., 2008; Gloff et al., 2015; Myers et al., 2007; Nelson & Sharp, 2016). A major change in the implementation of telemental health at this time was the increase in the availability of videoconferencing platforms that could be used with relative simplicity in the home. Subsequently, telemental health programs no longer required two medical spaces, and services could be provided within patients' homes. When a cost analysis of pediatric telemental health care included the savings to parents in time and travel, the per-session cost for telemental health services for children became significantly lower than in-person services (Spaulding et al., 2010).

Although the advanced technologies available for telemental health were increasingly reliable and affordable, negative attitudes toward remote mental health services, poor insurance reimbursement, and concerns about confidentiality continued to limit the dissemination of telemental health services (Payne et al., 2020). Not until March 11, 2020, when the World Health Organization declared the COVID-19 outbreak to be a pandemic and in-person interactions of all types were restricted or shutdown did telemental health truly surge into use (https://www.cdc.gov/museum/timeline/covid19.html). The US Department of Health and Human Services reported that Medicare visits via telehealth increased from 840,000 in 2019 to 52.7 million in 2020 (Samson et al., 2021). However, it wasn't the shutdown itself that brought about the spike in telemental health services, but rather the cascade of changes that followed. Under pressure from the provider community and government agencies, many insurance companies altered their billing policies to reimburse remote health care, a large and necessary step for widespread use of telemental health. At the same time, national and state licensure-regulating bodies began initiatives like PSYPACT and the Social Work Interstate Licensure Compact—which developed plans for licensure reciprocity for psychologists and social workers—allowing providers to offer services across state lines. As of July 1, 2024, 42 states were active in PSYPACT (https://psypact.org/mpage/psypactmap), and 18 states were participants in the Social Work Interstate Licensure Compact (https://www.socialworkers.org/Advocacy/Interstate-Licensure-Compact-for-Social-Work).

At the time of the abrupt pivot to telehealth services that occurred at the start of the COVID-19 pandemic, little thought was given to the evidence base of telemental health care. The prevailing attitude was that some care (even if diluted) was better than no care (Nealon, 2021). Since 2020, more work has been done to investigate the effectiveness of telemental health care in terms of intervention delivery and patient outcomes. Evidence suggests that telemental health services lead to lower no-show rates than in-person services (Eyllon et al., 2021; Tolou-Shams et al., 2022) and that children receiving telemental health services experience a strong therapeutic alliance (Frye et al., 2022). In one of the few controlled studies, children with severe anxiety and obsessive compulsive disorder experienced similar outcomes whether they received treatment in person or via telemental health (Stone et al., 2023). Further, a meta-analysis of telemental health studies found no significant differences in outcomes between services delivered via remotely or in person (Greenwood et al., 2022). It should be noted that even now well-controlled studies of telemental health are sparse—only 12 randomized control trials could be identified by Greenwood et al. (2022). As is typical of treatment outcome research generally, more studies have examined telemental health services for adults than for children.

Ethical Considerations in Telemental Health

Not until 2013 did the American Psychological Association (APA) publish initial guidelines for the ethical practice of telepsychology (Joint Task Force, 2013). Until that time, providers leaned on the recommendations of those relatively few providers with experience in the area (Nelson et al., 2011; Nelson et al., 2017). The 2013 guidelines covered the provision of any mental health services using distance communication devices such as telephone, mobile phone, videoconferencing platform, email, text, or Internet. Provider-patient communications that come under the guidelines include written materials and audio or visual communication, with therapeutic sessions that are synchronous or asynchronous. As many more therapists began to provide telemental health services during the pandemic, however, it became apparent that a new review of the ethical considerations was necessary. Thus, the guidelines were updated in 2024 (APA). Similar ethical and best-practice guidelines for telemental health have been published by other mental health professional organizations such as the National Association of Social Workers (https://www.socialworkers.org/About/Legal-Defense-Fund/HIPAA-Help-for-Social-Workers/Telemental-Health) and the American Psychiatric Association (https://www.psychiatry.org/psychiatrists/practice/telepsychiatry/toolkit/best-practices; Liem et al., 2020). We have summarized the core components of these guidelines below.

Competence of the Psychologist

With regard to telemental health, *competence* refers to the need for therapists to have skills in the use of the technology implemented in session and an understanding of how the technology might impact patients (e.g., whether the telehealth modality is appropriate for a given patient, if the patient can engage appropriately, etc.). For child and family telehealth, this may mean that the therapist not only pursues training experiences to understand the logistics of a telehealth platform (e.g., Zoom) but also that the therapist takes additional measures to assess the caregiver's and child's capacity to engage through telecommunication (e.g., whether there are cultural, language, or socioeconomic barriers that may interfere with treatment success). Additionally, therapists must assess whether children are at a developmental level that allows them to engage in the therapeutic process remotely.

Standards of Care

It is expected that psychologists maintain general ethical and professional standards throughout treatment, regardless of the use of technology. Providers are responsible for ensuring that telemental healthcare is an appropriate modality for patients and to conduct frequent assessment to ensure that telehealth services continue to be a good fit (APA, 2024). When considering standards of care, it is important to review potential risks and benefits of telehealth and for the therapist to assess the appropriateness of telehealth format throughout the duration of the intervention. For instance, if a family experiences a crisis (e.g., child self-harm, disclosure of abuse) during session, can the therapist adequately and appropriately manage the crisis over telehealth? Can the therapist manage other emergencies in session? These risks should be weighed against the potential benefits of telehealth (e.g., access to care that might not otherwise be available for a family). It is the duty of the therapist to terminate telehealth services if it is believed that remote services are no longer beneficial to the child or family.

Informed Consent

Although imperative in any modality of psychotherapy, obtaining informed consent can be more challenging when working with children and families via telehealth. At a minimum, obtaining informed consent for telehealth psychotherapy involves providing a description of the services being offered and a discussion of how technology will be involved in the treatment. Obtaining assent for telehealth services from minors can be tricky. The therapist should communicate the process of assessment or treatment, as well as any risks and benefits, in a developmentally appropriate manner to caregivers and to children. Some risks of treatment, such as Internet security concerns, may be dismissed by youth and may therefore require additional care to appropriately communicate the potential threats. Treatment boundaries should also be discussed (e.g., how will the therapist respond to electronic communication from caregivers). A therapist is obligated to provide caregivers and children with adequate information about the treatment format to give informed consent and assent.

Confidentiality of Data and Information/Secure Transmission and Disposal of Data

Maintaining confidentiality is a foundational ethical obligation of any mental health professional, but when working with children and families via telehealth, the issue can be multi-faceted. Psychotherapy within a child's home means therapists cannot control who may have access to the session. Others may be able to hear the child's conversation without the therapist even being aware of it. Therapists must consider who is present for the session and engage families in discussions regarding who will have access to the child's conversation. Parameters as to who will and will not be part of the session should be agreed upon with the family prior to beginning treatment. Relatedly, therapists should discuss with parents appropriate locations for telehealth sessions (e.g., in the home without visitors rather than in a coffee shop or park). Therapists should consider whether children feel comfortable divulging information if sessions might be overheard by others and resolve barriers to maintaining confidentiality.

The security of the platform used for sessions is also a necessary consideration. Using telecommunication technology increases the risk to confidentiality (APA, 2024). This may be particularly relevant when working with youth who are more and more technologically savvy and who have significant access to social media. Therapists should be mindful of privacy settings on social networking sites for their own professional and personal purposes.

Additional security measures are required to be in place when using telecommunication methods for psychotherapy to protect patient data from unintended access or disclosure. Strategies to reduce the potential for breaches of confidentiality (e.g., via hackers, theft) are imperative. Therapists must take reasonable steps to ensure security measures are in place to protect against data breaches. In doing so, therapists must also consider how to dispose of telepsychology data in a safe and appropriate way.

Testing and Assessment

In the selection of assessment tools to be used via telemental health, therapists are "encouraged to ensure that the integrity of the psychometric properties of the test and the conditions of administration indicated are preserved" (Joint Task Force, 2013, para. 7). Most psychological tests and assessment procedures have been developed for in-person administration. Therapists should understand a test's suitability for telehealth administration prior to use. Therapist must also consider how to maintain the integrity of the testing process in challenging situations. If, for instance, the child has access to a cell phone behind the computer screen of the telehealth session or a family member is watching television in an area out of view, the validity of the assessment results may be compromised.

Interjurisdictional Practice

State regulations regarding jurisdictional borders differ, and therapists must familiarize themselves with and comply with relevant laws and regulations when providing telehealth services across state lines. For instance, states may have differing requirements regarding the information required to be included in the informed consent process (APA, 2024). A therapist may encounter an ethical dilemma if the family they have been working with moves to another state and wants to continue services via telehealth. The therapist may be tempted to continue seeing the family but should first investigate whether they are considered credentialed to provide services in the new state. Ultimately, it is recommended that therapists monitor changes in licensure and jurisdictional requirements within their telehealth practice, as the requirements continue to evolve (APA, 2024).

Telemental Health Care: The New Normal

The levels of telemental health service use that spiked during the pandemic have not returned to pre-pandemic levels, and evidence suggests they will not. By early in 2021, 38% of Americans had participated in telemental health care, and 59% said they would be willing to participate in telemental health; both rates increased from 2020 (American Psychiatric Association, 2021). Notably, 43% of those questioned said they would like to continue using telehealth services after the pandemic ended.

At the same time, patterns of use also changed radically among mental health providers. By 2021, 96% of psychologists reported providing at least some telemental health services, and as of 2023, 67% reported they were providing hybrid services telemental health/in-person (American Psychological Association, 2021; APA, 2023). According to an analysis of healthcare encounters from 2019 to 2023 at the US Veterans Administration (VA), in 2019 less than 5% of mental health encounters were provided via video conferencing (Ferguson et al., 2024). During the pandemic the percentage rose to 34%, and as of July, 2023 remained at approximately the same percentage.

In short, advances in technology, changes in the attitudes of providers and patients, and new reimbursement policies of insurance companies have lastingly changed the way that telemental health care is used (USDHHS, 2023). This change renews the hope that telemental health may play a significant role in increasing access to quality mental health care for children and families in underserved communities. It is important therefore that therapists remain updated on the types of interventions for children and families that have demonstrated success when implemented remotely.

The following chapters focus on three key areas of pediatric telemental health services: psychological assessment, parenting and family interventions, and individual interventions for children and adolescents. Each chapter presents the intervention and adaptations necessary to administer it via telemental health, reviews the research base for the telemental health adaptation, and illustrates the use of the intervention with a case example.

References

American Psychiatric Association. (2021, May). *New Nationwide poll shows an increased popularity for telehealth services*. Retrieved May 29, 2024 from https://www.psychiatry.org/news-room/news-releases/new-nationwide-poll-shows-an-increased-popularity

American Psychological Association. (2021, October). *Worsening mental health crisis pressures psychologist workforce: 2021 COVID-19 Practitioner Survey*. Retrieved May 29, 2024 from: https://www.apa.org/pubs/reports/practitioner/covid-19-2021

American Psychological Association (2023). *Infographic: Percentage of psychologists offering remote or in-person treatment, 2020–2023*. https://www.apa.org/pubs/reports/practitioner/2023-infographics/telehealth-location

American Psychological Association. (2024). Guidelines for the practice of telepsychology. https://www.apa.org/practice/guidelines/telepsychology

Baer, L., Cukor, P., & Coyle, J. T. (1997a). Telepsychiatry: Application of telemedicine to psychiatry. In R. L. Bashshur, J. H. Sanders & G. W. Shannon (Eds.), *Telemedicine: Theory and practice* (pp. 265–288, chapter xviii, 435 pages).

Baer, L., Elford, R., & Cukor, P. (1997b). Telepsychiatry at forty: What have we learned? *Harvard Review of Psychiatry, 5*(1), 7–17. https://doi.org/10.3109/10673229709034720

Barak, A., Hen, L., Boniel-Nissim, M., & Shapira, N. A. (2008). A comprehensive review and a meta-analysis of the effectiveness of internet-based psychotherapeutic interventions. *Journal of Technology in Human Services, 26*, 109–160.

Bashshur, R. L., & Bashshur, M. J. (2023). Telemedicine, history of. In E. Y. Ho, C. L. Bylund, J. C. M. Van Weert, I. Basnyat, N. Bol, & M. Dean (Eds.), *The international encyclopedia of health communication*. https://doi.org/10.1002/9781119678816.iehc0623

Brown, F. W. (1998). Rural telepsychiatry. *Psychiatric Services, 49*(7), 963–964. https://doi.org/10.1176/ps.49.7.963

Bashshur, R. L., & Shannon, G. W. (2010). History of telemedicine: Evolution, context, and transformation. New Rochelle, NY: Mary Ann Liebert.

Campbell, J., Theodoros, D., Russell, T., Hartley, N., & Gillespie, N. (2021). Role and process change and satisfaction with an educational and developmental psychologist telehealth service for rural children. *The Educational and Developmental Psychologist, 38*(1), 143–157. https://doi.org/10.1080/20590776.2021.1915097

Chavez, N. (1997). Serving the underserved: Our societal responsibility. *Professional Psychology: Research and Practice, 28*(3), 203–204. https://doi.org/10.1037/0735-7028.28.3.203

Connolly, S. L., Miller, C. J., Lindsay, J. A., & Bauer, M. S. (2020). A systematic review of providers' attitudes toward telemental health via videoconferencing. *Clinical psychology: A publication of the Division of Clinical Psychology of the American Psychological Association, 27*(2). https://doi.org/10.1111/cpsp.12311

Conrad, K. (1998). Making telehealth a viable component of our national health care system. *Professional Psychology: Research and Practice, 29*(6), 525–526. https://doi.org/10.1037/h0092809

Dongier, M., Tempier, R., Lalinec-Michaud, M., & Meunier, D. (1986). Telepsychiatry: Psychiatric consultation through two-way television: A controlled study. *The Canadian Journal of Psychiatry/La Revue Canadienne de Psychiatrie, 31*(1), 32–34. https://doi.org/10.1177/070674378603100107

Dwyer, T. F. (1973). Telepsychiatry: Psychiatric consultation by interactive television. *The American Journal of Psychiatry, 130*(8), 865–869. https://doi.org/10.1176/ajp.130.8.865

Einthoven, W. (1957). The Telecardiogram (H. Blackburn, Trans.). *American Heart Journal* 53(4), pp. 602–615. (Original work published 1906).

Eyllon, M., Barnes, J. B., Daukas, K., Fair, M., & Nordberg, S. S. (2021). The impact of the covid-19-related transition to telehealth on visit adherence in mental health care: An interrupted time series study. *Administration and Policy in Mental Health and Mental Health Services Research, 49*, 453. https://doi.org/10.1007/s10488-021-01175-x

Ferguson, J. M., Wray, C. M., Van Campen, J., & Zulman, D. M. (2024). A new equilibrium for telemedicine: Prevalence of in-person, video-based, and telephone-based Care in the Veterans Health Administration, 2019-2023. *Annals of Internal Medicine, 177*(2), 262–264. https://doi.org/10.7326/M23-2644

Flaum, M. (2013). *Telemental health as a solution to the widening gap between supply and demand for mental health services* (pp. 11–25). Elsevier.

Frye, W. S., Gardner, L., & Mateus, J. S. (2022). Utilising telemental health in a paediatric outpatient psychology clinic: Therapeutic alliance and outcomes. *Counselling & Psychotherapy Research, 22*(2), 322–330. https://doi.org/10.1002/capr.12450

Graham, M. A. (1996). Telepsychiatry in Appalachia. *American Behavioral Scientist, 39*(5), 602–615. https://doi.org/10.1177/0002764296039005007

Greenwood, H., Krzyzaniak, N., Peiris, R., Clark, J., Scott, A. M., Cardona, M., Griffith, R., & Glasziou, P. (2022). Telehealth versus face-to-face psychotherapy for less common mental health conditions: Systematic review and meta-analysis of randomized controlled trials. *JMIR Mental Health, 9*(3), e31780. https://doi.org/10.2196/31780

Gloff, N. E., LeNoue, S. R., Novins, D. K., & Myers, K. (2015). Telemental health for children and adolescents. *International review of psychiatry* (Abingdon, England), *27*(6), 513–524. https://doi.org/10.3109/09540261.2015.1086322

Institute of Medicine (US) Committee on Evaluating Clinical Applications of Telemedicine. (1996). In M. J. Field (Ed.), *Telemedicine: A guide to assessing telecommunications in health care*. National Academies Press.

Joint Task Force for the Development of Telepsychology Guidelines for Psychologists. (2013). Guidelines for the practice of telepsychology. *The American Psychologist, 68*(9), 791–800. https://doi.org/10.1037/a0035001

Liem, A., Sit, H. F., Arjadi, R., Patel, A. R., Elhai, J. D., & Hall, B. J. (2020). Ethical standards for telemental health must be maintained during the COVID-19 pandemic. *Asian Journal of Psychiatry, 53*, 102218. https://doi.org/10.1016/j.ajp.2020.102218

McLaughlin, L. (1968, June 30). Big brother MD is watching over you. *The Boston Sunday Globe*, 206–207.

Myers, K., Valentine, J. M., & Melzer, S. M. (2007). Feasibility, acceptability, and sustainability of telepsychiatry for children and adolescents. *Psychiatric Services, 58*, 1493–1496.

Nealon, M. (2021, October 9). *The pandemic accelerant: How COVID-19 advanced our mental health priorities*. United Nations Chronicle. https://www.un.org/en/un-chronicle/pandemic-accelerant-how-covid-19-adv...

Nelson, E. L., Bui, T., Sharp, M., (2011). *Gregerson Technology Innovations for Behavioral Education Telemental Health Competencies: Training Examples from a Youth Depression Telemedicine Clinic*, Springer, 41–47.

Nelson E. L., & Sharp, S. (2016). A review of pediatric telemental health. *Pediatric Clinics of North America, 63*(5), 913–931. https://doi.org/10.1016/j.pcl.2016.06.011

Nelson, E., Cain, S., & Sharp, S. (2017). Considerations for conducting telemental health with children and adolescents. *Child and Adolescent Psychiatric Clinics of North America, 26*(1), 77–91. https://doi.org/10.1016/j.chc.2016.07.008

Oxford English dictionary (OED). (1989). (2nd ed.). Oxford University Press.

Payne, L., Flannery, H., Gedara, C. K., Daniilidi, X., Hitchcock, M., Lambert, D., Taylor, C., & Christie, D. (2020). Business as usual? Psychological support at a distance. *Clinical Child Psychology and Psychiatry, 25*(3), 672–686. https://doi.org/10.1177/1359104520937378

Pignatiello, A., Teshima, J., Boydell, K. M., Minden, D., Volpe, T., & Braunberger, P. G. (2011). Child and youth telepsychiatry in rural and remote primary care. *Child and Adolescent Psychiatric Clinics of North America, 20*(1), 13–28. https://doi.org/10.1016/j.chc.2010.08.008

Pignatiello, A., Stasiulis, E., Solimine, C., Ayad, O., & Boydell, K. M. (2019). Lessons learned in a physician referral to pediatric telemental health services program. *Journal of the Canadian Academy of Child and Adolescent Psychiatry/Journal De l'Académie Canadienne De Psychiatrie De l'Enfant Et De l'Adolescent, 28*(3), 99–104. https://cmich.idm.oclc.org/login?url=https://www.proquest.com/scholarly-journals/lessons-learned-physician-referral-pediatric/docview/2487173618/se-2

Samson, L. W., Tarazi, W., Turrini, G., & Sheingold, S. (2021). *Medicare beneficiaries' use of telehealth in 2020: Trends by beneficiary characteristics and location*. Retrieved from https://aspe.hhs.gov/reports/medicare-beneficiaries-use-telehealth-2020

Spaulding, R., Belz, N., DeLurgio, S., & Williams, A. R. (2010). Cost savings of telemedicine utilization for child psychiatry in a rural Kansas community. *Telemedicine and e-Health, 16*(8), 867–871. https://doi.org/10.1089/tmj.2010.0054

Stone, D. I., Elkins, R. M., Gardner, M., Boger, K., & Sperling, J. (2023). Examining the effectiveness of an intensive telemental health treatment for pediatric anxiety and ocd during the covid-19 pandemic and pediatric mental health crisis. *Child Psychiatry and Human Development*. https://doi.org/10.1007/s10578-023-01500-5

Strehle, E. M., & Shabde, N. (2006). One hundred years of telemedicine: Does this new technology have a place in paediatrics? *Archives of Disease in Childhood, 91*(12), 956–959. https://doi.org/10.1136/adc.2006.099622

Swinton, J. J., Robinson, W. D., & Bischoff, R. J. (2009). Telehealth and rural depression: Physician and patient perspectives. *Families, Systems & Health, 27*(2), 172–182. https://doi.org/10.1037/a0016014

Tolou-Shams, M., Folk, J., Stuart, B., Mangurian, C., & Fortuna, L. (2022). Rapid creation of child telemental health services during COVID-19 to promote continued care for underserved children and families. *Psychological Services, 19*(Suppl 2), 39–45. https://doi.org/10.1037/ser0000550

U.S. Department of Health and Human Services. (2023). *Fact sheet: End of the COVID-19 public health emergency*. Retrieved from https://www.hhs.gov/about/news/2023/05/09/fact-sheet-end-of-the-covid-19-public-health-emergency.html

Werner, A., & Anderson, L. E. (1998). Rural telepsychiatry is economically unsupportable: The Concorde crashes in a cornfield. *Psychiatric Services, 49*(10), 1287–1290. https://doi.org/10.1176/ps.49.10.1287

Part II
Assessment

Chapter 2
Remote Assessment of Child Cognitive Functioning: Virtually Standard?

Shalena Heard, Rebecca Warwick, and Alison Pritchard

Overview

Although telehealth options have been available for some mental health-related services for decades, cognitive assessment was largely limited to in-person methods until the COVID-19 pandemic. With the onset of the pandemic, a rapid transition to telehealth assessment services was adopted by some, and the full measure of the complexity of providing cognitive testing remotely became clear to all. In this chapter, we start by providing an overview of some basic information important to understanding cognitive assessment of children broadly, including its historical context, the breadth of cognitive skills that can be assessed, and the ways in which cognitive assessment is used. Next, we review two different models of remote cognitive assessment and discuss their pros and cons. We then spend substantial time on validity considerations with regard to remote assessment of cognitive functioning, as an understanding of the nuances of these issues is critical for any practitioner intending to undertake teletesting. This includes a discussion of the existing empirical literature examining the validity and utility of the practice. This is followed by a discussion of the practical and ethical concerns involved in remote assessment of cognitive functioning, as well as the characteristics of the client and the evaluation itself that may impact the feasibility and appropriateness of a remote testing

S. Heard · R. Warwick
Center for Neuropsychological and Psychological Assessment, Kennedy Krieger Institute, Baltimore, MD, USA

A. Pritchard (✉)
Center for Neuropsychological and Psychological Assessment, Kennedy Krieger Institute, Baltimore, MD, USA

Department of Psychiatry & Behavioral Sciences, Johns Hopkins University School of Medicine, Baltimore, MD, USA
e-mail: pritchard@kennedykrieger.org

L. N. Niec, C. E. Schoonover (eds.), *Telemental Health Care for Children and Families*,
https://doi.org/10.1007/978-3-031-69264-2_2

approach. Finally, we review the potential for remote assessment to address health-care disparities and offer guidance to practitioners who wish to receive training in remote assessment. A case study illustrating many of the practical and conceptual issues raised here rounds out the chapter.

A Brief History of Cognitive Assessment in Children

The history of cognitive assessment can be traced back to the sixteenth century when the earliest intelligence tests were developed (Kamphaus & Kamphaus, 2001); however, modern, standardized intelligence testing emerged in earnest in the nineteenth and twentieth centuries. Many scientists and researchers have since tried to measure intelligence in a wide variety of ways that ranged from Wilhelm Wundt and James Cattell's tests of sensory abilities and reaction time in 1879 to Alfred Binet and Theodore Simon's cognition and reasoning assessments in the early twentieth century (Kamphaus & Kamphaus, 2001). Binet and Simon are widely recognized as the developers of the first modern intelligence test for children, having created a measure in France in 1905 that was designed to determine which children might require more assistance in school (Feldman & Sutcliffe, 2009). Soon after, the "Binet and Simon Tests of Intellectual Capacity" were adapted for use in the United States by Henry Goddard and subsequently revised by Stanford's Lewis Terman in 1916, producing the Revised Stanford-Binet Scale (Becker, 2003). The new test was quickly adopted by public schools, in testing of immigrants at Ellis Island, and as evidence in courts of law (Benjamin Jr, 2009). Although it has undergone multiple revisions and updates over the century since its inception, the Stanford-Binet Intelligence Scales remain in use today (Roid, 2003) and share many characteristics with more recently developed and widely used intelligence tests, for example, the Wechsler Intelligence Scales for Children (Wechsler, 2014). Over the last century, many different theories of what constitutes intelligence have been put forth (e.g., Spearman's theory of general intelligence, Gardner's theory of multiple intelligences, and Cattell, Horn, and Carrol's hierarchical theory of intelligence), each of which has informed the development of cognitive measures (Gardner, 1998; Schneider & McGrew, 2012; Spearman, 1904). While this has resulted in the publication of many different cognitive measures, each of which is structured somewhat differently, at present, many of these measures largely assess the same skills and abilities, albeit in slightly different ways. Historical evaluations relied on various theories of psychology, which could be interpreted differently depending on the practitioner (Frick et al., 2020). Today's tests are, by design, independent of the psychologist, positioning them to serve as a more objective measure of a child's behavior (Schaffer & Rodolfa, 2016).

Skills and Abilities Typically Included in Cognitive Assessment of Children

Cognitive functioning involves the processes essential to how one perceives, registers, stores, retrieves, and uses information learned and accumulated from one's environment (Foreman et al., 1996). Cognitive assessment of children is very useful for identifying common developmental conditions, monitoring the course of disorder or an individual's readiness to learn, establishing treatment goals and plans, and measuring the effectiveness of a treatment intervention (Foreman et al., 1996; Lezak, 1983). Key components of functioning often measured in cognitive assessment include but are not limited to: reasoning/problem-solving, memory, attention, and executive functioning.

Reasoning/Problem-Solving

Reasoning and problem-solving skills are very commonly assessed in children, particularly as part of intelligence testing. The Wechsler scale, considered one of the most credible measures of cognitive strengths and areas of difficulty, based on its sound psychometric properties and utility for practitioners (Groth-Marnat, 2009; Groth-Marnat & Wright, 2016), contains several subtests measuring verbal and nonverbal reasoning and problem-solving skills. For example, the Fluid Reasoning Index score on the Wechsler Intelligence Scale for Children (Wechsler, 2014) measures mental operations required for novel tasks that cannot be done automatically, such as accurately perceiving relationships among patterns, drawing inferences, recognizing and forming concepts, problem-solving, understanding implications of decision-making, recognizing and transforming information, and extrapolating (Flanagan & Ortiz, 2001; Flanagan & Kaufman, 2004; Lichtenberger & Kaufman, 2013). Language-based reasoning is also commonly examined as part of cognitive functioning, given the extent to which language is used in the process of communication, teaching, and learning in our society.

Memory

When individuals or families are seeking cognitive assessment, a frequently reported symptom is poor memory (Kipps, 2005) or difficulty retaining learned information. These reported issues are often linked to the aspects of memory most relevant to cognitive assessment semantic memory and working memory (Kopelman, 2002). Semantic memory refers to memory for general, learned information (e.g., vocabulary, historical facts, math formulas). Familiar skills and tasks that require semantic memory include word reading and reading comprehension. Caregivers and educators may express concerns about, for instance, a child's ability to remember the meaning of learned vocabulary words when reading. Working memory refers to retention and manipulation of information for a brief period of time (Binder & Desai, 2011). A common activity that utilizes working memory is mathematics, and children with working memory difficulties may, for example, struggle to recall all of the components to solve a math word problem and to complete the necessary operations in the correct order. Learning and study strategies, such as chunking and utilizing mnemonics, are often suggested to aid children in enhancing their working memory capacity. Short-term memory is a component of working memory but is different in that it involves storing information temporarily but with minimal or no additional processing (Dehn, 2015).

Attention/Executive Functioning

Attention is a foundational ability, even underlying other fundamental skills such as working memory and reasoning. Attention is defined in the American Psychological Association's Dictionary of Psychology (Vanden Bos, 2015) as "a state in which cognitive resources are focused on certain aspects of the environment rather than on others and the central nervous system is in a state of readiness to respond to stimuli." Day-to-day indications of attention include the ability to concentrate, ignore distractions, and follow directions (Foreman et al., 1996). Difficulty with attention is a common presenting concern for children referred for evaluation and can be an indicator of a wide variety of developmental and mental health conditions (e.g., ADHD, anxiety, depression, learning disabilities).

Related to attention and similarly critical for day-to-day functioning are the skills commonly referred to as executive functions. These are higher-order cognitive processes that are essential to control thought and behavior. While there remains some disagreement on which specific higher-order skills comprise executive functions, in many cases working memory (described above), cognitive flexibility, planning, and inhibitory control are included (Baggetta & Alexander, 2016). For a thorough discussion of executive functions, visit the Harvard University Center on the Developing Child website: https://developingchild.harvard.edu/science/key-concepts/executive-function/.

Difficulties with both attention and executive functions are commonly seen across many developmental and mental health conditions; thus, assessing a child's cognitive abilities in these areas can be helpful for diagnostic decision-making and treatment planning for children.

IQ as a Special Issue

The terms "intelligence/IQ testing" and "cognitive testing" are sometimes used interchangeably; however, it is important to note that a unified definition of intelligence has been difficult to establish (Valencia & Suzuki, 2001). As mentioned previously, many theories of intelligence have been set forth, several of which have some strong evidence to support them, but none have yet to be accepted as the gold standard. Furthermore, IQ has been a controversial topic in the field of psychology (Bartholomew, 2004; Decker et al., 2013; Flanagan & Harrison, 2005; Weinberg, 1989). Specifically, there is a well-established history of a cultural bias in IQ testing toward members of particular minority groups (e.g., African Americans, Mexican Americans) who have traditionally scored lower on intelligence measures when compared to their White counterparts (Valencia & Suzuki, 2001). This cultural bias is but one indication that individuals possess a number of cognitive abilities that may not be fully measured using our current tests of intelligence. A common criticism of almost all intelligence tests is that they have an inherent bias toward scientific modes of thought (i.e., convergent, analytical), leaving those whose strengths lie in divergent, artistic, and imaginative modes of thought at a disadvantage (Flanagan et al., 2006, 2010; Groth-Marnat & Wright, 2016). Generally, intelligence tests tend to be heavily skewed toward measuring the types of skills that predict academic success and fail to measure other important abilities that are also essential for successfully navigating life (Gardner, 1998; Snyderman & Rothman, 1987; Sternberg, 2003), such as managing interpersonal relationships, social fluency, and adaptive living skills. Thus, the current chapter specifically focuses on assessing cognitive ability, broadly defined as opposed to restricting our discussion to intelligence alone.

The Purpose(S) of Cognitive Assessment of Children

In contemporary clinical practice, cognitive assessment plays a significant role in client care. In her overview of cognitive assessment, Ida Sue Baron (2004) emphasizes that, though it remains an important tool for practitioners, traditional cognitive testing is designed to be only one part of a holistic assessment, typically utilized in conjunction with other factors such as sociocultural context, medical history, and behavioral observations. Baron asserts that these assessments are meant to showcase both the strengths and weaknesses of the child being tested to gain a clearer understanding of their clinical presentation as a whole; further, child evaluations are designed to both explain and contextualize behavior in a way that will inform interventions and supports. A strength of modern cognitive assessment, which was absent in many of its historical iterations, is its relative objectivity and reliability, as today's assessments are standardized and based on normative data from a population sample (Ivnik et al., 2001).

Cognitive assessment is used in a wide variety of settings, where it is frequently considered the beginning of an individualized intervention path that is unique to each child. Referrals, which often serve as the impetus for child evaluation, can come from diverse settings that range from school to family to medical practitioners (Baron, 2004). Depending on the referral source and question, as well as available resources, cognitive testing may take place in any of several contexts. For children, the most common are the clinical setting and the school setting. Evaluations involving cognitive testing in a clinical setting are typically conducted by a psychologist or physician and often have the goal of clarifying the child's diagnostic profile and making recommendations for treatment and for educational services and supports. Evaluations conducted in the clinical setting may also serve to monitor a client's response to treatment or to support application for state and federal programs like DDA (Developmental Disabilities Administration) or SSI (Supplemental Security Income).

The Individuals with Disabilities Education Act (IDEA) of 1974 and its reauthorization in 2004 require schools in the United States to identify and support children with learning, behavioral, and emotional needs, which expanded cognitive assessment to include school-based diagnostic impressions and testing (Frick et al., 2020). Cognitive evaluations completed in the school setting are typically geared toward determining disability (and need for associated support) or gifted status and monitoring response to interventions. State-to-state and even district-to-district variability exists in requirements for and rules around cognitive testing in the school setting (including who can complete testing, whether diagnoses can be rendered, and what information is required to support disability or gifted status). Rarely does school-based testing result in recommendations for treatments or supports that a child might need outside of the school setting.

Though different scenarios require distinct assessment processes, many of them benefit from some type of cognitive testing in addition to other tools such as interviews and behavioral observations (Sattler, 2008; see Table 2.1). The cognitive testing completed as part of a full evaluation can range in nature from comprehensive

Table 2.1 Different types of assessments

Type of assessment	Definition
Screening assessment	An assessment designed to determine if a child is at risk for developing a disorder
Focused assessment	An assessment that looks in-depth at only one area of functioning
Diagnostic assessment	An assessment that answers clinical questions, aids in diagnosing disorders, and informs treatment plans
Counseling/rehabilitation assessment	An assessment to evaluate a child's ability to complete activities of daily living, likely following some treatment course
Progress evaluation assessment	A longitudinal assessment designed to examine changes and developments in a child
Problem-solving assessment	An assessment that seeks to solve a specific problem

(Adapted from Sattler, 2008)

testing of multiple areas of cognition (e.g., language- and visually based reasoning skills, memory, and attention) to a brief screening of a single cognitive function such as language or attention.

To be considered useful, cognitive assessments must be reliable and valid, meaning the population that generated the norming data must resemble the target client (Schaffer & Rodolfa, 2016). While most measures were traditionally normed on largely White samples, in recent decades, test developers and publishers have aimed to include proportional representation, informed by census data, of ethnic and racial minority groups in their standardization samples (Valencia & Suzuki, 2001). Further, some test developers have incorporated oversampling of minority groups to allow them to explicitly examine racial and ethnic group patterns (Wechsler, 1991). Additional considerations regarding the validity of tests include the earnestness and effort of the person being tested (Schaffer & Rodolfa, 2016). Many modern cognitive tests have embedded effort measures, which are meant to identify whether the client is putting forth at least a minimal level of effort on the test at hand (Sweet et al., 2021).

Results from cognitive testing can be interpreted in several different ways. Common methods of interpreting test results, as discussed by Baron (2004) and by Ivnik et al. (2001) include consideration of absolute scores, difference scores, profile variability, and change scores. Absolute scores rely on a single score or group of scores to indicate a diagnosis (e.g., a standard score below 80 on a word reading test as an indicator of dyslexia), while the difference score approach compares results of two or more tests to determine whether dysfunction is present (e.g., a standard score below 80 on a word reading test may indicate dyslexia only if the client has an IQ above 95). The profile variability approach examines performance across many tests in an effort to understand the client's strengths and weaknesses, with the assumption that dysfunction should manifest across multiple measures of different skills. Evaluation of change scores relies on repeated administration of the same (or very similar) tests to observe changes in a client's skills over time.

In summary, the purpose of, approach to, and interpretation of cognitive testing can vary depending on several factors, chief among these typically being the referral question and presenting problems.

Administration of Cognitive Measures for Children in Traditional Practice

The majority of standardized cognitive measures are designed for face-to-face, individual administration, though increasingly since the COVID-19 pandemic test developers and publishers have shown an interest in measures that have more flexibility in how they are administered.

Importance of Standardization and Norming

Many cognitive measures provide clear guidelines for administration and scoring that serve as the backbone of the standardized assessment process. Standardized administration practices increase the likelihood that a test is administered the same way from one practitioner to the next and from one client to the next. Only when test administration is standardized can scores for one client be compared to scores for another or to normative scores. In short, standardization of test administration allows for comparison of apples to apples. Critical aspects of standardization include:

- Reading task instructions verbatim during administration.
- Precisely timing responses when timing is required.
- Following specific subtest administration rules exactly, for example (Moon et al., 1991):
- Providing opportunities for the client to elaborate on a response that does not qualify for full credit, when allowed.
- Repeating items only when allowed for the specific subtest.
- Administering items at a specified rate of speed, when required.
- Recording verbal responses verbatim so that all relevant information is available for scoring.
- Properly orienting stimuli for visually based tasks and response booklets for paper-and-pencil tasks.

Before administering an unfamiliar measure, practitioners are encouraged to review the most common errors and recommended corrections for that measure to help ensure standardized administration (Groth-Marnat & Wright, 2016).

Many cognitive measures used in practice today are scored based on carefully constructed normative data. Interpreting performance on these tests involves comparing the client's score to scores generated by the normative sample. Normative samples are, ideally, chosen to accurately and thoroughly reflect the population of clients who will be using a test. Normative samples are often selected to represent the population on variables such as age, sex or gender, geography, race and ethnicity, and disability status; however, rarely are the samples used to gather normative data perfectly representative of the population of test users. For a discussion of the implications of this important issue, the reader is referred to Sattler (2008). For the purpose of this chapter, what is important is that a majority of cognitive measures have, to date, been normed using in-person testing procedures (Hewitt et al., 2020). This creates a concern when tests are administered remotely but scored based on in-person norms, as the practitioner is no longer able to make an apples-to-apples comparison. This issue will be discussed in greater detail in a subsequent section of this chapter.

Behavioral Observations

Behavioral observations are an essential part of traditional assessment practice. Practitioners are encouraged to document notable behavioral observations for each subtest in addition to general observations of the entire assessment administration. Subtest-level observations may be helpful in detailing the child's approach to problem-solving (e.g., use of self-talk, efforts to block out distractions such as covering ears and closing eyes) or distinguishing a child's difference in performance under timed versus untimed conditions, especially when the instructions state "work as fast as you can" or the child inquires about whether they are being timed. Careful observation of behavior during cognitive testing can not only support the practitioner's estimate of the validity of the testing but can also inform diagnosis and treatment recommendations.

Models for Remote Administration of Performance-Based Cognitive Tests

Using a telehealth format, there are two primary models for administering performance-based cognitive tests: a facilitated model and an independent model.

The Facilitated Teletesting Model

In the facilitated model, the practitioner and the client are in separate locations, and a facilitator is present at the client's location. The facilitator may not have an advanced degree or extensive clinical training; however, they should be specifically trained in how to manage behavior and assist with standardized test administration. In this model the practitioner administers the tests remotely, via videoconferencing software, and the facilitator assists with onsite observation and management of client behavior, as well as setup and presentation of manipulatives and other stimuli for testing. Facilitated remote testing may be particularly useful, for instance, in rural areas lacking qualified psychologists. In these cases, appropriate facilitators may be identified at a client's school (e.g., a teacher or paraprofessional who receives training in remote testing facilitation) or in the context of a community health center (e.g., a physician's assistant or nurse who receives training), and testing can be accomplished by a qualified psychologist at a remote location, with the help of the facilitator. Advantages of this model are highlighted in Table 2.1 and disadvantages in Table 2.2.

Table 2.2 Advantages of each teletesting model

	Facilitated teletesting (trained facilitator assists child)	Independent teletesting (caregiver assists child, if necessary)
Provision of cognitive assessment for children living in locations that otherwise would not have access to these services or would have to travel considerable distances to access them	X	X
Potential for client and family to miss less time from school or work for the assessment	X	X
Can administer all components of performance-based cognitive measures (even those that require manipulatives) remotely	X	
Similar control of testing environment to in-person testing	X	
Assurance that the technology being used by the client is of adequate quality for testing	X	
Similar opportunity for behavioral observations of the client to in-person testing	X	
Similar opportunity for behavioral management of the client to in-person testing	X	
Minimization of the possibility of cheating by the client	X	
Minimization of risks to test security	X	
Does not require involvement of a trained third party		X
Easily accessible for all clients who have access to a suitable computer and reliable internet connection		X
Potential for decreased anxiety for client as a result of increased familiarity with surroundings		X
Opportunity for practitioner to observe the client in their day-to-day home environment		X

The Independent Teletesting Model

An independent remote testing model involves only the psychologist and the client (though caregivers are also typically involved in the process for younger children). In this model, the psychologist administers those components of cognitive tests that are possible to administer remotely (i.e., those tasks that do not involve manipulatives or specialized stimuli that cannot be presented on a computer screen) to the client via videoconferencing software. Advantages of this approach are highlighted in Table 2.2 and disadvantages in Table 2.3.

Clearly both models of teletesting offer advantages and disadvantages, and the decision about which model to use will necessarily be based on the referral question

Table 2.3 Disadvantages of each teletesting model

	Facilitated teletesting	Independent teletesting
Not consistent with standardized administration on which norms are based	X	X
Time and expense of training facilitators in basic standardized testing practices	X	
Risk of inadequate training of facilitators, which may impact standardized administration of measures	X	
Requires twice as many person-hours to complete testing	X	
While caregivers can assist with behavioral management of client, they also can serve as a distraction or may inadvertently offer assistance to the client during testing		X
Potential for less thorough behavioral observations		X
Increased risk of challenges with technology when clients are using their own devices (e.g., unreliable internet connectivity, devices with insufficient screen size)		X
Without multiple devices connected simultaneously to videoconferencing software, it is challenging for the practitioner to adequately monitor for cheating		X
Behavioral management of child is more challenging		X
Lack of control of testing environment (increased potential for distractions)		X
Inability to administer all components of cognitive tests in a standardized way (i.e., those that require the use of manipulatives or stimuli that cannot be presented on a computer screen)		X

and the constraints of the specific situation in which the practitioner and practitioner find themselves.

Validity Considerations for Teletesting

One of the primary characteristics of cognitive testing that makes it so useful is its standardization. Ensuring that we are administering the same tasks in the same way to different individuals enables us to compare the performance of one person to another or—better yet—to a group of other people (a normative sample). This apples-to-apples comparison is where much of the useful information in cognitive testing lies, both for accurate diagnostic decision-making and for effective intervention planning. Given the importance of standardization in cognitive testing, and the fact that nearly all cognitive tests are currently normed under in-person testing conditions, it is easy to understand why the validity of teletesting has been called into question by practitioners and clients alike.

There are two related and critical considerations in any discussion of measurement validity. The first is that validity is not all-or-nothing; rather, it exists on a continuum. The second consideration is that the validity of a test or measure depends on several factors, some of which are intrinsic to the measure itself, and others that are related to the environment in which the measure is administered. Thus, for each testing situation, the practitioner must evaluate both the test and the way in which it is administered in order to make a judgment about whether the results are *valid enough* to be considered useful for a given client.

For independent teletesting specifically, validity is likely to depend on (a) the client's access to appropriate electronic devices and Internet connectivity, (b) the client and family's familiarity and comfort with using videoconferencing software, (c) the extent to which the client's environment can be controlled, and (d) the nature of the task being administered.

Access to and Familiarity with the Necessary Technology

Ensuring that the client has access to appropriate electronic devices and strong Internet connectivity prior to initiating teletesting is essential to validity. Interorganizational Practice Committee recommendations for teleneuropsychology (Bilder et al., 2020) recommend that clients use a desktop or laptop computer rather than a tablet or smartphone for participating in teletesting in order to ensure that clients can adequately view visual stimuli. They also recommend testing Internet connectivity, as well as audio and video quality, at the start of a teletesting session and saving timed tasks or tasks for which repetition of stimuli is prohibited for later in the testing session, once adequate connectivity has been reliably observed. If connectivity is problematic, but testing cannot be accomplished in person, telephone may offer a more reliable complement to videoconferencing, at least for auditory tasks. Even with adequate electronic devices and connectivity, however, validity of teletesting can be compromised if clients and families are less familiar/comfortable with using the necessary technologies.

Control of Testing Environment

Control of the testing environment is another critical aspect of teletesting validity. While a quiet, distraction-reduced testing environment is typically easy to establish in a practitioner's office and even in a facilitated teletesting situation, this is more challenging to assure for independent teletesting, which usually takes place in the client's home. The validity of performance-based measures may be reduced when independent testing conditions include third-party observers or when noise or distractions cannot be avoided (e.g., child cannot be in a separate room from siblings who are engaged in other activities, TV is on in the background, etc.). The presence of a third-party observer also raises the possibility of the client receiving assistance with the testing, either purposeful or inadvertent, from the observer. The setting also has clear implications for the validity of clinical interviews. The information obtained during an interview may be less useful in cases where privacy cannot be assured. Clients may be less forthcoming if they are concerned that their caregivers may hear their answers, and caregivers may not share the full nature or urgency of their concerns if they believe that their child could hear them.

In order to maximize validity of independent teletesting, it is essential for the practitioner to work with the client and their caregivers in advance of the appointment. Discussing with the client and caregivers ahead of time, the necessity of identifying a quiet and private space, with a comfortable desk and chair arrangement, is critical to ensuring an environment that enhances the testing validity. Clear expectations should be communicated to caregivers before the testing about their role and level of involvement in the testing process. Practitioners may wish to specify, for instance, that caregivers can assist the client with navigating the technology, as necessary, throughout the visit, but should not otherwise offer any encouragement or assistance to the child. Practitioners may also let caregivers know that assistance with behavior management will be explicitly requested, if necessary, and that they should refrain from intervening unless directly asked to do so by the practitioner. Further, to avoid inadvertently offering subtle nonverbal cues about the client's performance, such as facial expressions, in cases where the caregiver needs to remain in the room, the caregiver might be asked to turn their chair so as to face away from the client for the duration of the testing.

Nature of the Measure Being Administered

The nature of the tasks being administered is another important consideration in establishing the validity of your teletesting. The size and resolution of the video display, for instance, are critical to ensuring validity of teletesting visual tasks but are not particularly important for many tasks administered verbally. Table 2.4 offers a brief overview of these issues. Of note, some tasks are simply not well-suited to

Table 2.4 Brief overview of teletesting validity concerns and solutions

Nature of task	Validity concern	Potential solution
Visual	Differences in displays in terms of size and resolution of stimulus materials	Desktop or laptop computer is recommended
Verbal	Variability in audio quality or speed could invalidate speeded tasks or verbal memory task stimulus presentation	Recommend conducting these tasks by phone while maintaining video contact
Memory	Clients can cheat and write down information to be recalled	Recommend instructing clients to move themselves so that they are in full view of the camera, with hands visible

independent remote administration—measures of fine motor skills which often require manipulatives and close visual examination of the client's hands, are particularly challenging to administer remotely.

Existing Research in Teletesting Validity

In light of these considerations, and in response to the necessity for teletesting during the COVID-19 pandemic, a growing body of research has begun to examine the extent to which teletesting is or is not comparable to in-person testing. While this research remains largely in its infancy, and few cognitive measures have been prospectively normed and psychometrically validated for remote administration, the existing literature does offer some initial hope that even cognitive tests developed and normed for in-person administration may be able to be used with adequate reliability in teletesting circumstances.

Prior to the COVID-19 pandemic, most research into teletesting validity was conducted with adult clients, rather than children. A systematic meta-analysis of this literature indicated that verbally administered tasks (e.g., digit span, list learning, verbal fluency tasks) were minimally impacted by the teletesting format (Brearly et al., 2017); however, the majority of the studies included in this meta-analysis utilized a facilitated rather than an independent remote testing format. A separate systematic review of older adult studies suggested that some cognitive screeners, language tests, attention tasks, and memory tasks appear valid when administered remotely, though others lack sufficient support (Marra et al., 2020).

Fewer pediatric studies examining remote cognitive testing have been conducted, even when a broad view of what constitutes cognitive testing is taken. A systematic review of this area, conducted by Ruffini and colleagues and published in 2022, reported that the results of 23 studies generally supported similar performance between remote (both facilitated and independent remote testing) and in-person testing modalities for youth. The reader is referred to the systematic review for details; however, it is worth noting that the studies included in this review assessed the validity of remote administration of a broad range of measures tapping receptive and expressive language, verbal and nonverbal reasoning skills, math and reading skills, and short-term and working memory. Participants in these studies ranged from preschool-aged to young adults and included both typically developing youth and those with a variety of neurodevelopmental disabilities.

In the 2 years since the publication of this review, several additional studies comparing in-person and remote testing modalities have been published. A brief overview of the methods and findings of these studies is presented in Table 2.5. Overall, these more recent studies seem to support the conclusions of the earlier systematic review: while remote and in-person administrations of cognitive measures for children are not perfectly equivalent, most measures appear to demonstrate similar psychometric properties and result in similar scores regardless of administration method. In sum, the existing literature, though still far from conclusive, offers good

Table 2.5 Brief overview of studies comparing in-person and remote testing modalities

Study	Sample and method	Measures	Findings
Ahmed et al. (2022)	97 preschoolers Independent remote testing	Day-night Stroop task Dimensional change card Sort Digit span Head toes knees shoulders task WJ-IV letter-word and applied problems subtests	Scores on all tasks were normally distributed (except digit span backward), and all tasks demonstrated good internal consistency (except digit span forward)
Ashworth et al. (2021)	40 children ages 10–11 years with Williams syndrome – 26 in-person testing – 14 independent remote testing	Raven's colored progressive matrices British picture vocabulary scales (BPVS)	No differences in Raven's scores across testing method, but higher BPVS scores among children tested remotely
Gnambs and Lenhard (2023)	1590 8-year-olds – 1183 independent remote testing – 407 in-person testing	ELFE-II (German reading comprehension measure)	Slightly higher scores found for about one-fourth of the test items when remotely administered Children with lower reading proficiency had larger score differences between in-person and online testing
Magimairaj et al. (2022)	357 school-aged children, all independent remote testing Scores compared to in-person normative data	Test of narrative language, second edition (TNL-2)	No significant differences between remote administration and in-person normative sample scores in internal consistency, interrater reliability, or measurement invariance
McDermott et al. (2023)	896 youth with ADHD, ages 5–21 – Half independent remote testing – Half (matched sample) in-person testing	WISC-V similarities, vocabulary, matrix reasoning, visual puzzles, and digit span subtests KTEA-3 letter-word ID, nonsense word, math concepts and applications, and Reading comprehension subtests D-KEFS or NEPSY-2 verbal fluency subtest	No significant differences on any measure across remote and in-person testing
Ng et al. (2023)	35 youth with low to average intellectual functioning – Initially underwent in-person testing and then independent remote testing	WISC-V or WAIS-IV similarities, matrix reasoning, and digit span subtests	Strong correlations between in-person and remote testing scores for all subtests

(continued)

Table 2.5 (continued)

Study	Sample and method	Measures	Findings
Rivella et al. (2023)	1288 Italian youth aged 6–14 years – 554 underwent in-person testing – 734 underwent independent remote testing	TeleFE—a measure of executive functions designed for online administration consisting of a go/no-go task, a flanker task, an N-back task, and a "daily planning task"	No significant differences in scores found between remote and in-person administrations
Worhach et al. (2021)	46 youth ages 8–19: 18 with narcolepsy, 6 with daytime sleepiness, and 22 healthy controls All completed both in-person and independent remote testing, conditions counterbalanced	WASI-II vocabulary, matrix reasoning, and block design subtests	Good reliability between administration methods found for the vocabulary subtest, moderate reliability for matrix reasoning, and poor reliability for block design (though very small sample)

preliminary support for the validity of both facilitated and independent remote testing methods.

Practical and Ethical Concerns with Teletesting

Since teletesting became more commonplace during COVID-19, the practical and ethical concerns with the method have been discussed in detail in multiple forums. Bilder et al. (2020), Hewitt et al. (2020), and Pritchard et al. (2020) together offer a thorough review of practical and ethical concerns with teletesting, as well as recommended solutions. Here we highlight some of the most important practical and ethical issues for practitioners engaging in teletesting to consider, discussed with respect to the relevant APA ethical guidelines (Joint Task Force for the Development of Telepsychology Guidelines for Psychologists, 2013).

Boundaries of Competence

APA ethical principle 2.01 mandates that psychologists must practice within their areas of competence. Given the unique demands and limitations of teletesting, in order for psychologists to be competent in this area, they must seek out teletesting-specific training, rather than simply assuming that their competence with in-person testing transfers to teletesting. Direct instruction/training in teletesting methods, validity, and limitations has only recently begun to be offered on a large scale and formally as part of psychology training programs.

Established Scientific and Professional Knowledge and Use of Assessments

Per ethical principle number 2.04, psychologists' work should be based upon established scientific and professional knowledge of the discipline. Principle 9.02 specifies that psychologists should use assessments with established reliability and validity and that, if evidence of these is unavailable, the potential consequences of this must be addressed with the client. As is evident from the previous section of this chapter, the field's scientific knowledge regarding the validity of teletesting is still limited (although promising). Professionals engaging in teletesting must educate themselves using the available literature on the validity of remote administration for the measures that they intend to use. If no such literature is available, then they are required to discuss this as a potential limitation to the validity of the testing that was completed and to indicate its impact on their interpretation of the assessment findings (per APA principle 9.06).

Informed Consent

The ethical obligation that psychologists obtain informed consent prior to evaluating or treating clients (APA principle 3.10) requires some additional consideration when teletesting is involved. In order to truly obtain informed consent from clients and caregivers regarding teletesting, we must acknowledge the potential limitations of this format up front with families. We need to be clear with them before we start an evaluation about what we can and cannot measure well when using this testing format, implications that testing in this format may have for the findings of the evaluation, what technologies the family needs to have access to in order to participate successfully in teletesting, and what support may be needed from caregivers in order for the child to complete a telehealth assessment successfully. Perhaps most important among these limitations is the possibility that individual schools or even the entire districts may reject the validity of telehealth assessment outright and therefore may refuse to consider the findings and recommendations of your assessment, even if you as the practitioner believe them to be valid. Anecdotally, we have fortunately found that the latter is rarely an issue in practice. Other things that may need to be acknowledged in the process of obtaining informed consent include:

- The fact that standard test administration will be modified, and this might affect the results in ways that we still don't fully understand.

- That involvement of a third party (such as a caregiver) in teletesting may add concerns about the impact of observation on performance.
- That error may be compounded when teletesting procedures are used with people who come from culturally and linguistically diverse populations or who have limited experience with the technology that's being used.
- That there may be a loss of some qualitative data usually obtained during an in-person examination.
- That teletesting may pose additional risks to privacy and confidentiality.

Maintaining Confidentiality

Ethical principle 4.01 states that psychologists have a primary obligation and take reasonable precautions to protect confidential information obtained through or stored in any medium. The use of an independent teletesting format complicates the maintenance of confidentiality considerably, given that others may be present in the home or even in the same room as the client and can overhear information that should be confidential. In order to minimize this risk, practitioners should regularly inquire about who else is in the home before beginning an assessment and ask whether the client and caregiver are comfortable with others in the home potentially overhearing what is discussed. Even with this caveat, when a private space is unavailable during clinical interviewing, caregivers and children may be less willing to discuss sensitive topics. If this is the case, this should be thoroughly discussed, including the implications that it may have for the evaluation findings (e.g., the practitioner may not be confident in their differential diagnosis if they suspect that the client or caregiver withheld sensitive information due to lack of privacy), in the validity section of the report.

Maintaining Test Security

Per ethical principle 9.11, psychologists are required to make reasonable efforts to ensure the integrity and security of test materials and techniques. When considering test security and client privacy, a primary factor is the platform on which teletesting will occur. Most video conferencing or telehealth platforms offer a variety of options that can be used to enhance security and privacy. Be sure to check the various levels of accounts offered by the video conferencing platform that you are using, as different levels may have different privacy safeguards associated with them. In addition to specific platform-based considerations, client confidentiality and test security can be protected by securing formal agreement from the client and family at the beginning of the session that they will refrain from recording throughout the visit. In addition to agreement from the client and family, some platforms allow the practitioner to restrict recording unless, as the host, they specifically grant permission for the client or family to do so. Other platforms can alert the host when the participant is recording.

Client and Evaluation Characteristics That May Impact Teletesting

Based on our clinical experience, as there is not available research in this area as yet, there are several characteristics of clients that are important to consider in determining whether teletesting is likely to work well for a given case:

1. Older children tend to do better with the teletesting format than do very young children. They often require less third-party involvement, are more familiar with the necessary technologies, and have a greater capacity for behavioral regulation.
2. Similarly, less behaviorally dysregulated children, regardless of age, are usually a better fit for teletesting, given the limited degree to which the practitioner is able to control the client's home environment and the fact that caregivers may vary in their ability to effectively manage their child's behavior.
3. Clients who have access to a private, quiet space with a desk and chair are a better fit for teletesting. Testing a child at their kitchen table with siblings going in and out of the room and the TV on in the background will likely result in an underestimate of the child's true abilities—though it may give the practitioner a good idea of how the child is functioning in their typical day-to-day environment.
4. Youth and families who are more familiar with and have better access to technology, as well as a reliable Internet connection, are also a better fit for teletesting, for obvious reasons.

The nature and purpose of the evaluation are also important considerations in determining whether teletesting is appropriate for a given client. Teletesting is ideal for evaluations that consist of structured or unstructured diagnostic interviews, and that may include self-, parent-, and teacher-report ratings. Performance-based assessment of language skills, visual reasoning, memory, speed of processing, and most academic skills is also easily accomplished in the teletesting format, as can some components of attention. Motor functioning and writing can be more challenging to assess in a valid way remotely, though with a bit of creativity and careful attention to detail these are not impossible. Finally, the purpose of the evaluation must be considered: in high-stakes evaluations, such as those that make an initial determination of service eligibility (e.g., for DDA applications, new IEPs, etc.), completing the evaluation remotely carries with it the risk that the service agency may refuse to consider the evaluation results or deny eligibility out of hand, given that the data supporting the validity of teletesting remain limited. However, this risk is easily mitigated by simply contacting the relevant agency in advance of the evaluation to inquire about whether they accept the results of remote evaluations.

In our practice, we have developed a tiered approach to assessment that takes these factors into account. The reader is referred to Pritchard et al. (2020) for a full description of this model and examples of its application. In short, Tier 1 evaluations are comprised of a comprehensive interview and review of records and can be accomplished entirely remotely; Tier 2 evaluations include a comprehensive interview, review of records, and targeted teletesting; and Tier 3 evaluations are those that require a comprehensive interview, review of records, and in-person testing.

Tier 1 evaluations work well for clients with less complex presentations, those with more complex presentations but for whom some components are already being addressed in treatment, clients who have many records available for review (particularly recent testing), and clients who present with psychiatric concerns that are well-suited to a structured or semi-structured diagnostic interview. Tier 2 evaluations are most appropriate for re-evaluations, evaluation of response to intervention, and some specific differential diagnosis or questions about function. Tier 3 evaluations are reserved for those clients with very complex neurocognitive, emotional, and/or behavioral presentations, as these clients often require comprehensive testing of most domains of functioning in order for effective differential diagnosis and treatment recommendations to be made.

Does Telehealth Improve Access to Care?

The telehealth modality would seem to offer considerably easier access to care for some client populations that have traditionally struggled to access medical and psychological services—those living in rural locations, for instance. Existing research, however, indicates that this issue is less straightforward than it may seem. For a recent overview of the literature regarding cultural, socioeconomic, geographic, and age-related disparities in telehealth use during the COVID-19 pandemic, see Pritchard et al. (2023). To sum up this overview:

- The majority of studies indicate that White clients and clients whose preferred language is English used telehealth services more than non-White or Hispanic clients and clients whose preferred language is not English during the pandemic.
- Higher socioeconomic status tends to be associated with greater telehealth service use.
- The evidence is limited regarding geographic disparities, with two studies suggesting that clients living in rural areas were less likely to use telehealth during COVID-19 but another study finding the opposite.
- Most studies of age disparities in telehealth use found less use among older adults than younger adults.

These findings must be considered in light of two important factors, however: first, the vast majority of these studies examined adult rather than pediatric clients, and second, these studies were almost exclusively evaluating the use of telehealth services in medicine, rather than in psychological practice. None specifically examined cognitive assessment, except for the novel study reported in the manuscript. For this study, Pritchard et al. (2023) examined the demographic and clinical characteristics of over 2000 pediatric clients with ADHD who were seen for psychological evaluation in person before the COVID-19 pandemic and those tested via telehealth and in person during the pandemic. Comparison of these groups revealed that youth evaluated via telehealth during the pandemic were significantly older, had fewer comorbid conditions, lived farther from the clinic, and were more likely to be White than youth evaluated in person before the pandemic. The groups had similar sex ratios, socioeconomic status, and ethnicities. The authors conclude that, while offering some benefit for particular types of clients, telehealth has not eliminated barriers to care for pediatric clients receiving psychological evaluations.

Thus, while the telehealth modality seems to have a great potential for improving access to care, and may do so in certain circumstances, with particular types of clients or services, the existing literature does not offer a clear indication that its potential is currently being realized.

Guidelines for Training in Teletesting

Prior to the COVID-19 pandemic and the widespread surge in telepsychology services, the American Psychological Association (APA) launched a task force that developed telepsychology guidelines for psychologists (Joint Task Force for the Development of Telepsychology Guidelines for Psychologists, 2013). These guidelines indicate that practitioners must seek appropriate training before providing telehealth services, with Guideline 7 specifying that practitioners should have ample knowledge of ways to address unique issues that may arise when applying a remote testing format to test instruments and assessment approaches designed for face-to-face administration. Practitioners preparing to offer telehealth assessments must also consider common logistic challenges cited in various studies, and mentioned earlier in this chapter, prior to conducting a remote assessment (Bilder et al., 2020; Hewitt et al., 2020; Houser et al., 2023; Pritchard et al., 2020; Schoebel et al., 2021). Thus, when administering cognitive assessments through telehealth, the practitioner must not only be comprehensively trained in valid and standardized face-to-face administration of the necessary measures, but they should also be trained in and practice administration of these measures in a virtual format in order to maximize reliability and validity of the telehealth administration.

Currently, while there are no formal standards for training in teletesting, many continuing education courses and workshops are available online for practitioners seeking training in this area. In fact, the current interjurisdictional compact (PsyPact) that allows practitioners to provide telehealth services to clients in some other states under certain conditions requires that members receive regular continuing education training in telehealth specifically. Both the American Psychological Association (APA) and the Buros Center for Testing offer online continuing education courses and webinars designed to familiarize practitioners with a wide variety of issues (practical, ethical, and clinical) relevant to remote assessment. In our large clinical practice, we have developed a teletesting training workshop for new trainees and practitioners. This workshop covers the following areas:

1. APA guidelines for teletesting.
2. Test publisher-specific guidelines for teletesting.
3. Basic and advanced videoconferencing functions, settings, troubleshooting, and tips (e.g., enabling the "waiting room" function, use of the annotation, and remote control functions).
4. Best practices around test security and maintaining the client's privacy and confidentiality when using online testing platforms (e.g., using a unique numeric identifier rather than the client's name for online rating scales).
5. Specific measures and scoring systems that are available for telehealth use (e.g., PARiConnect, Q-global), including telehealth-friendly protocols, norms, audio files, and stimuli.
6. Information on where and how to score questionnaires depending on if they are digital versus paper administrations.
7. General remote administration tips relevant across measures (e.g., eliminating miscellaneous sounds, webcam setups that allow for adequate behavioral observation).

While specific training in teletesting is necessary, such training often follows the same basic framework as training for in-person cognitive assessment. Although the following five-step mastery model (Fantuzzo, 1984) was designed to prepare individuals for in-person administration of the Wechsler child and adult measures, the following list has been modified below to apply to any cognitive assessment and to incorporate the nuance of remote assessment and attention to technology:

1. **1 to 2 h studying the manual**—*A thorough review of the administration manual for measuring your plan to administer is vital for in-person and remote assessment.*
2. **Viewing a recording of an error-free remote cognitive assessment administration**—*It is suggested that a full administration of an error-free remote cognitive assessment be viewed for training purposes; when a recording is not possible, a live observation of a remote administration may be adequate.*
3. **Understanding major pitfalls of remote administration**—*Viewing a recorded or live presentation or reading an article on the common errors and considerations for remote administration of a given measure helps set you up for success.*
4. **Successfully detecting errors in a recording of a flawed remote cognitive assessment administration**—*In addition to observing an error-free administration, it is also useful to view a flawed remote administration and to test your knowledge by identifying the flaws you observed.*
5. **Administering a remote cognitive assessment and have your administration formally evaluated**—Sattler's (2008) *"General Test Administration Practices Checklist" can be useful as an evaluation tool, though other carefully developed tools are acceptable as well.*

Thus, as the field evolves to expand the scope and reach of telehealth and remote assessment administration, training programs, clinical sites, supervisors, and individual practitioners hold a responsibility to stay abreast of the latest information, measures, technologies, and approaches to providing telehealth assessments.

A Case Study

Mae, a 14-year-old Black girl, is referred to a practitioner for evaluation by her school. During the intake interview, completed via Zoom, her parents report concerns around attention, anxiety, and reading. They note that Mae has been struggling academically since the start of middle school and that now, as a ninth grader, her grades have declined precipitously. In elementary school, she struggled briefly with reading, but with supplemental reading, support was reported to be reading on the grade level by the fourth grade. She now reports that she has to re-read passages three to four times in order to understand them. As a younger child, Mae experienced some separation anxiety for which her parents sought treatment, but she was otherwise well-adjusted throughout elementary school. Starting in the sixth grade, Mae's grades declined somewhat largely as a result of missing and late assignments, and organization and time management were a significant challenge for her throughout middle school. In addition to the further decline in her grades, once she entered high school, Mae started complaining to her parents about having trouble falling asleep at night, and they noticed a pattern of frequent stomachaches and headaches without obvious physical causes, as well as reluctance to leave the house, even for activities that she used to eagerly anticipate, such as her art classes at the local art institute. With the exception of what her parents characterize as typical adolescent irritability, Mae's mood is usually upbeat and happy. No concerns about her eating habits were noted. Socially, Mae gets along well with peers. While she tends to be somewhat shy and slow to warm up to new people, she has several close friendships that she has maintained since elementary school. Her parents' goal for the evaluation is to ensure that Mae receives any supports or interventions that she might need to do her best in school and feel good about herself.

Based on her demographic and clinical characteristics, the practitioner thinks that Mae could be a good fit for a telehealth evaluation, rather than coming into the office in person. At the age of 14, Mae is likely quite comfortable with and capable of using technology. The practitioner noted during the intake interview that the family's Internet connection appeared stable throughout the hour that they were together on Zoom. Mae is an only child and has her own bedroom with a desk, as well as a laptop computer that she uses for school, so the practitioner feels confident that teletesting could be accomplished with minimal distractions and in a conducive environment. Her teachers and parents report that Mae is, behaviorally, a model student, who is compliant and has no difficulty sitting still through classes, so the practitioner has a reason to believe that she will be able to engage effectively in testing remotely and will be responsive to redirection, if necessary, requiring little involvement of her parents in the evaluation beyond their input in the diagnostic interview and their completion of behavior ratings for Mae. Given the concerns for anxiety and her recent reluctance to spend time outside of her home, testing Mae in a familiar environment rather than in the practitioner's office could reduce her anxiety, enhancing the validity of your findings. Furthermore, Mae's mother is able to work from home at times, but otherwise neither parent has much flexibility in their work schedules, so a telehealth assessment would have significant practical advantages for the family.

The nature of the clinical concerns is also well-suited to a telehealth evaluation. A brief screening of IQ is easily accomplished remotely with a two-subtest Wechsler Abbreviated Scales of Intelligence, Second Edition (WASI-II Vocabulary and Matrix Reasoning subtests; (Wechsler, 2011). Both foundational reading skills and reading comprehension are easily assessed remotely with performance-based testing (e.g., Wechsler Individual Achievement Test, Fourth Edition [WIAT-4] Word Reading, Pseudoword Decoding, and Reading Comprehension subtests) (Wechsler, 2020). You choose measures sensitive to attention that can be administered remotely (e.g., Wechsler Intelligence Scales for Children, Fifth Edition [WISC-5] Working Memory subtests, Delis-Kaplan Executive Functioning System [D-KEFS] Verbal Fluency subtest; Test of Everyday Attention for Children [TEA-Ch] Score!, and ScoreDT subtests) (Delis et al., 2001; Manly et al., 2016; Wechsler, 2014) and send links to online ratings of ADHD symptoms (e.g., Conners, Fourth Edition) Conners, 2022) and executive functioning skills (e.g., Behavior Rating Inventory of Executive Functions, Second Edition [BRIEF-2]; Gioia et al., 2015) to parents, teachers, and Mae herself. You also send Mae a link to a self-report of anxiety symptoms that she can complete online (e.g., Multidimensional Anxiety Scale for Children, Second Edition [MASC-2]; (March, 2012)).

On the day of the evaluation, the practitioner notes that Internet connectivity is good and that Mae settles into the remote testing process without difficulty, even noting that it reminds her somewhat of the distance learning that she did during COVID-19, which she enjoyed. Before starting testing, the practitioner ensures that Mae places her webcam in a position that allows for an adequate view of her upper body, including her hands, to ensure that the practitioner is able to capture necessary behavioral observations and prevent cheating. The practitioner also reminds Mae that she is not allowed to record or photograph any portion of the evaluation. Some of the performance-based measures that the practitioner selected require screen or audio sharing, which was practiced beforehand, so that goes smoothly. After completing the performance-based testing successfully and without any involvement of her caregiver, who was home but in another room at the time, the practitioner finds Mae to be open and at ease during the clinical interview. She notes that she feels most comfortable at home and that her anxiety is significantly worse when in unfamiliar environments. The practitioner is able to develop a nice rapport with Mae and feels a good estimate of her skills, and a representative observation of her behavior was obtained. Even so, the practitioner is careful, in their written report and when providing feedback to Mae and her parents about the findings of the evaluation, to note the limitations of the telehealth evaluation and possible ways in which the findings could have been different had the evaluation been completed in person.

Summary

Cognitive assessment of children has developed over more than a century from largely subjective interpretations of intelligence, rooted in varied psychological theories, to a set of standardized, norm-referenced, and more objective measures of a breadth of cognitive skills. Practitioners now have a broad array of standardized assessment tools at their disposal and can strategically select specific tools that are most appropriate to the referral question and purpose of the assessment, to the client's functional abilities and limitations, and to a face-to-face versus a remote assessment modality. Reasoning, problem-solving ability, memory, attention, and executive functioning are commonly assessed domains of cognitive functioning, and performance in these areas can be used to inform diagnosis, treatment and educational planning, response to interventions, and eligibility for services.

Two major models of remote assessment exist—a facilitated model and an independent model. As each model offers advantages and disadvantages, practitioners are expected to reference telehealth guidelines for ethical practice, developing research, and to utilize their professional judgment in identifying the best method given the referral question and presenting concerns. Ensuring the validity of the assessment should always be a top concern for the practitioner, and remote assessment presents unique challenges in this area that must be addressed, sometimes with creative problem-solving. Fortunately, a growing literature suggests that remote administration of even measures that were developed for face-to-face testing seems to produce valid results, regardless of whether a facilitated or an independent testing model was used.

While there are, at present, no formal standards for training in remote assessment, several continuing education courses and workshops are available online for practitioners seeking training in this area, as are several excellent peer-reviewed publications. Training in remote assessment should consider the ethical, legal, practical, and clinical concerns outlined in this chapter, and practitioners are ethically obligated to undergo training before providing this service.

As the field evolves to expand the scope and reach of telehealth broadly and remote assessment specifically, we anticipate that research on its validity and utility will increase, and formal training methods will become available within graduate programs and at the continuing education level to help practitioners integrate this method into their clinical practice. In the meantime, practitioners continue to hold a responsibility to stay abreast of the latest information, measures, technologies, and approaches to providing remote assessments.

Key Takeaways

1. Whether administering a cognitive assessment face to face or remotely, the practitioner should keep in mind the referral question and purpose of their assessment and the specific areas of cognitive functioning that are most important to evaluate and track over time (e.g., reasoning, problem solving ability, memory, attention, and executive functioning).
2. Remote assessment can be accomplished independently or using a facilitated model. Each model has its particular advantages and disadvantages.
3. Remote cognitive assessment for children has unique clinical, practical, ethical, and legal considerations that must be addressed in order for the assessment to be valid.
4. A growing literature supports the validity of teletesting for children, even when measures developed for face-to-face administration are used.
5. Before undertaking remote assessment, practitioners are ethically obligated to undergo adequate training, which may include review of the existing telehealth guidelines and empirical research, as well as formal coursework or workshops on the topic.

References

Ahmed, S. F., Skibbe, L. E., McRoy, K., Tatar, B. H., & Scharphorn, L. (2022). Strategies, recommendations, and validation of remote executive function tasks for use with young children. *Early Childhood Research Quarterly, 60*, 336–347. https://doi.org/10.1016/j.ecresq.2022.03.002

Ashworth, M., Palikara, O., Burchell, E., Purser, H., Nikolla, D., & Van Herwegen, J. (2021). Online and face-to-face performance on two cognitive tasks in children with Williams syndrome. *Frontiers in Psychology, 11*, 594465. https://doi.org/10.3389/fpsyg.2020.594465

Baggetta, P., & Alexander, P. A. (2016). Conceptualization and operationalization of executive function. *Mind, Brain, and Education, 10*(1), 10–33. https://doi.org/10.1111/mbe.12100

Baron, I. S. (2004). *Neuropsychological evaluation of the child*. Oxford University Press.

Bartholomew, D. J. (2004). *Measuring intelligence: Facts and fallacies*. Cambridge University Press.

Becker, K. A. (2003). *History of the Stanford-Binet intelligence scales: Content and psychometrics*. (Stanford- Binet intelligence scales, fifth edition assessment service bulletin no. 1). Riverside Publishing.

Benjamin, L. T., Jr. (2009). Time capsule: The birth of American intelligence testing. *Monitor on Psychology, 40*(1), 20.

Bilder, R. M., Postal, K. S., Barisa, M., Aase, D. M., Cullum, C. M., Gillaspy, S. R., Harder, L., Kanter, G., Lanca, M., Lechuga, D. M., Morgan, J. M., Most, R., Puente, A. E., Salinas, C. M., & Woodhouse, J. (2020). Inter organizational practice committee recommendations/guidance for teleneuropsychology (TeleNP) in response to the COVID-19 pandemic. *The Clinical Neuropsychologist, 34*(7–8), 1314–1334. https://doi.org/10.1080/13854046.2020.1767214

Binder, J. R., & Desai, R. H. (2011). The neurobiology of semantic memory. *Trends in Cognitive Sciences, 15*(11), 527–536. https://doi.org/10.1016/j.tics.2011.10.001

Brearly, T. W., Shura, R. D., Martindale, S. L., Lazowski, R. A., Luxton, D. D., Shenal, B. V., & Rowland, J. A. (2017). Neuropsychological test administration by videoconference: A systematic review and meta-analysis. *Neuropsychology Review, 27*(2), 174–186. https://doi.org/10.1007/s11065-017-9349-1

Conners, K. (2022). *Conners* (4th ed.). Multi-Health Systems.
Decker, S. L., Hale, J. B., & Flanagan, D. P. (2013). Professional practice issues in the assessment of cognitive functioning for educational applications. *Psychology in the Schools, 50*(3), 300–313. https://doi.org/10.1002/pits.21675
Dehn, M. J. (2015). *Essentials of working memory assessment and intervention*. Wiley.
Delis, D., Kaplan, E., & Kramer, J. (2001). *Delis-Kaplan executive function scale*. The Psychological Corporation.
Fantuzzo, J. (1984). Mastery: A competency-based training model for clinical psychologists. *The Clinical Psychologist, 37*(1), 29–30.
Feldman, H. M., & Sutcliffe, T. L. (2009). The history of developmental-behavioral pediatrics. In *Developmental-behavioralPediatrics*(pp.1–12).Elsevier.https://doi.org/10.1016/B978-1-4160-3370-7.00001-8
Flanagan, D. P., & Harrison, P. L. (Eds.). (2005). *Contemporary intellectual assessment: Theories, tests, and issues* (2nd ed.). Guilford Press.
Flanagan, D. P., & Kaufman, A. S. (2004). *Essentials of WISC-IV assessment*. Wiley.
Flanagan, D. P., & Ortiz, S. O. (2001). *Essentials of cross-battery assessment*. Wiley.
Flanagan, D. P., Ortiz, S. O., Alfonso, V. M., & Mascolo, J. T. (2006). *The achievement test desk reference: A guide to learning disability identification* (2nd ed.). Wiley.
Flanagan, D. P., Fiorello, C. A., & Ortiz, S. O. (2010). Enhancing practice through application of Cattell–Horn–Carroll theory and research: A "third method" approach to specific learning disability identification. *Psychology in the Schools, 47*(7), 739–760. https://doi.org/10.1002/pits.20501
Foreman, M. D., Fletcher, K., Mion, L. C., Simon, L., & Faculty, N. (1996). Assessing cognitive function. *Geriatric Nursing, 17*(5), 228–232. https://doi.org/10.1016/S0197-4572(96)80210-2
Frick, P. J., Barry, C. T., & Kamphaus, R. W. (2020). *Clinical assessment of child and adolescent personality and behavior* (4th ed.). Springer. https://doi.org/10.1007/978-3-030-35695-8
Gardner, H. (1998). *Frames of the mind: The theory of multiple intelligences* (10. anniversary ed.). [Nachdr.]). Basic Books.
Gioia, G. A., Isquith, P. K., Guy, S. C., & Kenworthy, L. (2015). *Behavior rating inventory of executive function* (2nd ed.). The Psychological Corporation.
Gnambs, T., & Lenhard, W. (2023). Remote testing of reading comprehension in 8-year-old children: Mode and setting effects. *Assessment, 107319112311593*. https://doi.org/10.1177/10731911231159369
Groth-Marnat, G. (2009). The five assessment issues you meet when you go to heaven. *Journal of Personality Assessment, 91*(4), 303–310. https://doi.org/10.1080/00223890902935662
Groth-Marnat, G., & Wright, A. J. (2016). *Handbook of psychological assessment* (6th ed.). Wiley.
Hewitt, K. C., Rodgin, S., Loring, D. W., Pritchard, A. E., & Jacobson, L. A. (2020). Transitioning to telehealth neuropsychology service: Considerations across adult and pediatric care settings. *The Clinical Neuropsychologist, 34*(7–8), 1335–1351. https://doi.org/10.1080/13854046.2020.1811891
Houser, S. H., Flite, C. A., & Foster, S. L. (2023). Privacy and security risk factors related to telehealth services—A systematic review. *Perspectives in Health Information Management, 20*(1), 1f.
Ivnik, R. J., Smith, G. E., Cerhan, J. H., Boeve, B. F., Tangalos, E. G., & Petersen, R. C. (2001). Understanding the diagnostic capabilities of cognitive tests. *The Clinical Neuropsychologist, 15*(1), 114–124. https://doi.org/10.1076/clin.15.1.114.1904
Joint Task Force for the Development of Telepsychology Guidelines for Psychologists. (2013). Guidelines for the practice of telepsychology. *American Psychologist, 68*(9), 791–800. https://doi.org/10.1037/a0035001
Kamphaus, R. W., & Kamphaus, R. W. (2001). *Clinical assessment of child and adolescent intelligence /c Randy W. Kamphaus* (2nd ed.). Allyn and Bacon.
Kipps, C. M. (2005). Cognitive assessment for clinicians. *Journal of Neurology, Neurosurgery & Psychiatry, 76*(suppl_1), i22–i30. https://doi.org/10.1136/jnnp.2004.059758

Kopelman, M. D. (2002). Disorders of memory. *Brain, 125*(10), 2152–2190. https://doi.org/10.1093/brain/awf229

Lezak, M. D. (1983). *Neuropsychological assessment* (2nd ed.). Oxford University Press.

Lichtenberger, E. O., & Kaufman, A. S. (2013). *Essentials of WAIS-IV assessment* (2nd ed.). Wiley.

Magimairaj, B. M., Capin, P., Gillam, S. L., Vaughn, S., Roberts, G., Fall, A.-M., & Gillam, R. B. (2022). Online administration of the test of narrative language–second edition: Psychometrics and considerations for remote assessment. *Language, Speech, and Hearing Services in Schools, 53*(2), 404–416. https://doi.org/10.1044/2021_LSHSS-21-00129

Manly, T., Crawford, J., George, M., Underbjerg, M., Robertson, I. H., & Anderson, V. (2016). *TEA-Ch 2: Test of everyday attention for children* (2e édition). Pearson clinical.

March, J. S. (2012). Multidimensional anxiety scale for children-2nd edition: Technical manual. *Multi-Health Systems*. https://doi.org/10.1037/t05050-000

Marra, D. E., Hamlet, K. M., Bauer, R. M., & Bowers, D. (2020). Validity of teleneuropsychology for older adults in response to COVID-19: A systematic and critical review. *The Clinical Neuropsychologist, 34*(7–8), 1411–1452. https://doi.org/10.1080/13854046.2020.1769192

McDermott, S. M., Sweeney, K., Jacobson, L. A., Lieb, R. W., Wexler, D., & Pritchard, A. E. (2023). Does assessment format matter? A comparison of in-person versus Teletesting scores for youth with ADHD. *Journal of Attention Disorders, 27*(2), 152–158. https://doi.org/10.1177/10870547221129311

Moon, G. W., Blakey, W. A., Gorsuch, R. L., & Fantuzzo, J. W. (1991). Frequent WAIS-R administration errors: An ignored source of inaccurate measurement. *Professional Psychology: Research and Practice, 22*(3), 256–258. https://doi.org/10.1037/0735-7028.22.3.256

Ng, R., Ludwig, N. N., Peterson, R. K., & Jacobson, L. A. (2023). Clinical utility of teleneuropsychology among pediatric patients with broadly average and low intellectual functioning. *Child Neuropsychology, 29*(8), 1388–1397. https://doi.org/10.1080/09297049.2023.2170996

Pritchard, A. E., Sweeney, K., Salorio, C. F., & Jacobson, L. A. (2020). Pediatric neuropsychological evaluation via telehealth: Novel models of care. *The Clinical Neuropsychologist, 1–13*. https://doi.org/10.1080/13854046.2020.1806359

Pritchard, A. E., Northrup, R. A., Peterson, R., Lieb, R., Wexler, D., Ng, R., Kalb, L., Ludwig, N., & Jacobson, L. A. (2023). Can we expand the pool of youth who receive telehealth assessments for ADHD? Covariates of service utilization. *Journal of Attention Disorders, 27*(2), 159–168. https://doi.org/10.1177/10870547221129304

Rivella, C., Ruffini, C., Bombonato, C., Capodieci, A., Frascari, A., Marzocchi, G. M., Mingozzi, A., Pecini, C., Traverso, L., Usai, M. C., & Viterbori, P. (2023). TeleFE: A new tool for the tele-assessment of executive functions in children. *Applied Sciences, 13*(3), 1728. https://doi.org/10.3390/app13031728

Roid, G. H. (2003). *Stanford-Binet intelligence scales* (5th ed.). Riverside Publishing.

Ruffini, C., Tarchi, C., Morini, M., Giuliano, G., & Pecini, C. (2022). Tele-assessment of cognitive functions in children: A systematic review. *Child Neuropsychology, 28*(6), 709–745. https://doi.org/10.1080/09297049.2021.2005011

Sattler, J. M. (2008). *Assessment of children: Cognitive foundations* (5th ed.). Sattler Publication.

Schaffer, J., & Rodolfa, E. (2016). *A student's guide to assessment and diagnosis using the ICD-10-CM: Psychological and behavioral conditions*. American Psychological Association.

Schneider, W. J., & McGrew, K. S. (2012). The Cattell-horn-Carroll model of intelligence.

Schoebel, V., Page, C., Beck, A., Buche, J., Gaiser, M., Wayment, C., & Mauri, A. (2021). "We have to meet those clients where They're at"–Michigan behavioral health providers' responses to telehealth policy changes during COVID -19. *Health Services Research, 56*(S2), 42–43. https://doi.org/10.1111/1475-6773.13807

Snyderman, M., & Rothman, S. (1987). Survey of expert opinion on intelligence and aptitude testing. *American Psychologist, 42*(2), 137–144. https://doi.org/10.1037/0003-066X.42.2.137

Spearman, C. (1904). "General Intelligence," Objectively Determined and Measured. The American Journal of Psychology, 15(2), 201. doi:https://doi.org/10.2307/1412107.

Sternberg, R. J. (2003). *Wisdom, intelligence and creativity synthesized*. Cambridge University Press.

Sweet, J. J., Heilbronner, R. L., Morgan, J. E., Larrabee, G. J., Rohling, M. L., Boone, K. B., Kirkwood, M. W., Schroeder, R. W., Suhr, J. A., & Conference Participants. (2021). American Academy of Clinical Neuropsychology (AACN) 2021 consensus statement on validity assessment: Update of the 2009 AACN consensus conference statement on neuropsychological assessment of effort, response bias, and malingering. *The Clinical Neuropsychologist, 35*(6), 1053–1106. https://doi.org/10.1080/13854046.2021.1896036

Valencia, R., & Suzuki, L. (2001). *Intelligence testing and minority students: Foundations, performance factors, and assessment issues*. Sage. https://doi.org/10.4135/9781452231860

Vanden Bos, G. R. (2015). *APA dictionary of psychology* (2nd ed.). American psychological association.

Wechsler, D. (1991). *Weschler intelligence scale for children* (3rd ed.). The Psychological Corporation.

Wechsler, D. (2011). *Wechsler abbreviated scale of intelligence: WASI-II ; Manual*. Pearson. https://books.google.com/books?id=MjarjwEACAAJ

Wechsler, D. (2014). *Wechsler intelligence scale for children-fifth edition*. Pearson.

Wechsler, D. (2020). *Wechsler individual achievement test* (4th ed.). Pearson.

Weinberg, R. A. (1989). Intelligence and IQ: Landmark issues and great debates. *American Psychologist, 44*(2), 98–104. https://doi.org/10.1037/0003-066X.44.2.98

Worhach, J., Boduch, M., Zhang, B., & Maski, K. (2021). Remote assessment of pediatric patients with daytime sleepiness and healthy controls: A pilot study of feasibility and reliability. *Child Neurology Open, 8*, 2329048X2110480. https://doi.org/10.1177/2329048X211048064

Part III
Child-Focused Interventions

Chapter 3
Guidance for the Telehealth Delivery of Cognitive-Behavioral Therapy for Anxiety Disorders in Youth

Ovsanna Leyfer, Alyssa M. Farley, Rachel A. Merson, and Donna B. Pincus

Introduction

Anxiety disorders are the most prevalent psychiatric disorder in youth, with community prevalence rates ranging from 2.2 to 9.5% and lifetime prevalence rates as high as 28.8% (e.g., Merikangas et al., 2010). Anxiety disorders are also highly comorbid, both with each other and with other psychiatric disorders (Essau, 2003). Evidence indicates that anxiety disorders may be chronic and recurrent conditions with lengthy, even lifelong durations, in the absence of effective treatment. For example, Keller et al. (1992) found that in youth ages 6–19 years, the average duration of an anxiety disorder was 4 years and that approximately 46% of these children were still experiencing anxiety symptoms 8 years after the anxiety disorder onset. In fact, many adult anxiety disorders have their onset in childhood or adolescence (Burke et al., 1990). Anxiety disorders cause high levels of impairment in social, academic, and family functioning and can predict later negative outcomes such as substance abuse, educational underachievement, and difficulty transitioning into adulthood (Booth et al., 2004; Costello et al., 2003; Grills-Taquechel & Ollendick, 2013).

Cognitive-behavioral therapy (CBT), which focuses on identifying and modifying thoughts and behavioral patterns that lead to and maintain emotional difficulties, has been found efficacious for the treatment of anxiety disorders in children and adolescents (e.g., Walkup et al., 2008). Several randomized control trails have compared CBT treatment with waitlist control conditions, demonstrating its efficacy in youth with typical development (e.g., Kendall, 1994; Rapee, 2000). Kendall (1994) found that most of the children in his treatment group no longer met the criteria for an anxiety disorder at the post-treatment follow-up, a finding that was replicated and

O. Leyfer (✉) · A. M. Farley · R. Merson · D. B. Pincus
Center for Anxiety and Related Disorders, Boston University, Boston, MA, USA
e-mail: oleyfer@bu.edu

L. N. Niec, C. E. Schoonover (eds.), *Telemental Health Care for Children and Families*,
https://doi.org/10.1007/978-3-031-69264-2_3

extended in a second clinical trial (Kendall et al., 1997), which demonstrated the maintenance of treatment gains 12 months later. Similarly, in their clinical trial of CBT for children with anxiety disorder, Wood et al. (2006) reported a remission rate of 79% post-treatment. Furthermore, the treatment gains also were maintained at the 1-year follow-up (Wood et al., 2009). Overall, research has shown that the improvement from CBT is durable over time (e.g., Barrett et al., 2001; Kendall et al., 2004), with longer-term longitudinal studies reporting maintenance of improvement as long as 6 and 7 years after treatment, respectively. It has also been found that the CBT-induced decreases in anxiety are associated with improvement in social maladjustment and academic achievement (e.g., Wood et al., 2006). Finally, Walkup et al. (2008) demonstrated that in children, CBT produces effect sizes similar to effect sizes produced by selective serotonin reuptake inhibitors (SSRIs).

Despite the well-documented efficacy of these treatments, fewer than 20% of adolescents receive services for anxiety-related problems (Merikangas et al., 2011). The reasons for such low service utilization among anxious youth are multifold. One of them is low availability of and high demand for specialty services, which results in long waitlists (Moore & Gammi, 2018). This is particularly true for youth in remote or underserved areas. Other barriers include difficulties scheduling multiple weekly sessions over extended periods of time when following the traditional weekly clinic-based treatment model, transportation to appointments, and securing childcare for siblings as well as stigma related to visits to a mental health clinic (Booth et al., 2004; Salloum et al., 2016). To address the gaps in service availability and accessibility, delivering treatment via innovative formats has become critical.

Following the start of the COVD-19 pandemic, telehealth interventions have become a prominent part of healthcare (Sasangohar et al., 2020), and they may offer transformative solutions to overcoming some of the barriers to effective and equitable care for anxiety disorders in youth. In fact, telehealth delivery can bring treatment to underserved communities and meet youth where they are, addressing the issue of lack of specialized services, burden of travel and scheduling, and the potential discomfort with visits to a mental health clinic. For example, in a study of parent-child interaction therapy, families in the telehealth condition reported fewer barriers to accessing treatment than the families in the clinic-based condition (e.g., transportation, scheduling, and child care concerns; Comer et al., 2017a). Second, conducting exposures, i.e., the practice of facing anxiety-provoking situations and sensations, in the child's natural setting may give clinicians access to stimuli that may be unavailable or difficult to simulate in the clinic (e.g., the scary corner of the basement). Telehealth also enables the clinician to observe the child in their home and to develop better understanding of the family dynamics and functioning. Finally, delivering treatment in the natural setting of the child and the family may aid the generalization of the skills learned in therapy (Islam et al., 2023).

There are also potential challenges to providing CBT for anxiety disorders to youth via telehealth. They include difficulties with rapport-building and developing a relationship with the therapist, issues with privacy, and distractors in the environment as well as technical difficulties and lack of reliable Internet connection for some households. It may be easier for youth to avoid engagement in session by staying off camera, playing games or reading material in other computer windows, or logging off of sessions prematurely. In this chapter we review CBT for anxiety disorders in youth, the evidence base for telehealth delivery of CBT for anxiety disorders, and offer guidelines on delivering CBT for anxiety via telehealth. We conclude with a case study illustrating the points discussed.

Components of CBT for Youth with Anxiety

Typical CBT for anxiety disorders consists of the following techniques: psychoeducation, cognitive restructuring, exposure to anxiety-provoking situations and sensations, and relaxation (Kendall, 1994). Psychoeducation focuses on increasing the youth's understanding of the components of anxiety (thoughts, physiological sensations, and behaviors) and their interaction, how anxiety is maintained, and how the treatment works. It also allows time to set goals and expectations for the treatment. Cognitive restructuring focuses on challenging the maladaptive beliefs and cognitions and replacing them with alternative thoughts. Relaxation exercises teach youth how to better manage the uncomfortable physiological experiences associated with anxiety. Finally, exposure consists of facing or experiencing anxiety-provoking situations and sensations in order to allow the individual to experience their anxiety in an objectively safe situation (Kendall et al., 2005). Exposure is arguably the most important component of CBT for anxiety, with a meta-analysis of 75 studies of CBT for anxious children and adolescents demonstrating that higher amounts of in-session exposures were related to greater effect sizes between the treatment and the control groups (Whiteside et al., 2019). We address delivering these components via telehealth later in the chapter.

Telehealth Delivery of CBT for Anxiety Disorders in Youth

Rapid growth in access to Internet and communication technologies in the recent years has opened the door to broad delivery of telehealth treatments. In fact, as of 2021, 93% of Americans have access to Internet (Pew Research Center, 2021), which suggests that telehealth-based treatments have the potential of being accessed almost anywhere. Despite the growing popularity and advantages of delivering CBT for anxiety via telehealth, only a handful of studies have examined the delivery of CBT via videoconferencing in children with anxiety. Carpenter et al. (2018) conducted a multiple baseline trial of telehealth-delivered CBT in 13 children with anxiety (mean age 9.9 years), using family-based CBT (Howard et al., 2000). The results demonstrated that the treatment was feasible to conduct and acceptable to the families, and it yielded high levels of satisfaction. They also reported symptom improvement post-treatment as well as maintenance of gains at 3 months of follow up.

Similar findings were reported by Comer et al. (2021) in young children with social anxiety (ages 3–8) in a waitlist control trial of a family-based behavioral intervention. Forty children were randomized to either treatment or waitlist condition. At post-treatment, the children in the treatment group demonstrated significantly greater decreases in fear, discomfort, and social impairment, in comparison to the control group. The families also reported a high level of treatment satisfaction.

Gittins Stone et al. (2023) compared outcomes of an intensive (4+ weeks, daily meetings) CBT for children and adolescents with anxiety and obsessive-compulsive disorder (mean age = 13.81) delivered either via videoconferencing or in person. While the results need to be interpreted with caution due to the fact that the participants were not randomized to the conditions, and the treatment dose differed depending on the presenting problems, the study found no difference between the groups in the degree of reduction in the symptoms of anxiety at post-treatment.

There is an additional body of research supporting the use of telehealth in pediatric obsessive-compulsive disorder. Several studies examined CBT delivered via teleconferencing specifically in pediatric obsessive-compulsive disorder (OCD). Although OCD is not classified as an anxiety disorder, the treatment applies the same CBT principles, including psychoeducation, cognitive work, and exposure (e.g., Lack, 2012). Storch et al. (2011) randomized 31 children and adolescents (7–16 years) with OCD to either telehealth-delivered family-based CBT or a waitlist control, demonstrating that the treatment condition was superior to the waitlist. Comer et al. (2017b) expanded these findings further by comparing the outcomes of 22 children (ages 4–8 years) randomized to either videoconferencing or in-person treatment, finding no significant difference between the two groups and similar maintenance of gains at the 6-month follow-up.

Overall, evidence demonstrates no difference in treatment outcomes between in-person and telehealth conditions in anxiety and OCD in youth (e.g., Carpenter et al., 2018). This is further supported by meta-analyses of studies of children and adults with a variety of presenting emotional disorders which illustrate that therapy delivered via telehealth (i.e., videoconferencing) produces treatment effects comparable to those of therapy delivered in-person (Batastini et al., 2020; Fernandez et al., 2021). Additionally, the studies reviewed in this section demonstrate that it is feasible and acceptable to families to receive CBT treatment via telehealth, and families generally report a high level of satisfaction with such services (e.g., Comer et al., 2021). Finally, it has been shown that telehealth delivery of interventions has in fact increased access to effective care (Shore et al., 2018). However, it is important to acknowledge that very few randomized controlled trials have been conducted, particularly in children and adolescents, directly comparing in-person and telehealth treatment formats. Larger randomized controlled studies are needed to produce more generalizable findings and also cast a more nuanced look at the groups for whom telehealth works better or worse and under what conditions. Furthermore, because telehealth has become such a large part of the clinical practice, it is critical to make sure that clinicians are trained to provide evidence-based treatments responsibly via telehealth and taking advantage of the benefits it has to offer.

Guidance for Clinicians

Throughout the course of virtual CBT for youth anxiety, clinicians can utilize and leverage the virtual format to provide effective care. The following section offers suggestions for how clinicians can try to overcome some of the frequent challenges in virtual treatment for youth anxiety such as logistical issues, rapport-building, and session engagement. Next, the section provides guidance on ways to deliver the core components of CBT for youth anxiety when providing virtual treatment.

Common Challenges

Logistical Issues When providing virtual treatment, families may experience technical difficulties that interfere with treatment sessions. Clinicians must provide families with clear instructions on how to access their videoconferencing program. When possible, clinicians should allow additional time for sessions early in their course of treatment in case families face delays or require assistance accessing the videoconferencing program. If the family lacks a reliable Internet connection in their household, the clinician should work with the family to identify a location in their community where they can privately access the Internet. For example, individuals are frequently able to reserve private rooms within their local public library to conduct therapy sessions. At times, schools also allow youth to participate in virtual therapy sessions during the school day and provide a private space for these sessions. When a youth is participating in sessions from their home but does not have a private room there, their clinician may need to help them brainstorm creative solutions. For instance, youth might be able to find a private space in the bathroom, a larger closet, their family's car, or their yard. They might consider reducing others' ability to hear them by playing music or white noise in the background. The youth might wear headphones to remove family members' ability to overhear what the clinician is saying, or they might ask nearby family members to wear earplugs or noise-canceling headphones while they are conducting their sessions (Eiseman, 2020). Finally, caregivers or older siblings can entertain younger siblings outside or in another area of the home during the session.

Rapport-Building Building rapport is an essential step in youth anxiety treatment. Clinicians and clients sometimes feel this is more challenging during virtual than in-person treatment. Still, many rapport-building activities developed for in-person treatment lend themselves well to the virtual format, including some suggested in the foundational manual on CBT for children with anxiety (Coping Cat). For example, the Coping Cat manual suggests playing a "Personal Facts" game, which involves the client and clinician answering the same friendly questions (e.g., "How many siblings do you have?"; "What is your favorite food?") and then playfully quizzing each other on the answers (Kendall & Hedtke, 2006). Other clients might enjoy asking and/or answering various "Would You Rather…?" questions with their clinician.

If a client would benefit from a rapport-building activity involving physical movement, their clinician might suggest playing "Feelings Charades," during which the client and clinician take turns acting out different feelings, guessing the feelings, and discussing what signs helped them guess (e.g., the person's actions or facial expressions) (Beidas et al., 2010). Alternatively or additionally, the client and clinician might play "Jump," during which the clinician asks the client to jump twice if the answer to a personally relevant question is *yes* and stand still if the answer is *no* (e.g., "Jump up and down two times if you have a pet"). Another popular option that takes advantage of the client's environment is "Show and Tell." During this activity, the clinician and client each find nearby items to share and discuss. For example, the clinician and client might each find an item in their home that is important to them, or they might each bring an item that fits into a certain predesignated category (e.g., something red, something soft, something you like to play with) (Lowenstein, n.d.).

At times, youth with anxiety may be more reserved during their initial sessions and require rapport-building that does not necessarily involve verbal communication or sharing of personal information. In such cases, activities to consider include playing virtual games, such as a computer version of Uno, and drawing together, such as by jointly watching and following a learn-to-draw video. The clinician and client can then share their drawings with each other, and the clinician can use the opportunity to praise the client's work. Finally, when working with a younger child, the clinician and the child's caregiver might choose to arrange for the child to play with their toys in the camera's view. While the child is playing, the clinician should practice using skills that support the child's confidence and help foster their relationship, such as the PRIDE skills—Praise, Reflection, Imitation, Description, and Enthusiasm—from parent-child interaction therapy (Funderburk & Eyberg, 2011). In such situations, it is ideal for the clinician to have some similar toys on their end of the videoconferencing session so they can approximately imitate the child's play.

Session Engagement At times, it can be harder to sustain youths' engagement throughout sessions when conducting treatment virtually rather than in-person. Youth with anxiety may be more susceptible to avoidance and disengagement during sessions because session content may provoke their anxiety (e.g., due to nervousness when interacting with their therapist, talking about their fears, or facing their fears). To proactively address this barrier, clinicians should aim to structure sessions with content that is engaging, interactive, and varied to sustain their clients' attention. They should also receive their clients' and caregivers' agreement about session expectations as early as possible during the course of treatment, ideally during the first session. For instance, the clinician might explicitly state the expectations that the client will (1) keep their video and microphone on, (2) keep their entire face within the camera's view, and (3) avoid engaging in other activities on their screen throughout sessions. Establishing these expectations early gives the clinician permission to remind the client about them later if needed. If a client is persistently engaging in other activities during virtual sessions, and this is interfering with treatment, the clinician might consider whether it would be appropriate to involve (a) caregiver(s) in their sessions or institute regular caregiver check-ins during sessions to support the client's attention. If a client is unable to maintain their focus for the full length of the session, the clinician might schedule briefer meetings (e.g., twice-weekly 25-min sessions with the client; 25 min of each session spent with the client and the other 25 min spent with their caregiver[s]). Lastly, if a client is unable to engage in virtual sessions for any amount of time, the clinician might offer a caregiver-only course of treatment. For example, research has indicated that a parent-only treatment for youth anxiety (Supportive Parenting for Anxious Childhood Emotions) is as efficacious as traditional CBT with sessions primarily involving children (Lebowitz et al., 2020).

Core Components of CBT for Youth Anxiety

Psychoeducation Virtual treatment can excellently facilitate psychoeducation because CBT for youth anxiety typically involves the use of worksheets and visual aids. Clinicians should share their screen to present relevant worksheets, such as those showing the cognitive-behavioral model, an anxiety rating scale, and vignettes about other children who are experiencing anxiety. Clinicians should also electronically write on worksheets or their virtual white board when discussing examples presented by the client—for instance, when applying the cognitive-behavioral model to an example anxiety-provoking situation from the client's life. Finally, youth tend to engage well with videos that provide psychoeducation about anxiety, such as the videos from Anxiety Canada that discuss the fight/flight/freeze response (Anxiety Canada, 2019a, b).

Cognitive Restructuring Like during psychoeducation, it is often beneficial to use visual aids and written information when conducting cognitive restructuring. Using a worksheet or virtual white board, the client or clinician might write down the client's anxiety-provoking thought, the evidence supporting or refuting that thought, and any more helpful/realistic thoughts they generate based on the evidence provided. The decision about whether the client or clinician writes down this information should depend on consideration of the client's developmental level, learning style, and cognitive profile. If factual information might be useful to incorporate into the evidence for assessing the validity of a thought (e.g., the frequency of shark attacks where the client will be swimming), the clinician might deem it appropriate to jointly research such information online. In such instances, the client or clinician can share their screen while researching their question(s). If the client and clinician successfully address one of the client's recurring anxious thoughts during a virtual session and the written information (e.g., the completed worksheet) is on the clinician's computer, the clinician can electronically send the client this information so the client can save or print it and then refer to it when needed. Another option is to create a shared folder online to store de-identified copies of therapy materials so they are accessible for the youth, their clinician, and their caregivers (if applicable) throughout the course of treatment.

Relaxation Relaxation is a helpful tool in youth anxiety treatment, and it often works well to teach relaxation in a virtual format. Clinicians can use video and/or audio aids when presenting relaxation skills including diaphragmatic breathing and progressive muscle relaxation and then practice them alongside their clients during sessions. When practicing, to the extent possible, clinicians should carefully monitor their clients to confirm appropriate skill implementation (e.g., expanding the stomach when inhaling during diaphragmatic breathing, squeezing muscles tightly during progressive muscle relaxation). Clinicians can also ask their clients to practice the relaxation skills in locations where they would especially benefit from using them, such as in their bed if they tend to experience nighttime worries. Clinicians should electronically share any video or audio aids that were helpful during sessions to facilitate clients' ongoing practice between sessions.

Exposures Exposure is an essential component of CBT for youth anxiety (Ale et al., 2015), and it can require creativity on the part of clinicians who are delivering treatment virtually. However, virtual treatment can also provide many opportunities for valid and useful exposures given the ability for clients to conduct them in their home and community while receiving live coaching from their clinician. In this way, virtual treatment overcomes some of the limitations of office treatment sessions, because the clinician can give real-time support to their client in locations where they would not traditionally have access.

If providing treatment to a youth attending sessions from their home, the clinician might help them address fears that arise in that setting. For example, when working with an adolescent with contamination-related fears, a clinician challenged her to bring her school supplies into her bedroom without wiping them down first and to practice sitting on her bed without changing out of her school clothes beforehand. When treating a child with separation anxiety, a clinician supported him with going to the second floor of his home independently and with remaining in his home while his mother retrieved an item from their car in the driveway.

Virtual treatment can also support in-session community exposures, with clinicians tagging along via portable device (e.g., smartphone, tablet) while their clients practice facing their fears in public settings. This can be more discreet than having the clinician join in person, which can help the exposure to feel more natural and similar to the client's everyday activities. It can also help the clinician join their client at places their client goes frequently in their community, which might be different from those near the clinician's therapy office (which is where they would typically be able to go during in-person sessions). For instance, when working with a child with social anxiety, a clinician virtually coached the child and his father to help the child approach a librarian and ask the librarian various questions. When treating an adolescent with a phobia of dogs, a clinician virtually joined the adolescent as they visited a dog park, allowed dogs to approach them, and asked dog owners to pet their dogs.

Virtual treatment can also be useful for having additional people join sessions so that clients can complete exposures with them. Coming together virtually can often be more feasible than in-person, which can ultimately allow the client to gain additional practice. When working with a child with selective mutism, a clinician helped the child practice her "brave talking" (a) with her friend while they had a play date and (b) with her grandparents who lived in China while they joined by videoconferencing. Moreover, when an adolescent with generalized anxiety worried about messing up during an interview, a clinician asked a colleague to join their virtual session, act as a mock interviewer, and give feedback on the interview afterward. In the following section, we present a case of a young child with generalized anxiety disorder to illustrate the delivery of CBT via telehealth.

Background and Case Presentation

Clare is a 9-year-old, White female who presented for treatment at a university-based, specialty clinic in June 2020, due to a long-standing history of anxiety. Her parents described her as being fearful for as long as they could remember, noting that she had previously received mental health services from three other providers. Reportedly, Clare "spent most of her time worried" and experienced "intense spikes of anxiety" several times a week, marked by irritability, significant dysregulation, and at times unsafe behavior (e.g., running into the street). Although Clare's worries spanned a range of topics, they generally centered on concerns about her safety and security as well as the well-being of her family. Specific worries included a burglar breaking into the family's home in a relatively safe, upper middle-class suburb, the house catching on fire while her mother cooked dinner, her parents getting into an accident, getting in trouble from the police for minor infractions (e.g., playing music too loudly in the car), and getting hurt, especially when she was not with her parents. She regularly engaged in reassurance seeking (e.g., asking many questions about things like the schedule for each day and what her parents were cooking for dinner) and was highly rule-oriented, often "policing" the behavior of her younger sister. At the time of the intake, she required a parent to lay with her for upwards of an hour before she fell asleep, and multiples times a week she woke up in the middle of the night and went into her parent's room, falling back asleep on a mattress on their floor. Clare presented with the core belief "the world is an unsafe place," which led to associated thoughts like, "I need to make sure adults are there to protect me," "I need to do my part to protect others," and "Rules must be followed to keep everyone safe." Given the interference associated with these worries as well as their long duration, Clare was diagnosed with generalized anxiety disorder. Although a comorbid diagnosis of separation anxiety disorder was considered, her separation-specific symptoms were conceptualized more parsimoniously as part of a broader generalized anxiety presentation.

Treatment Plan

A cognitive-behavioral treatment plan was developed, with the following goals:

- Increase Clare's ability to fall asleep independently and sleep through the night in her own bedroom.
- Reduce excessive worry about situations including fire alarms, thunderstorms, following rules, and parental well-being.
- Reduce excessive reassurance seeking.
- Engage in age-appropriate activities with greater independence (e.g., riding her bike around the neighborhood with a friend, going to dance class without a parent sitting in the waiting room).
- Increase self-efficacy, particularly with regard to her ability to cope with strong emotions.

Planned interventions, which were all expected to be delivered via telehealth, included psychoeducation about the nature and function of anxiety, cognitive restructuring, in vivo and imaginal exposure, relaxation and distress tolerance skills, parent anxiety management strategies, and sleep training/hygiene interventions. Because of the virtual format of treatment, as well as the addition of several components not included in traditional CBT for anxiety manuals (e.g., distress tolerance skills, sleep interventions), it was projected that Clare's treatment would be delivered over 20–24 sessions.

Execution of the Treatment Plan

Given Clare's age, the nature of her presenting problems, and the telehealth format of treatment, it was decided to front-load parent training sessions. Thus, four parent-only sessions were held at the beginning of the treatment, which focused on providing psychoeducation about anxiety and common parental responses to anxious behavior and teaching skills including increasing empathy, using labeled praise, implementing active ignoring, and setting up a behavior reward chart. These sessions also included a thorough assessment of the family's sleep concerns and Clare's bedtime routine, leading to the establishment of an initial plan for increasing her independence at night.

Despite the virtual nature of treatment, Clare generally was a thoughtful and active participant in therapy sessions. Although she was only 9 years old, she was able to stay engaged and focused for periods of 30–40 min at a time, which provided sufficient time in session to work directly with Clare and to meet regularly with her parents to reinforce their use of new skills, problem-solve, and engage in exposure planning. Initial sessions with Clare focused on rapport-building and anxiety psychoeducation. CBT skills including cognitive restructuring and relaxation training (e.g., diaphragmatic breathing) were then introduced. The screen share feature of the telehealth software was used to present visual aids, handouts, and worksheets, and the annotate feature allowed Clare and the therapist to complete worksheets and forms collaboratively. Because Clare quickly became dysregulated when anxious, additional distress tolerance skills also were incorporated into the beginning stage of treatment. Clare was eager to earn in-session rewards for homework completion and task engagement; these included watching short YouTube videos together and playing online games.

Exposures focused on several domains of anxiety, including (a) Clare's difficulty sleeping alone, (b) Clare's fear of spending time outside of the house without a parent nearby, and (c) Clare's fear of the smoke alarm going off and the house catching on fire. Exposures related to sleep and activities outside of the home were generally planned in session but executed independently by the family. With regard to sleep, Clare was expected to spend more time alone in bed at night before a parent came in to support her, with the goals of increasing her comfort alone in her room, ultimately allowing her to fall asleep on her own. Given her high level of distress, this plan was implemented extremely gradually, as initially Clare was only willing to spend 60 seconds alone. However, within several weeks, Clare was able to increase this to almost 20 min, and within 2 months, she was falling asleep independently about 50% of the time. While Clare was motivated to be able to fall asleep without her parents, as she wanted to have a sleepover with friends, she also often pushed back when her parents tried to increase the time she was spending in her room alone. The incorporation of a reward system through which Clare earned points for staying in bed that she could later "cash in" for a desired prize or privilege helped increase her motivation as did cognitive work around her nighttime fears.

Exposure planning also focused on increasing Clare's engagement in activities outside of the house and without her parents. This included outings with her babysitter at increasingly distant places, riding her bike with friends out of eyesight of her house, and spending more time at friends' houses. As Clare was a naturally social child and her relationships with friends were important to her, she accomplished these challenges fairly easily, quickly climbing up her fear ladder. Although she reported significant anticipatory anxiety before these events, she found that her anxiety generally was low while actually engaging in the activities and their intrinsically rewarding nature further increased her approach behavior.

In-session exposures primarily focused on Clare's fear of the smoke alarm going off, especially while her mother was cooking dinner. In completing lower-level exposures, Clare listened to recordings and watched videos of different smoke alarms going off but reported low distress as she knew they were not in her house. Thus, in vivo exposures quickly switched to incorporate her home's actual smoke alarms. Exposures included listening to the alarm being set off in a planned way, listening to the alarm being set off unexpectedly, and lastly having the alarm go off while her mother was cooking dinner. For these exposures, the telehealth nature of treatment proved particularly helpful.

As treatment ended, Clare's parents reported that she had been consistently falling asleep independently and staying in her own room throughout the night, independently going to friends' houses, and even staying calm when the smoke alarm accidentally went off. Furthermore, Clare had started regularly riding her bike with friends around the neighborhood, started a new extracurricular activity and pushed through going, despite being nervous, and stopped repeatedly checking in when her mother was out in the evening.

Advantages of Providing Treatment via Telehealth

In the case of Clare, treatment via telehealth proved to have many advantages. From a logistical perspective, it enabled both of her parents to participate in parent-only sessions, despite the fact that they were often not in the same location. Had these sessions taken place in person, it is likely that only one parent would have been able to attend, as the other would have needed to be home to provide childcare.

Although some youth may struggle to connect online, rapport was established easily with Clare. She enjoyed getting to complete worksheets electronically and having the chance to type into the fields directly. The novelty of this—as compared to filling out a worksheet with pencil and paper, a task that feels more "school like"—may have facilitated her attention and engagement. Additionally, at the end of each session, all forms were electronically sent to Clare's parents, which increased their accessibility and eliminated the problem of homework and handouts getting lost or forgotten at home between clinic appointments. As Clare's "toolbox" grew, she decorated a poster with reminders of her coping strategies, which she then hung up next to her bed in session.

Telehealth also provided an opportunity for the clinician to coach Clare in using her skills in the environments in which she most often needed them. Specifically, the clinician had Clare lay down in bed and practice skills like diaphragmatic breathing and muscle relaxation, in order to more strongly link the skills with one of the settings in which they could be most useful. The ability of the clinician to guide exposures in Clare's home environment also was an important advantage of telehealth, as it is unlikely that simulating smoke alarm exposures in the clinic environment would have triggered Clare's fear in the same way.

Disadvantages of Telehealth

In this case, the primary disadvantage of telehealth treatment was that it was sometimes difficult for Clare (and her mother, during parent portions of sessions) to find a private place at home to meet. Clare's younger sister periodically interrupted sessions, and at times, her mother sat on the family's basement steps in order to be able to talk out of earshot of her children. Furthermore, clinic-based sessions may have made it easier to conduct additional separation-focused exposures.

Conclusion

Considering the high levels of impairment associated with anxiety disorders, it is timely that telehealth has expanded the options on the "menu" of care for youth and families. Given the many barriers that could prevent affected youth such as Clare from receiving evidence-based care, telehealth offers one transformative method to begin to address gaps in accessibility and service availability. Telehealth, even with its challenges, has the potential to break down some of the logistical barriers to youth receiving evidence-based care. As described in detail in this chapter, by using techniques to tailor and adapt cognitive behavioral strategies to a telehealth format, clinicians can be equipped to deliver treatments to youth with diverse presenting problems right to their homes, so that the treatments are more accessible. By making some creative modifications in the delivery of treatment (such as sharing screens to teach psychoeducation concepts, using a virtual white board to teach youth skills, creating new rapport-building strategies that are suitable for a telehealth format, trouble-shooting technical issues when needed, etc.), clinicians can open up the possibility of more youth and families receiving much needed services. Furthermore, the existing evidence to date indicates that patients appear to be highly satisfied with the telehealth-based format of intervention (Waite et al., 2022). Virtual/telehealth treatments also offer many advantages over in-person sessions. For example, as described in this chapter, telehealth-delivered treatment has been associated with lower no-show rates than in-person treatment, it offers patients the ability to have others join sessions easily and can support in-session community exposures, and it may allow the clinician to observe a child or adolescents' home environment.

As seen in the case of Clare, it is feasible to make adaptations to standard CBT to tailor treatment to a virtual format. Clare was able to successfully meet all of her therapy goals—increasing her ability to fall asleep independently in her own bedroom, decreasing her excessive worry about unpredictable situations such as thunderstorms or fire alarms, and tolerating uncertainty about parental well-being. After her course of treatment, she was able to increase her age-appropriate independence, her feelings of self-efficacy, and her ability to cope with strong emotions. Although telehealth does come with its disadvantages (such as finding a private meeting space without interruptions, dependence on a reliable internet connection), the benefits of having telehealth as an option for therapeutic delivery appear to far outweigh the logistical inconveniences, and clinicians are continually developing new methods/strategies for overcoming any disadvantages.

As we look toward the future, the mental health field has numerous tasks ahead. First, although telehealth approaches to delivering CBT offer a new menu option for delivering care, it has not yet greatly expanded the numbers of families receiving care. Youth from low-income, underserved, and disadvantaged backgrounds continue to have low access to mental health service and may have extensive logistical barriers that make even telehealth-delivered care difficult (Green et al., 2000; Douthit et al., 2015). Thus, increased training of clinicians in delivering child anxiety treatment in a variety of community settings may be needed to "move the needle" on increasing and expanding the "reach" of care. There also may be perceptions that persist that Internet-based treatment is less effective than in-person treatment. Nevertheless, telehealth-delivered CBT is starting to become a more widespread option at community clinics, and those seeking immediate care may be served more quickly by agreeing to be seen "virtually." As we work together with our community partners, we should strive to better understand the barriers that might prevent the uptake of telehealth-based care. Furthermore, it is necessary to conduct future research to better discern reasons for patient and clinician preferences for telehealth or in-person treatment. Currently, there is limited practical guidance for methods to decide whether or not care should be delivered via telehealth or in person and little data on when to use a "hybrid" approach where part of the treatment is delivered via telehealth and part in person. Recent work has offered some clinical considerations for determining the optimal treatment modality for youth with anxiety, based on factors such as clinical severity of the presenting problem, the nature of the exposures that are required, the patient's motivation, co-occurring symptoms, and patient age (Islam et al. (2023). Continued work is still needed to understand which patients might benefit most from which treatment modality. Furthermore, continued work should compare the efficacy of telehealth, in-person, and hybrid approaches or moderators that might impact treatment outcomes. This will help inform clinical recommendations that treatment providers make when treating youth with anxiety. Ultimately, the goal is to harness telehealth and other types of technology to increase the numbers of youth who receive care and to help youth return to healthy everyday functioning.

References

Ale, C. M., McCarthy, D. M., Rothschild, L. M., & Whiteside, S. P. (2015). Components of cognitive behavioral therapy related to outcome in childhood anxiety disorders. *Clinical Child and Family Psychology Review, 18*, 240–251.

Anxiety Canada. (2019a, March 25). Fight flight freeze—A guide to anxiety for kids [Video]. *YouTube*. https://www.youtube.com/watch?v=1VQUOr-R3eA.

Anxiety Canada. (2019b, March 25). Fight flight freeze—Anxiety explained for teens [Video]. *YouTube*. https://www.youtube.com/watch?v=rpolpKTWrp4

Barrett, P. M., Duffy, A. L., Dadds, M. R., & Rapee, R. M. (2001). Cognitive-behavioral treatment of anxiety disorders in children: Long-term (6-year) follow-up. *Journal of Consulting and Clinical Psychology, 69*(1), 135–141.

Batastini, A. B., Paprzycki, P., Jones, A. C. T., & MacLean, N. (2020). Are videoconferenced mental and behavioral health services just as good as in-person? A meta-analysis of a fast-growing practice. *Clinical Psychology Review, 83*, 101944. https://doi.org/10.1016/j.cpr.2020.101944

Beidas, R. S., Benjamin, C. L., Puleo, C. M., Edmunds, J. M., & Kendall, P. C. (2010). Flexible applications of the coping cat program for anxious youth. *Cognitive and Behavioral Practice, 17*(2), 142–153. https://doi.org/10.1016/j.cbpra.2009.11.002

Booth, M. L., Bernard, D., Quine, S., Kang, M. S., Usherwood, T., Alperstein, G., & Bennett, D. L. (2004). Access to health care among Australian adolescents young people's perspectives and their sociodemographic distribution. *Journal of Adolescent Health*. https://doi.org/10.1016/S1054-139X(03)00304-5

Burke, K. C., Burke, J. D., Jr., Regier, D. A., & Rae, D. S. (1990). Age at onset of selected mental disorders in five community populations. *Archives of General Psychiatry, 47*(6), 511–518. https://doi.org/10.1001/archpsyc.1990.01810180011002

Carpenter, A. L., Pincus, D. B., Furr, J. M., & Comer, J. S. (2018). Working from home: An initial pilot examination of videoconferencing-based cognitive behavioral therapy for anxious youth delivered to the home setting. *Behavior Therapy, 49*(6), 917–930. https://doi.org/10.1016/j.beth.2018.01.007

Comer, J. S., Furr, J. M., Miguel, E. M., Cooper-Vince, C. E., Carpenter, A. L., Elkins, R. M., Kerns, C. E., Cornacchio, D., Chou, T., Coxe, S., DeSerisy, M., Sanchez, A. L., Golik, A., Martin, J., Myers, K. M., & Chase, R. (2017a). Remotely delivering real-time parent training to the home: An initial randomized trial of internet-delivered parent–child interaction therapy (I-PCIT). *Journal of Consulting and Clinical Psychology, 85*(9), 909–917. https://doi.org/10.1037/ccp0000230

Comer, J. S., Furr, J. M., Kerns, C. E., Miguel, E., Coxe, S., Meredith Elkins, R., et al. (2017b). Internet-delivered, family-based treatment for early-onset OCD: A pilot randomized trial. *Journal of Consulting and Clinical Psychology, 85*(2). https://doi.org/10.1037/ccp0000155

Comer, J. S., Furr, J. M., del Busto, C., Silva, K., Hong, N., Poznanski, B., Sanchez, A., Cornacchio, D., Herrera, A., Coxe, S., Miguel, E., Georgiadis, C., Conroy, K., & Puliafico, A. (2021). Therapist-led, internet-delivered treatment for early child social anxiety: A waitlist-controlled evaluation of the iCALM telehealth program. *Behavior Therapy, 52*(5). https://doi.org/10.1016/j.beth.2021.01.004

Costello, E. J., Mustillo, S., Erkanli, A., Keeler, G., & Angold, A. (2003). Prevalence and development of psychiatric disorders in childhood and adolescence. *Archives of General Psychiatry*. https://doi.org/10.1001/archpsyc.60.8.837

Douthit, N., Kiv, S., Dwolatzky, T., & Biswas, S. (2015). Exposing some important barriers to health care access in the rural USA. *Public Health, 129*(6), 611–620. https://doi.org/10.1016/j.puhe.2015.04.001

Eiseman, J. (2020, March 27). *9 ways to create a private space for tele-therapy*. Mental Health Match. Retrieved July 11, 2023, fromhttps://mentalhealthmatch.com/articles/coronavirus/private-space-teletherapy

Essau, C. A. (2003). Comorbidity of anxiety disorders in adolescents. *Depression and Anxiety*. https://doi.org/10.1002/da.10107

Fernandez, E., Woldgabreal, Y., Day, A., Pham, T., Gleich, B., & Aboujaoude, E. (2021). Live psychotherapy by video versus in-person: A meta-analysis of efficacy and its relationship to types and targets of treatment. *Clinical Psychology & Psychotherapy, 28*(6). https://doi.org/10.1002/cpp.2594

Funderburk, B. W., & Eyberg, S. (2011). Parent–child interaction therapy. In J. C. Norcross, G. R. Vanden Bos, & D. K. Freedheim (Eds.), *History of psychotherapy: Continuity and change* (pp. 415–420). American Psychological Association.

Gittins Stone, D. I., Elkins, R. M., Gardner, M., Boger, K., & Sperling, J. (2023). Examining the effectiveness of an intensive Telemental health treatment for pediatric anxiety and OCD during the COVID-19 pandemic and pediatric mental health crisis. *Child Psychiatry & Human Development, 29*(2). https://doi.org/10.1007/s10578-023-01500-5

Green, J. G., McLaughlin, K. A., Fillbrunn, M., Fukuda, M., Jackson, J. S., Kessler, R. C., Sadikova, E., Sampson, N. A., Vilsaint, C., Williams, D. R., Cruz-Gonzalez, M., & Alegría, M. (2000). Barriers to mental health service use and predictors of treatment drop out: Racial/

ethnic variation in a population-based study. *Administration and Policy in Mental Health, 47*(4), 606–616. https://doi.org/10.1007/s10488-020-01021-6

Grills-Taquechel, A. E., & Ollendick, T. H. (2013). *Phobic and anxiety disorders in children and adolescents*. Hogrefe Publishing.

Howard, B., Chu, B. C., Krain, A. L., Marrs-Garcia, A. L., & Kendall, P. C. (2000). *Cognitive behavioral family therapy for anxious children: Therapist manual* (2nd ed.). Workbook Publishing.

Islam, S., Sanchez, A. L., McDermott, C. L., Clapp, D., Worley, J., & Becker-Haimes, E. M. (2023). To proceed via telehealth or not? Considerations for pediatric anxiety and related disorders beyond COVID-19. *Cognitive and Behavioral Practice*. https://doi.org/10.1016/j.cbpra.2023.01.004

Keller, M. B., Lavori, P. W., Wunder, J., Beardslee, W. R., Schwartz, C. E., & Roth, J. (1992). Chronic course of anxiety disorders in children and adolescents. *Journal of the American Academy of Child and Adolescent Psychiatry*. https://doi.org/10.1097/00004583-199207000-00003

Kendall, P. C. (1994). Treating anxiety disorders in children: Results of a randomized clinical trial. *Journal of Consulting and Clinical Psychology, 62*(1), 100–110.

Kendall, P. C., & Hedtke, K. A. (2006). *Cognitive-behavioral therapy for anxious children: Therapist manual*. Workbook Publishing.

Kendall, P. C., Flannery-Schroeder, E., Panichelli-Mindel, S. M., Southam-Gerow, M., Henin, A., & Warman, M. (1997). Therapy for youths with anxiety disorders: A second randomized clinical trial. *Journal of Consulting and Clinical Psychology, 65*(3), 366–380.

Kendall, P. C., Safford, S., Flannery-Schroeder, E., & Webb, A. (2004). Child anxiety treatment: Outcomes in adolescence and impact on substance use and depression at 7.4-year follow-up. *Journal of Consulting and Clinical Psychology, 72*(2), 276–287.

Kendall, P. C., Robin, J. A., Hedtke, K. A., Suveg, C., Flannery-Schroeder, E., & Gosch, E. (2005). Considering CBT with anxious youth? Think exposures. *Cognitive and Behavioral Practice, 12*(1), 136–150.

Lack, C. W. (2012). Obsessive-compulsive disorder: Evidence-based treatments and future directions for research. *World Journal of Psychiatry, 2*(6), 86. https://doi.org/10.5498/wjp.v2.i6.86

Lebowitz, E. R., Marin, C., Martino, A., Shimshoni, Y., & Silverman, W. K. (2020). Parent-based treatment as efficacious as cognitive-behavioral therapy for childhood anxiety: A randomized noninferiority study of supportive parenting for anxious childhood emotions. *Journal of the American Academy of Child & Adolescent Psychiatry, 59*(3), 362–372. https://doi.org/10.1016/j.jaac.2019.02.014

Lowenstein, L. (n.d.). *Creative interventions for online therapy with children: Techniques to build rapport*. Liana Lowenstein, MSW, RSW, CPT-S. http://www.lianalowenstein.com/artcileProfTeleplayLowenstein.pdf

Merikangas, K. R., He, J.-P., Burstein, M., Swanson, S. A., Avenevoli, S., Cui, L., et al. (2010). Lifetime prevalence of mental disorders in U.S. adolescents: results from the National Comorbidity Survey Replication—Adolescent Supplement (NCS-A). *Journal of the American Academy of Child and Adolescent Psychiatry, 49*(10), 980–989. https://doi.org/10.1016/j.jaac.2010.05.017

Merikangas, K. R., He, J. P., Burstein, M., Swendsen, J., Avenevoli, S., Case, B., et al. (2011). Service utilization for lifetime mental disorders in U.S. adolescents: Results of the national comorbidity survey adolescent supplement (NCS-A). *Journal of the American Academy of Child and Adolescent Psychiatry*. https://doi.org/10.1016/j.jaac.2010.10.006

Moore, A. & Gammi, J. (2018). Revealed: Hundreds of children wait more than a year for specialist help. Health Service Journal. (https://www.hsj.co.uk/quality-and-performance/revealed-hundreds-of-children-wait-more-than-a-year-for-specialist-help/7023232.article)

Pew research Center. (2021). *Internet/broadband fact sheet*. Pew Research Center: Internet, Science & Tech. https://www.pewresearch.org/internet/fact-sheet/internet-broadband

Rapee, R. M. (2000). Group treatment of children with anxiety disorders: Outcome and predictors of treatment response. *Australian Journal of Psychology, 52*(3), 125–130. https://doi.org/10.1080/00049530008255379

Salloum, A., Johnco, C., Lewin, A. B., McBride, N. M., & Storch, E. A. (2016). Barriers to access and participation in community mental health treatment for anxious children. *Journal of Affective Disorders*. https://doi.org/10.1016/j.jad.2016.02.026

Sasangohar, F., Bradshaw, M. R., Carlson, M. M., Flack, J. N., Fowler, J. C., Freeland, D., et al. (2020). Adapting an outpatient psychiatric clinic to telehealth during the COVID-19 pandemic: A practice perspective. *Journal of Medical Internet Research*. https://doi.org/10.2196/22523

Shore, J. H., Yellowlees, P., Caudill, R., Johnston, B., Turvey, C., Mishkind, M., Krupinski, E., Myers, K., Shore, P., Kaftarian, E., & Hilty, D. (2018). Best practices in videoconferencing-based Telemental health April 2018. *Telemedicine and e-Health, 24*(11), 827–832. https://doi.org/10.1089/tmj.2018.0237

Storch, E. A., Caporino, N. E., Morgan, J. R., Lewin, A. B., Rojas, A., Brauer, L., Larson, M. J., & Murphy, T. K. (2011). Preliminary investigation of web-camera delivered cognitive-behavioral therapy for youth with obsessive-compulsive disorder. *Psychiatry Research, 189*(3), 407–412. https://doi.org/10.1016/j.psychres.2011.05.047

Waite, M. R., Diab, S., & Adefisoye, J. (2022). Virtual behavioral health treatment satisfaction and outcomes across time. *Journal of Patient-Centered Research and Reviews., 9*(3), 158–165. https://doi.org/10.17294/2330-0698.1918

Walkup, J. T., Albano, A. M., Piacentini, J., Birmaher, B., Compton, S. N., Sherrill, J. T., et al. (2008). Cognitive behavioral therapy, sertraline, or a combination in childhood anxiety. *The New England Journal of Medicine, 359*(26), 2753–2766. https://doi.org/10.1056/NEJMoa0804633

Whiteside, S. P., Sim, L. A., Morrow, A. S., Farah, W. H., Hilliker, D. R., Murad, M. H., & Wang, Z. (2019). A meta-analysis to guide the enhancement of CBT for childhood anxiety: Exposure over anxiety management. *Clinical Child and Family Psychology Review, 23*(1), 102–121. https://doi.org/10.1007/s10567-019-00303-2

Wood, J. J., Piacentini, J. C., Southam-Gerow, M., Chu, B. C., & Sigman, M. (2006). Family cognitive behavioral therapy for child anxiety disorders. *Journal of the American Academy of Child and Adolescent Psychiatry, 45*(3), 314–321. https://doi.org/10.1097/01.chi.0000196425.88341.b0

Wood, J. J., McLeod, B. D., Piacentini, J. C., & Sigman, M. (2009). One-year follow-up of family versus child CBT for anxiety disorders: Exploring the roles of child age and parental intrusiveness. *Child Psychiatry and Human Development, 40*(2), 301–316. https://doi.org/10.1007/s10578-009-0127-z

Chapter 4
Telehealth Delivery of Trauma-Focused Cognitive-Behavioral Therapy

Regan Stewart, Rosaura Orengo-Aguayo, and Caroline Shanholtz

Each year, approximately one billion youth worldwide will experience a traumatic event (e.g., physical, emotional, or sexual abuse, neglect, community or family violence, traumatic loss, disaster; Hillis et al., 2016). Exposure to traumatic events increases the risk of developing posttraumatic stress disorder (PTSD), depression, behavior problems, substance use disorders, and suicidal ideation/self-harm (Fairbank & Fairbank, 2009; Lai et al., 2017). Trauma exposure is also associated with poor academic and occupational achievement and adverse physical health outcomes that can last a lifetime (Carliner et al., 2016; Holt et al., 2007; McLaughlin et al., 2012; Ormel et al., 2008). The COVID-19 pandemic further increased the risk of trauma exposure for already vulnerable youth and families (Khan et al., 2020; Xiong et al., 2020).

Despite high rates of trauma exposure and subsequent mental health outcomes, many children in need of mental health care still do not receive it, receive an inadequate "dose" of sessions, or do not receive evidence-based care (Comer & Barlow, 2014; Merikangas et al., 2009; Whitney & Peterson, 2019). Even greater disparities in access to care are seen across geographies (e.g., rural locations) and among marginalized racially and ethnically diverse youth and those whose primary language is not English (Alegria Vallas & Pumariega, 2010; Merikangas et al., 2011; Rodgers et al., 2022). Specific barriers to accessing and engaging in evidence-based trauma-focused treatment include logistical factors (e.g., lack of transportation, scheduled work hours and leave restrictions, limited availability of services in rural and

R. Stewart (✉) · R. Orengo-Aguayo
Department of Psychiatry and Behavioral Sciences, Medical University of South Carolina, Charleston, SC, USA
e-mail: stewartr@musc.edu

C. Shanholtz
Department of Psychology, University of California, Los Angeles, CA, USA

L. N. Niec, C. E. Schoonover (eds.), *Telemental Health Care for Children and Families*,
https://doi.org/10.1007/978-3-031-69264-2_4

underserved urban areas) and engagement factors (e.g., stigma about mental health treatment; National Research Council and Institute of Medicine, 2009).

Telehealth (also referred to as telemental health, telemedicine, and telepsychology) offers an innovative way to address significant gaps in access to care and is being used to deliver a variety of treatments for children and adolescents (Centers for Medicare and Medicaid, 2019; Comer et al., 2017; McCarty et al., 2014). Telehealth can reduce barriers in access to care for populations that need mental health treatment but may not typically receive it due to lack of available providers or costs associated with traveling long distances for appointments (Comer & Barlow, 2014). For example, telehealth reduces travel time and thus can decrease interference with caregiver work schedules and missed school time for children. In addition to the distance and time barriers, children and families also report that they utilize telehealth to decrease costs associated with traveling long distances for care and to decrease stigma by connecting to child-friendly locations such as schools and primary care centers (Gloff LeNoue et al., 2015). Current research provides support that mental health services delivered via telehealth are effective in addressing a number of mental health disorders in children and adolescents, including posttraumatic stress disorder (PTSD; Gloff LeNoue et al., 2015; Myers & Comer, 2016; Myers et al., 2017; Stewart et al., 2020b).

Trauma-focused cognitive-behavioral therapy (TF-CBT; Cohen et al., 2017) is an evidence-based, manualized treatment protocol designed to treat posttraumatic stress and co-occurring symptoms such as depression and anxiety in trauma-exposed children and youth ages 3–18 and their supportive and non-offending caregivers. TF-CBT is divided into nine cognitive and behavioral components, all of which incorporate gradual exposure to trauma memories and reminders. These components are summarized by the acronym PRACTICE: (1) psychoeducation, (2) parenting skills, (3) relaxation skills, (4) affective modulation skills, (5) cognitive processing skills, (6) trauma narration and processing, (7) in vivo mastery of trauma reminders, (8) conjoint child-parent sessions, and (9) enhancing future safety and development. TF-CBT is typically delivered in 12–25 weekly sessions (via a combination of individual, caregiver and conjoint sessions) (see Table 4.1 for further description of TF-CBT components).

TF-CBT is traditionally delivered by professionals with at least a master's degree in a mental health-related field (i.e., psychology, social work) who have an active professional license (https://tfcbt.org/certification). However, it is rare that clinicians learn the necessary skills to deliver TF-CBT during their graduate education, so additional training is needed to deliver TF-CBT with fidelity. First, clinicians should receive training in the developmental, biological, and psychological impact of trauma. Additionally, clinicians should be well versed in common reactions to trauma and the symptoms associated with PTSD. Next, clinicians need training on TF-CBT specifically. There are several opportunities to receive this training. First, there is an online course in English (https://tfcbt2.musc.edu/) and Spanish (https://tfcbt-es.musc.edu) in which clinicians can learn about each component of TF-CBT and how to deliver it with video examples. This online course is considered an introduction to TF-CBT, and it is recommended that clinicians follow this introductory

Table 4.1 Overview of trauma-focused cognitive-behavioral therapy (TF-CBT)

TF-CBT treatment phase	TF-CBT component	Component description
Stabilization phase	Psychoeducation	Provide information on the traumatic event, traumatic stress symptoms, and treatment
	Parenting skills	Help the parent address any behavioral concerns with effective techniques and improve caregiver-child relationship quality
	Relaxation	Teach skills to reduce the physiological impact of stress and trauma
	Affect identification and modulation	Help youth identify, express, and regulate their emotions
	Cognitive coping	Help youth identify their thoughts, recognize the relationship between thoughts and feelings, and begin to understand how to challenge irrational or unhelpful thoughts
Trauma narration phase	Trauma narrative and processing	Exposure to desensitize the traumatic event, identify and correct unhelpful or inaccurate beliefs, and learn how to share difficult experiences with their caregiver
Integration/ consolidation phase	In vivo exposures	Reduce fear and avoidance of trauma-related reminders
	Conjoint sessions	Improve caregiver-child communication, allow the caregiver to apologize of correct any inaccuracies, and set a precedence for the child to communicate future victimization
	Enhancing safety	Make a plan to prevent future revictimization and create a safety plan if symptoms return

[a]The stabilization phase components can be done in any order but must come before the trauma narration phase. Additionally, the parenting skills and enhancing safety components may be done at any point and throughout therapy to reduce the likelihood of revictimization. Finally, mastery of the stabilization phase components is not necessary to move to subsequent components

training with a live 2-day TF-CBT training. Subsequently, clinicians can become certified and rostered TF-CBT therapists (https://tfcbt.org).

Over 23 randomized controlled trials across the United States and the globe have documented TF-CBT's effectiveness at treating posttraumatic stress symptoms (PTSS) in children and adolescents (Cohen et al., 2017, pp. 74–80; de Arellano et al., 2012). These studies include youth in low- and middle-income countries like Zambia (Murray et al., 2013), the Democratic Republic of the Congo (McMullen et al., 2013; O'Callaghan et al., 2013), and Kenya and Tanzania (Dorsey et al., 2020). In the United States, TF-CBT applications have also been developed for Hispanic youth (de Arellano et al., 2012) and American Indians and Alaska Natives (BigFoot & Schmidt, 2010). In Central America, TF-CBT was culturally and linguistically tailored by Stewart et al. (2020, b) and shown to be effective at reducing posttraumatic stress, depression, and anxiety symptoms with a community-based sample of trauma-exposed youth and supportive caregivers in El Salvador (Stewart, Orengo-Aguayo, Villalobos, et al., 2020). In the Caribbean, TF-CBT was shown to be effective at reducing PTSD, depression, and anxiety symptoms in disaster-exposed youth in Puerto Rico who received treatment in person and transitioned to telehealth delivery due to the COVID-19 pandemic (Orengo-Aguayo et al., 2022). TF-CBT has also been shown to be feasible and effective when delivered via telehealth with Caucasian, African American, and Hispanic trauma-exposed youth via published case studies (Stewart et al., 2017; Stewart et al., 2021; Stewart, Orengo-Aguayo, Young, et al., 2020).

Telehealth Considerations

Telehealth Outreach Model

When delivering TF-CBT via telehealth, it is important to consider an implementation model that incorporates an evidence-based treatment model along with engagement strategies. One such model is the Telehealth Outreach Program Model (TOP Model), which was developed by Regan Stewart at the Medical University of South Carolina (MUSC) and is based partly on an outreach model developed by De Arellano and collogues (2005). Dr. Stewart uses this Telehealth Outreach Program Model in her Telehealth Outreach Program for Traumatic Stress (TOP-TS). TOP-TS at MUSC is where the original research on delivering evidence-based trauma treatment via telehealth to children and families was conducted. The model has a three-pronged approach to treatment: (1) telehealth delivery of services, (2) evidence-based treatment, and (3) evidence-based engagement strategies and intensive case management. The three-pronged approach is important because it includes not only telehealth delivery of evidence-based treatment but also utilizing additional engagement strategies, such as using reminder phone calls and text messages, directly addressing caregiver concerns and barriers at the time of the initial appointment and throughout treatment, and addressing beliefs and attitudes related to mental health treatment. Further, the model also addresses additional child and family needs through case management to connect the family with needed resources such as food, clothing, and rent assistance to improve stability. The model also utilizes engagement strategies within the telehealth therapy sessions to engage the child via the telehealth delivery format. Similar to in-person therapy, telehealth sessions should be interactive and engaging in order to build rapport and keep the child actively engaged in the therapy sessions. Telehealth allows the clinician to use online interactive tools and electronic therapy resources, as well as traditional psychotherapy tools such as feelings cards and books. For example, there are several interactive games using Microsoft PowerPoint that clinicians can use during treatment to deliver psychoeducation and teach therapy skills. These resources are freely available for download in both English and Spanish at www.telehealthfortrauma.com.

Telehealth Best Practices

When delivering TF-CBT via telehealth, it is also important for clinicians to follow the best practices for telehealth work. Many clinicians may not have had previous training in conducting telehealth therapy, and thus seeking out specific training for this modality will be important. There have been several recommendations to conduct effective telehealth services for youth, including recommendations from several professional organizations such as the American Psychiatric Association, American Telemedicine Association (Myers et al., 2017; Shore et al., 2018), and the American Psychological Association (American Psychological Association, 2013). Several articles and book chapters have also been written related to specific competencies and strategies to deliver trauma-focused treatment via telehealth for youth (e.g., Dueweke et al., 2020; Herting et al., 2023; Ros-Demarize et al., 2022). Recommendations for telehealth best practices include things such as explaining telehealth equipment and platforms to clients during the first session (Dueweke et al., 2020). Clinicians should orient clients to telehealth services and model proper use of the telehealth equipment. Next, clinicians should identify a private space with reliable Internet connection and establish safety protocols with the youth and family (Dueweke et al., 2020). Clinicians should work collaboratively with the family to find a private place to conduct sessions. Additionally, within the first session, a safety plan should be established for any safety issues that may arise (Dueweke et al., 2020). Clinicians should talk with the youth and caregiver about the limits of confidentiality and the plan if the youth is in danger and explain to the caregiver that they need to be home during sessions with access to the phone in case the video call gets disconnected, and the clinician needs to get in touch with the caregiver. Subsequently, there are a variety of best practice recommendations for engaging youth via telehealth (Dueweke et al., 2020; Ros-Demarize et al., 2022). Clinicians should use interactive activities via the telehealth platform. This can mean sharing your screen, playing games on the computer, or using interactive tools to build rapport and deliver coping skills. Clinicians can adapt typical in-person worksheets to be delivered online via Microsoft Word or PowerPoint. Further information on the best practices and practical applications via telehealth can be found at https://tfcbt.org/telehealth-resources/, in Table 4.2, and described in the case study below.

Ethical and Legal Issues to Consider

Some clinicians may be wary about conducting trauma treatment via telehealth. They often express concerns over building adequate rapport with youth via telehealth (Rees & Stone, 2005) and fear of not being able to adequately address safety concerns for youth and families (Capner., 2000; Mielonen et al., 2000). Fortunately, many of these concerns can be adequately addressed via telehealth. There are several legal and ethical considerations that clinicians should be aware of. First, it is

Table 4.2 Practical applications for implementing TF-CBT via telehealth

Environment	TF-CBT should be conducted in an environment where the child and parent can speak to the clinician privately, without being disturbed. Clinicians should work collaboratively with the parent to find a private place in the home with good internet connection for the youth to conduct therapy. Helpful tips include: Help the family choose a quiet spot. This may include asking other family members to go to other areas of the home during session or keeping pets in a different room. Ensure there is adequate lighting so that you can see the youth's face and they can see yours. You may need to ask them to bring a lamp in. The environment should not be too distracting. If the youth is in a room with a lot of their toys and they cannot focus on therapy, you may need to find a different location. Ask the family to limit distractions by turning off the television or radio. The clinician should assess if there is an outlet and if the youth have access to a charging cable in case of low battery on their equipment. Youth should be sitting at a desk or table. They should not be laying down in bed. Consider asking the family to purchase a small white noise machine to increase privacy.
Equipment	The clinician should assess if the family has appropriate telehealth equipment prior to scheduling the first appointment. This can be something as simple as a smartphone or as complex as a desktop set up with webcam, speakers, and headphones with a microphone. One of the most important pieces of equipment to assess for is reliable internet. This can include helping the client position the camera angle so that you can see at least their full face. You should teach the youth and parent how to mute and unmute themselves, how to join the meeting, how to turn their camera on and off, and how to troubleshoot any internet issues. Orienting the client to telehealth services can reduce barriers to accessing telehealth services and prevent wasted time adjusting equipment set up in the future
Safety planning	The clinician should work collaboratively with the family to establish a plan should any safety concerns arise. The clinician should explain to the caregivers that they should be at the location the therapy is taking place all sessions. At the start of each session, the clinician should obtain the physical address of the client and at least two phone numbers of people in the home in case of emergency or the video call gets disconnected
Engagement	The clinician should use interactive activities to keep youth engaged. Additionally, taking frequent screen breaks can help the youth remain focused. The clinician can also use their environment by having the youth show them their room or favorite toy

important to obtain informed consent to ensure that the child and family understand the treatment they are about to receive (Joint Task Force for the Development of Telepsychology Guidelines for Psychologists, 2013). Informed consent should review the service being provided via telehealth, the limits of confidentiality and local regulations specific to telehealth, risks associated with telehealth (e.g., loss of connection/sound/video), and the plan for addressing technology issues. Local laws, regulations, medical insurance guidelines, and licensing board requirements should be consulted when developing this informed consent document (Joint Task Force for the Development of Telepsychology Guidelines for Psychologists, 2013).

Privacy and confidentiality are paramount regardless of the modality through which mental health services are delivered. Both clinicians and clients may have additional concerns about confidentiality during telehealth sessions because there is less control over the environment. However, there are various strategies that can be implemented to increase confidentiality of the session. To maximize privacy and confidentiality, clinicians should help the child and caregiver identify a private and safe space where the therapy session can be conducted (Dueweke et al., 2020; Joint Task Force for the Development of Telepsychology Guidelines for Psychologists, 2013). Also, clinicians should use videoconferencing software that complies with the Health Insurance Portability and Accountability Act (HIPAA). Before beginning telehealth sessions, explain the importance of not being in a public place during session. If necessary, problem-solve how to create a private space in the home: perhaps the client uses headphones and microphone to limit background noise and ensure privacy when communicating. Also, discuss with the youth and caregiver the limits to confidentiality and mandated reporting requirements.

Additionally, some adolescents may experience thoughts of self-harm or suicidal ideation. To manage emergencies or crises via telehealth, the best practices suggest that clinicians develop a telehealth emergency protocol for each client that outlines the expectations of the client's caregiver during a telehealth session, gathers emergency contact information, and informs the caregiver of the clinician's response to emergency situations. When providing mental health services over telehealth to minors, it is recommended that a designated adult is present in the home during the entire duration of the sessions. It is recommended to verify that an adult is present at the beginning of each session and verify the location of the client and then record the address and location within the home where the client is located. The beginning of session safety check helps ensure the clinician is prepared in case of an emergency. In the event emergency services need to be called, the clinician has all the information needed to provide to emergency responders.

Finally, it is important to know state and federal regulations for providing telehealth services. Different states have different professional licensing requirements for services provided via telehealth. Additionally, providers need to be aware of their state's requirements for provider and client location. For example, one state may require that the provider is licensed in the state just where the provider is located, just in the state where the client is located, or in both the state where the provider is located and where the client is located. Additionally, some insurance companies do not fully fund telehealth services. Understanding the laws and regulations by both states and insurance companies is essential in providing the best care.

Case Study

Delivering TF-CBT via Telehealth with an Adolescent: A Case Example

The following case example will describe the delivery of TF-CBT via telehealth with an adolescent by detailing the overarching goals/objectives of each component of the therapeutic model (in this case, TF-CBT) and describing the delivery of this therapy via telehealth (please refer to Table 4.1 for more information about the treatment components of this modality for more information).

Background Information of the Client

Sandra (pseudonym) was a 15-year-old, Hispanic female living with her mother and biological older sister in the southern, rural United States. Sandra and her family's primary language was English. Sandra was referred to treatment by her guidance counselor at school due to experiencing sexual abuse by her maternal uncle over a period of 2 years, from the ages of 12–14. Sandra also had a history of traumatic loss from her grandparents dying in a tornado. Sandra and her mother lived with her grandparents around the time of the tornado; however, Sandra was not in the home at the time of the tornado. She learned of her grandparents' death several hours after the tornado. Her grandparents' death occurred when Sandra was 15 years old and 8 months prior to beginning treatment. After the sexual abuse, Sandra had difficulty concentrating in school, trouble sleeping, and nightmares and developed negative thoughts about herself (i.e., "I deserved what happened") and others (i.e., "I cannot trust anyone") which strained her relationships with her friends. Prior to the sexual abuse, Sandra received passing grades in all of her classes, but after the abuse, she began failing several classes. Sandra lived in an area with limited access to mental health providers and would have to travel over an hour to see a mental health provider in a clinic. Using telehealth services reduced these barriers to treatment for Sandra. Further, Sandra and her family had access to Internet and a laptop computer at home, so Sandra was able to connect with the clinician in a relatively private location. Sandra's family qualified for free mental health services through our community outreach program for grant-funded services. Sandra completed 18 therapy sessions via telehealth, each lasting approximately 50 min. Sandra received home-based telehealth services by a masters-level mental health clinician. Sandra was located at her home, and the clinician was located at an academic medical center approximately 2 h away from Sandra's home.

Intake Assessment: Session 1

Goals/Objectives The purpose of the intake assessment in TF-CBT is to gather the key diagnostic, cultural, and historic background of the client. This is also the time when informed consent is obtained, and clinicians can begin to instill hope and build rapport with the client. Prior to the intake session, the clinician should conduct a virtual test call with the family to explain equipment use, troubleshoot any technology issues, help the family find a location conducive to participating in therapy, and discuss the safety protocol.

Delivery via Telehealth The intake assessment interview was conducted via a secure telehealth platform. The link to access the telehealth session was sent to the caregiver who connected via laptop. Clinician gave an overview of the purpose of the intake to both the client and caregiver and explained confidentiality and the limits of confidentiality. The clinician then asked to interview each individually. First, the client stepped out of the room so the clinician could interview her mother. Clinician asked the mother if she thought the client could still overhear them and the mother said "no." Once the mother's interview was completed, the clinician asked the mother to step out of the room and have the client complete her interview alone. The clinician asked the mother to go to a part of the house where she could not overhear the client to permit her privacy.

Sandra completed an intake assessment in which she was asked questions about her psychosocial history, family history, physical health and mental health history, and current symptomatology. Sandra completed two empirically validated measures to assess her trauma symptoms and co-occurring mental health symptoms, including the Child PTSD Symptom Scale for DSM-5 and the Revised Children's Anxiety and Depression Scale. The assessment measures were administered by using the screen-sharing function in the videoconference platform. The clinician opened a PDF version of the instrument on the clinician's computer and then shared the screen so that Sandra could see the measure with the questions. The clinician verbally read aloud each question-and-answer choice; Sandra selected her answer choice, and the clinician recorded each answer on a paper copy of the measure. Assessment measures can also be administered via a secure online survey link or by emailing the measures to clients to complete and return via secure email. Sandra's mother completed a similar intake assessment about Sandra and completed parent versions of the instruments using the same procedure. Sandra's scores on the measures indicated clinically significant PTSD symptoms. Specifically, Sandra endorsed intrusive distressing memories of the trauma, psychological distress, and physiological reactions to trauma cues, avoidance of trauma reminders, self-blame for the trauma, diminished interest in significant activities, hypervigilance, and exaggerated startle response. Sandra and her mother were both motivated for treatment. The mother expressed readiness to participate in treatment with Sandra and stated that she was prepared to support Sandra in any way that she could during treatment.

Psychoeducation: Session 2

Goals/Objectives In TF-CBT, after an initial assessment, the therapist provides the first component of treatment, psychoeducation. The goal of the psychoeducation module is to teach caregivers and youth about common reactions that people experience after a traumatic event and to introduce the purpose of treatment.

Delivery Via Telehealth The clinician helped Sandra set up her web camera to the best angle. Sandra used headphones with a microphone so she could appropriately hear the clinician and the clinician could hear the client well. As this was the first session after the intake, the clinician began the session by reviewing the results of the intake and setting Sandra's expectations for therapy (i.e., that Sandra would meet with the clinician once per week online, timeline for completion, etc.). Next, the clinician discussed psychoeducation related to Sandra's trauma, including common reactions to traumatic events, PTSD and common symptoms, and safety (i.e., validation of Sandra's safety concerns and providing enhanced safety-seeking skills). All of this information was presented via graphics and games shared via the screen-sharing function. Specifically, the clinician utilized a Jeopardy-style (trivia) PowerPoint game and informational worksheets. The clinician also read a trauma-specific children's book with Sandra. The clinician utilized an electronic version of the book (via Kindle App on the clinician's computer; other electronic versions of books could also be used). The clinician shared the screen with Sandra, scrolling through the book page by page as the clinician read the book to Sandra. The clinician then brought Sandra's mother into the session to review the intake results with her and to provide psychoeducation related to Sandra's traumas. The clinician also explained to both Sandra and her mother what Sandra's mother's role in therapy would be and the best ways to support Sandra while in therapy. Sandra's mother was also given the opportunity to ask questions, and clinician corrected any misconceptions regarding Sandra's trauma. Throughout the psychoeducation section, the clinician continuously checked for understanding through asking Sandra and her mother to summarize what was said and answer questions about the material provided. The clinician paid particular attention to body language and facial expressions during psychoeducation and throughout all sessions. When working with children via telehealth, it can be particularly important to pay close attention to body language and facial expressions to ensure that these things are noticed through the camera. It may also be helpful for clinicians to be more animated via telehealth than they may be in person to ensure that their emotion is relayed via telehealth.

Parenting Skills: Session 3

Goals/Objectives The ultimate goal of the parenting skills component is to help caregivers address any behavioral concerns with effective behavioral management techniques and improve the caregiver-child relationship quality.

Delivery via Telehealth During the technology equipment assessment when scheduling the appointment, the clinician learned that Sandra's mother did not have access to a printer. Typically, session resources would be emailed to a family for them to print out for use during telehealth sessions. Since the family did not have access to a printer, the clinician mailed the worksheets and tools that would be used in session to the mother after the psychoeducation session.

Given that Sandra was a 15-year-old, parenting skills were targeted for adolescents and tailored to specific issues that Sandra's mother reported she was experiencing with Sandra. Specifically, the mother reported that Sandra was not completing her chores. The clinician taught the mother how to use a reward chart, which was mailed to her, and discussed with Sandra what would be a motivating reward for her to complete her chores. The clinician spoke with Sandra and her mother at the same time to choose the rewards. The clinician asked the pair to position the web camera so that the clinician could see them both and they could both see the clinician. The clinician explained to the mother that she wanted Sandra to achieve her reward to increase buy-in of the reward chart and motivate her to continue using it. The mother started with easy tasks such as having Sandra put her dishes in the sink after dinner three times in 1 week to earn a reward (i.e., having a friend sleep over) and gradually increased the tasks and frequency to earn rewards agreed upon by Sandra and her mother. Each week, Sandra and her mother showed the clinician the completed reward chart by holding up the document in front of the web camera. The clinician also emailed several informational handouts with parenting tips to the mother. Parenting skills were taught early in the course of treatment and refined over time.

Relaxation: Session 4

Goals/Objectives The second component of TF-CBT is relaxation. The goal of the relaxation module is to teach youth how to reduce the physiological impact of stress and trauma.

Delivery via Telehealth The clinician explained to Sandra the purpose of relaxation is to reduce the physiological response to stress and trauma and taught Sandra three relaxation skills to use to regulate her physiological responses. First, the clinician taught breathing exercises. To aid in the teaching of this skill, the clinician used the screen-sharing feature and brought up a gif image that would help Sandra time her inhales and exhales. She would breathe in for 3 s and breathe out for 4 s. Sandra preferred to put one hand on her heart and one hand on her stomach to feel her stomach rise and fall. The clinician asked Sandra to adjust the camera angle so that the clinician could see her stomach and ensure Sandra was performing the breathing exercise correctly. The next technique was progressive muscle relaxation. The clinician moved her chair away from the computer a bit so that Sandra could see the clinician's entire body. The clinician asked Sandra to set up the web camera and position her chair so she could also see Sandra's entire body so that the clinician could monitor the progressive muscle relaxation exercise. Then the clinician taught Sandra how to tense and relax each major muscle group starting from her toes and going all the way up to her head. Sandra would hold the tension for at least 4 s and then release. The final technique was tailored to Sandra's enjoyment of mindfulness activities in which she visualized her favorite location (a field near a river) paired with her breathing technique. After this session in which Sandra learned these techniques, she was assigned to practice each technique once to three times per day, every day until the next session. Sandra and the clinician planned when she would practice these techniques and used her phone to set an alarm to remind her to practice. Sandra and the clinician also identified potential barriers to practicing her homework and potential solutions to those barriers to increase Sandra's likelihood of completing her homework assignment.

Affect Identification and Modulation: Session 5

Goals/Objectives The third component of TF-CBT is affect identification and modulation. The goal of the affect identification and modulation module is to help youth identify, express, and regulate their emotions.

Delivery via Telehealth The clinician introduced the affect identification and modulation module through exploring one of Sandra's most distressing symptoms, her feelings of sadness when she thought about the death of her grandparents in the tornado. When reviewing physiological responses to emotions, the clinician utilized a worksheet that asked the client to indicate where in her body she felt specific emotions. The clinician utilized a PDF version of the document and shared the document via screen-sharing function. The clinician utilized the whiteboard function in the videoconference platform to allow Sandra to write and color on the worksheet. The clinician was able to see Sandra draw on the worksheet in real time through the whiteboard function. Additionally, to help Sandra identify emotions, Sandra and the clinician played a game called Feelings Charades. Using the screen-sharing function, the clinician shared a PowerPoint game in which each number corresponded to an emotion that Sandra and the clinician took turns acting out. The clinician and Sandra took turns choosing the number and acting out the emotion while the other person had to identify that emotion. During the session, the clinician also used an electronic version of the subjective units of distress scale (SUDs) on a 0 (not intense emotion) to 10 (very intense emotion) displayed as a thermometer to visualize more intense examples of sadness and less intense levels of sadness. Using the screen-sharing function helps the client visualize what the clinician is describing. Sandra established anchors at 1, 5, and 10 to be able to compare her current feelings to previous strong and weak emotional states. The clinician repeated the activity for the feelings of anger, fear, and happiness. The clinician explained how they would use the scale to gauge how strongly Sandra was feeling specific emotions when talking about her previous trauma. Again, the clinician used the screen-sharing function to show the thermometer and typed out Sandra's anchors. The clinician then saved each thermometer to use later in treatment. For homework, the clinician asked Sandra to track the intensity of her emotions at various points throughout the week. Again, Sandra and the clinician planned when she would complete the homework and used her phone to set an alarm to remind her to complete her homework assignment.

Cognitive Coping: Session 6

Goals/Objectives The fourth component of TF-CBT is cognitive coping. The goal of the cognitive coping component is to help youth (1) identify their thoughts, (2) recognize the relationship between thoughts feelings and behaviors, and (3) begin to understand how to challenge irrational or unhelpful thoughts.

Delivery via Telehealth The clinician taught Sandra cognitive coping using a Microsoft Word worksheet that included a cognitive triangle demonstrating the relationship between thoughts, feelings, and actions. The worksheet was fillable, and the clinician probed for Sandra's thoughts, feelings, and behaviors related to non-trauma-related examples from Sandra's own life and typed Sandra's responses directly into the worksheet. For example, to explain how thoughts can impact feelings and behaviors, the clinician used a scenario in which Sandra walked into the cafeteria in school and saw her friends start laughing when she walked in. Sandra reported that if she was in that scenario, she would probably think that they were laughing at her and feel sad. She reported that if she thought and felt that way, she might not sit with them at lunch or avoid talking to them the rest of the day. We conducted a thought experiment in which instead of thinking that her friends were laughing at her, she thought that someone had just told a funny joke at the exact same moment that she walked in. Sandra reported that if she had that thought, she would feel curious and walk over to her friends and ask what the joke was. As Sandra reported each different component, the clinician typed her answers directly into the worksheet. Sandra was able to see what the clinician was typing in real time via the screen-sharing function. The clinician also taught Sandra about common cognitive distortions, such as all-or-nothing thinking and catastrophizing through using a Jeopardy-style (trivia) PowerPoint game using the screen-sharing feature (multiple PowerPoint therapy games available at www.telehealthfortrauma.com/resources).

Trauma Narration and Processing: Sessions 7–10

Goals/Objectives After the child and caregiver have learned and practiced the first four components of TF-CBT (psychoeducation, relaxation, affect identification and modulation, and cognitive coping), they are ready to move into the second phase of treatment which starts with a trauma narration and processing component. The trauma narration and processing component has three main objectives: first, the trauma narrative is an exposure exercise aimed to desensitize the youth to the memory of the event which is causing distress; second, the trauma narrative helps the youth identify and correct unhelpful or inaccurate beliefs that are impacting their daily functioning; and finally, sharing the trauma narrative with a trusted caregiver provides an opportunity for the youth to learn that they can share things with their caregiver and receive supportive feedback.

Delivery via Telehealth The clinician explained the rationale for conducting a trauma narrative through using a scary movie analogy. The clinician asked Sandra what the scariest movie she ever saw was and then asked her on her fear levels on the intensity of emotions scale (0–10) developed in the affect identification and modulation (i.e., SUDs). She stated a 9. The clinician then asked her how scary the movie was the second time she saw it. She stated a 7. By the third time, she said it was only a 2. The clinician explained that her previous trauma was like a scary movie that she saw for the first time, but the more that she "sees," or talks about, the trauma memory, it will become less scary, just like the scariest movie she ever saw. Sandra understood this analogy and was ready to start her narrative. She requested that the clinician types her trauma narrative so that the clinician could use the screen-sharing function, and both she and the clinician could see it on the screen. The clinician accomplished this by opening a Microsoft Word document and increasing the font size of the type to a size that Sandra could easily see. The clinician used the screen-sharing function so that Sandra was able to see the Word document. Then, Sandra dictated what she wanted to say, the clinician typed what Sandra said, and Sandra could see the typing in the Word document in real time. Sandra's trauma narrative was set up in a book format with multiple chapters, one for each of her trauma types (tornado, sexual abuse); an introductory "About Me" chapter that listed her age, information about her hobbies, and her family; and a chapter about her future.

For each chapter, Sandra would dictate what to write, and the clinician would type what Sandra said into the document. Then Sandra would re-read the document aloud to the clinician multiple times. During each time re-reading the document aloud, the clinician would ask for additional details and thoughts and feelings that Sandra had at the time of the trauma and would type those into the document. The clinician then had Sandra read the chapter out loud with the new additions. Sandra then selected specific colors for thoughts and emotions in the narrative (green and purple) and assisted the clinician in finding these throughout the narrative. The clinician highlighted each thought and emotion and changed the color to correspond to the color Sandra had selected. Sandra and the clinician challenged Sandra's unhelpful or inaccurate thoughts. The clinician asked Sandra to report her SUD rating during each time she told the story. During her first reading of each chapter, her SUDs were quite high (i.e., 8) but gradually decreased by the final reading of each chapter (i.e., 3).

The clinician and Sandra worked on the trauma narrative over several weeks. Each week, the clinician saved the trauma narrative in a password-protected file on the clinician's computer, which was in a secure location. At the end of treatment, the clinician deleted the file from her computer. The clinician also emptied the trash on her computer to ensure that the file was completely deleted. Alternatively, you can also store the file on a secure cloud storage platform. Be sure to check with your local regulations to ensure that any type of cloud storage meets legal requirements in your state.

In Vivo Exposures: Sessions 11–13

Goals/Objectives An optional component of TF-CBT is called in vivo exposures. The purpose of in vivo exposures is to reduce fear and avoidance of trauma reminders when they are interfering everyday activities of the client.

Delivery via Telehealth After the trauma narration and processing, Sandra's symptoms were reassessed, and the clinician learned that she was still avoiding certain things that reminded her of tornados. Specifically, Sandra was afraid of sleeping with the lights off and would become distressed whenever there was a thunderstorm. The clinician worked with Sandra to create a fear hierarchy and asked Sandra to list her fear intensity (0–10) for each item related to the dark and thunderstorms. The fear hierarchy was created in a Microsoft Word document in which the clinician typed in Sandra's feared activities and corresponding distress level. Some items on Sandra's fear hierarchy were sleeping in her room with the lights off when no one is home and being home alone during a thunderstorm. Sandra and the clinician generated activities that were less distressing that Sandra could do to work up to her most fearful situations, such as being at home during a thunderstorm while being on the phone with her mother and sitting in her room with her mother with the lights off. During a session, the clinician played YouTube videos of a thunderstorm and a tornado. During Sandra's at-home practice of feared situations, the clinician was able to be present on the video call with Sandra for certain feared situations such as sitting in her room with the lights off. For this exposure activity, Sandra connected with the clinician via the videoconference platform and then turned the lights off in her room and closed the room-darkening curtains, which made the room quite dark. The clinician was able to verbally talk with Sandra and assist her with the exposure exercise. These in-session exposure activities helped Sandra work toward practicing other items on her fear hierarchy independently.

Conjoint Sessions: Sessions 14–16

Goals/Objectives The conjoint session is where the client shares their trauma narrative with a trusted and safe adult, usually a caregiver. The goals of these sessions are to (1) improve caregiver-child communication about the traumatic events and the child's reactions and (2) help caregivers develop skills for responding appropriately when children discuss traumatic events.

Delivery via Telehealth Sandra reported that she wanted to share her narrative with her mother. The clinician began meeting individually with Sandra's mother to prepare her for Sandra to share her trauma narrative. The clinician read chapters of the trauma narrative to the mother and processed her reactions and emotions with her. The mother became emotional and began crying when first hearing the trauma narrative. The clinician helped Sandra's mother process how she was feeling and how she could regulate those feelings. The clinician explained that if Sandra thinks that she is upsetting her mother by reading the trauma narrative, she will not feel comfortable sharing with her. The clinician shared some relaxation techniques that the mother could use when Sandra was reading, such as deep breathing. The mother and the clinician practiced exactly the message that the mother wanted to send Sandra when she was reading her trauma narrative to the mother. Sandra's mother wanted her to know that she loved her and supported her.

These meetings with the mother took place directly after Sandra's sessions for approximately 30 min. The clinician ensured that Sandra was out of the room and could not hear the discussion before meeting with the mother. When providing home-based telehealth services, it is important to ensure privacy for the individuals with whom you are meeting. It can be easy to overhear conversations through walls or if a door in left open. To help with this, the clinician asked Sandra's mother to purchase an inexpensive battery-powered white noise machine (available via Amazon or other retailer) to place next to the door to assist with sound travel. The clinician also asked that family members who were not in the therapy session move to rooms that were as far away as possible from the room where the therapy session was taking place.

Finally, when time for the conjoint session where Sandra would read her trauma narrative to her mother, the clinician first had the client and her mother set up the camera so that the clinician could see both of them. It is important to be able to see each person's face completely. To achieve this, you may need to have the family sit farther away from the camera or position the camera in a way that everyone is visible. Sandra read her trauma narrative, and her mother listened without interrupting and responded with the wording that was practiced. Sandra's mother did tear up but explained that it was because she was proud of Sandra and thanked her for trusting them enough to share her story with them.

Enhancing Safety: Sessions 3 and 17

Goals/Objectives The final component of TF-CBT (which can be done sooner or covered throughout the course of treatment as needed), is enhancing safety. The goal of the enhancing safety component is to help prevent future revictimization, identify fears the child may have for their future safety, and develop safety plans for specific areas of danger or fear.

Delivery via Telehealth Around Sandra's third therapy session, Sandra's mother reported that Sandra has started dating a new boy that she met at work and was concerned that Sandra would be involved in an unhealthy relationship. In response to that information, Sandra and the clinician discussed the traits that she was looking for in a romantic partner and the differences between a healthy relationship and unhealthy relationship. The clinician utilized a PDF handout describing unhealthy and controlling ways in which a romantic partner may act. The clinician shared the worksheet via the screen-sharing function in the videoconference platform. The clinician used this worksheet to start a conversation with Sandra about healthy and unhealthy relationships. Sandra and the clinician made a plan for how Sandra would choose relationship partners. Sandra and the clinician also role-played how Sandra could break up with an unhealthy relationship partner because Sandra expressed feeling nervous about breaking up with future partners. Sandra's mother also informed the clinician that Sandra was engaging in risky behavior online by sharing private personal information with strangers. The clinician created an Internet Safety PDF handout and shared it via screen-sharing to facilitate talking with Sandra about Internet safety.

In the final session, Sandra reviewed the coping skills that she had learned and how she could apply them should she experience any potentially traumatic events in the future or if her symptoms returned. In the final session, the clinician celebrated Sandra's completion of treatment with Sandra and her family. Often times, clinicians will hold "graduation" ceremonies or bring in special treats for children at the completion of treatment. The clinician mailed a certificate to Sandra ahead of the last session so that the parents could present it to Sandra during the session. The clinician also arranged with the mother to bake cupcakes, which they ate during the session to celebrate. Coordination of these logistics can sometimes be difficult via telehealth, but coordinating with caregivers to have a youth's favorite treat or mail them a certificate to present the youth can help make termination feel like a celebration.

Summary of Key Takeaways

Overall, it is feasible and effective to deliver TF-CBT via telehealth. Further, telehealth can significantly reduce barriers to care for many families. Clinicians must obtain the appropriate training to deliver TF-CBT and should have adequate knowledge of trauma, PTSD, and telehealth practices before starting. Clinicians should also be aware of their location's legal and ethical considerations when delivering TF-CBT via telehealth. It is especially important to use videoconferencing software that complies with confidentiality standards (HIPAA-compliant) and work collaboratively with the youth and family to find a private space to conduct therapy. It is important to note that the standard of care is the same for telehealth as it is for in-person services. Therapists should deliver TF-CBT with fidelity to the model while tailoring the activities and resources used during sessions to an electronic delivery format. When utilizing telehealth with children and adolescents, clinicians should work to engage youth and caregivers through interactive activities, using the screen-sharing function and communicating with both the youth and caregiver via telehealth. It is encouraged to use things such as videos, online assessments, and computer-based games to engage patients. There are many recommendations for the best practices for telehealth delivery included in this chapter, and its references, which clinicians can use to enhance their provision of trauma treatment for youth via telehealth. We encourage clinicians to try the tools that have been shown to be effective in delivering TF-CBT from the various websites provided above and determine which is the most engaging for your client. While there are many benefits to delivering TF-CBT via telehealth, it is also important for clinicians to manage risk by obtaining the location of the client at the beginning of each session in case of emergency and creating a safety plan before starting treatment in case of emergencies. Further, clinicians should be careful to set up secure and confidential videoconference sessions and have a plan if confidentiality is breached. These techniques can help mitigate the risks associated with telehealth. In conclusion, delivering TF-CBT via telehealth can improve the mental health of trauma-impacted youth around the world.

References

Alegria Vallas, M., & Pumariega, A. J. (2010). Racial and ethnic disparities in pediatric mental health. *Child and Adolescent Psychiatric Clinics of North America, 19*(4), 759–774. https://doi.org/10.1016/j.chc.2010.07.001

American Psychological Association. (2013). Guidelines for the practice of tele psychology. *American Psychologist, 68*(9), 791–800. https://doi.org/10.1037/a0035001

BigFoot, D., & Schmidt, S. (2010). Honoring children, mending the circle: Cultural adaptation of trauma-focused cognitive behavioral therapy for American Indian and Alaska native children. *Journal of Clinical Psychology, 66*(8), 847–856. https://doi.org/10.1002/jclp.20707

Capner. (2000). Videoconferencing in the provision of psychological services at a distance. *Journal of Telemedicine and Telecare, 6*(6), 311–319. https://doi.org/10.1258/1357633001935969

Carliner, H., Keyes, K. M., McLaughlin, K. A., Meyers, J. L., Dunn, E. C., & Martins, S. S. (2016). Childhood trauma and illicit drug use in adolescence: A population-based national comorbidity survey replication–adolescent supplement study. *Journal of the American Academy of Child & Adolescent Psychiatry, 55*(8), 701–708. https://doi.org/10.1016/j.jaac.2016.05.010

Centers for Medicare and Medicaid Services. (2019). *Telehealth services*. https://www.cms.gov/outreach-and-education/medicare-learningnetworkmln/mlnproducts/downloads/telehealth-srvcsfctsht.pdf

Cohen, J. A., Mannarino, A. P., & Deblinger, E. (2017). *Treating trauma and traumatic grief in children and adolescents* (2nd ed.). Guilford Press.

Comer, J. S., & Barlow, D. H. (2014). The occasional case against broad dissemination and implementation: Retaining a role for specialty Care in the Delivery of psychological treatments. *The American Psychologist, 69*(1), 1–18. https://doi.org/10.1037/a0033582

Comer, J. S., Furr, J. M., Kerns, C. E., Miguel, E., Coxe, S., Elkins, R. M., Carpenter, A. L., Cornacchio, D., Cooper-Vince, C. E., DeSerisy, M., Chou, T., Sanchez, A. L., Khanna, M., Franklin, M. E., Garcia, A. M., & Freeman, J. B. (2017). Internet-delivered, family-based treatment for early-onset OCD: A pilot randomized trial. *Journal of Consulting and Clinical Psychology, 85*(2), 178–186. https://doi.org/10.1037/ccp0000155

De Arellano, M. A., Waldrop, A. E., Deblinger, E., Cohen, J. A., Danielson, C. K., & Mannarino, A. R. (2005). Community outreach program for child victims of traumatic events: a community-based project for underserved populations. *Behavior modification, 29*(1), 130–155. https://doi.org/10.1177/0145445504270878

de Arellano, M. A., Danielson, C. K., & Felton, J. W. (2012). Children of Latino descent: Culturally modified TF-CBT. In J. A. Cohen, A. P. Mannarino, & E. Deblinger (Eds.), *Trauma-focused CBT for children and adolescents: Treatment applications* (pp. 253–279). Guilford Press.

Dorsey, S., Lucid, L., Martin, P., King, K. M., O'Donnell, K., Murray, L. K., Wasonga, A., Itemba, D. K., Cohen, J., Manongi, R., & Whetten, K. (2020). Effectiveness of task-shifted trauma-focused cognitive behavioral therapy for children who experienced parental death and post-traumatic stress in Kenya and Tanzania: A randomized clinical trial. *JAMA Psychiatry*. https://doi.org/10.1001/jamapsychiatry.2019.4475

Dueweke, A. R., Wallace, M. M., Nicasio, A. V., Villalobos, B. T., Hernandez Rodriguez, J., & Stewart, R. W. (2020). Resources and recommendations for engaging children and adolescents in telemental health interventions during COVID-19 and beyond. *The Behavior Therapist*.

Fairbank, J. A., & Fairbank, D. W. (2009). Epidemiology of child traumatic stress. *Current Psychiatry Reports, 11*(4), 289–295. https://doi.org/10.1007/s11920-009-0042-9

Gloff LeNoue, S. R., Novins, D. K., & Myers, K. (2015). Telemental health for children and adolescents. *International Review of Psychiatry (Abingdon, England), 27*(6), 513–524. https://doi.org/10.3109/09540261.2015.1086322

Herting, N., Condol, P., & Stewart, R. W. (2023). Increasing access and decreasing barriers to mental health services at CACs through telehealth. in A. St-Amand, P. Rimer, D. Nadeau, J. Herbert, & W. Walsh (Eds.), *Contemporary and innovative practices in child & youth advocacy centre models*. [Presses de l'Université de Québec University of Quebec Press].

Hillis, S., Mercy, J., Amobi, A., & Kress, H. (2016). Global prevalence of past-year violence against children: A systematic review and minimum estimates. *Pediatrics, 137*(3), e20154079. https://doi.org/10.1542/peds.2015-4079

Holt, M. K., Finkelhor, D., & Kantor, G. K. (2007). Multiple victimization experiences of urban elementary school students: Associations with psychosocial functioning and academic performance. *Child Abuse & Neglect, 31*(5), 503–515. https://doi.org/10.1016/j.chiabu.2006.12.006

Joint Task Force for the Developmentof Telepsychology Guidelines for Psychologists. (2013). Guidelines for the practice of telepsychology. *The American psychologist, 68*(9), 791–800.

Khan, K. S., Mamun, M. A., Griffiths, M. D., & Ullah, I. (2020). The mental health impact of the COVID-19 pandemic across different cohorts. *International Journal of Mental Health and Addiction*. https://doi.org/10.1007/s11469-020-00367-0

Lai, B. S., Lewis, R., Livings, M. S., La Greca, A. M., & Esnard, A.-M. (2017). Posttraumatic stress symptom trajectories among children after disaster exposure: A review. *Journal of Traumatic Stress, 30*(6), 571–582. https://doi.org/10.1002/jts.22242

McCarty, C. A., Vander Stoep, A., Violette, H., & Myers, K. (2014). Interventions developed for psychiatric and behavioral treatment in the Children's ADHD Telemental health treatment study. *Journal of Child and Family Studies, 24*(6), 1735–1743. https://doi.org/10.1007/s10826-014-9977-5

McLaughlin, K. A., Green, J. G., Gruber, M. J., Sampson, N. A., Zaslavsky, A. M., & Kessler, R. C. (2012). Childhood adversities and first onset of psychiatric disorders in a national sample of US adolescents. *Archives of General Psychiatry, 69*(11), 1151–1160. https://doi.org/10.1001/archgenpsychiatry.2011.2277

McMullen, J., O'Callaghan, P., Shannon, C., Black, A., & Eakin, J. (2013). Group trauma-focused cognitive-behavioural therapy with former child soldiers and other war-affected boys in the DR Congo: A randomized controlled trial. *Journal of Child Psychology and Psychiatry, 54*(11), 1231–1241. https://doi.org/10.1111/jcpp.12094

Merikangas, K. R., Nakamura, E. F., & Kessler, R. C. (2009). Epidemiology of mental disorders in children and adolescents. *Dialogues Clinical Neuroscience, 11*(1), 7–20. https://doi.org/10.31887/DCNS.2009.11.1/krmerikangas

Merikangas, K. R., He, J. P., Burstein, M., Swendsen, J., Avenevoli, S., Case, B., Georgiades, K., et al. (2011). Service utilization for lifetime mental disorders in U.S. adolescents: Results from the National Comorbidity Survey Adolescent Supplement (NCS-A). *Journal of the American Academy of Child and Adolescent Psychiatry, 50*, 32–45. https://doi.org/10.1016/j.jaac.2010.10.006

Mielonen, M. L., Ohinmaa, A., Moring, J., & Isohanni, M. (2000). Psychiatric inpatient care planning via telemedicine. *Journal of Telemedicine and Telecare, 6*(3), 152–157. https://doi.org/10.1258/1357633001935248

Murray, L., Familiar, I., Skavenski, S., Jere, E., Cohen, J., Imasiku, M., Mayeya, J., Bass, J. K., & Bolton, P. (2013). An evaluation of trauma focused cognitive behavioral therapy for children in Zambia. *Child Abuse & Neglect, 37*(12), 1175–1185. https://doi.org/10.1016/j.chiabu.2013.04.017

Myers, K., & Comer, J. S. (2016). The case for Telemental health for improving the accessibility and quality of Children's mental health services. *Journal of Child and Adolescent Psychopharmacology, 26*(3), 186–191. https://doi.org/10.1089/cap.2015.0055

Myers, K., Nelson, E. L., Hilty, D., Baker, D., Barnwell, S. S., Boyce, G., et al. (2017). American telemedicine association practice guidelines for Telemental health with children and adolescents. *Telemedicine and e-Health, 23*(10), 779–804. https://doi.org/10.1089/tmj.2017.0177

National Research Council and Institute of Medicine. (2009). *Adolescent health services: Missing opportunities*. Committee on adolescent health care services and models of Care for Treatment, prevention, and healthy development. In R. S. Lawrence, J. A. Gootman, & L. J. Sim (Eds.), *Board on children, youth, and families. Division of behavioral and social sciences and education*. The National Academies Press.

O'Callaghan, P., McMullen, J., Shannon, C., Rafferty, H., & Black, A. (2013). A randomized controlled trial of trauma-focused cognitive behavioral therapy for sexually exploited, war affected Congolese girls. *Journal of the American Academy of Child & Adolescent Psychiatry, 52*(4), 359–369. https://doi.org/10.1016/j.jaac.2013.01.013

Orengo-Aguayo, R., Dueweke, A., Nicasio, A., de Arellano, M. A., Rivera, S., Cohen, J., Mannarino, A. P., & Stewart, R. W. (2022). Trauma-focused cognitive behavioral therapy with Puerto Rican youth in a post-disaster context: Tailoring, implementation, and program evaluation outcomes. *Child Abuse and Neglect, 129*, 105671. https://doi.org/10.1016/j.chiabu.2022.105671

Ormel, J., Petukhova, M., Chatterji, S., Aguilar-Gaxiola, S., Alonso, J., Angermeyer, M. C., et al. (2008). Disability and treatment of specific mental and physical disorders across the world. *The British Journal of Psychiatry, 192*(5), 368–375. https://doi.org/10.1192/bjp.bp.107.039107

Rees, C. S., & Stone, S. (2005). Therapeutic Alliance in face-to-face versus Videoconferenced psychotherapy. *Professional Psychology, Research and Practice, 36*(6), 649–653. https://doi.org/10.1037/0735-7028.36.6.649

Rodgers, C. R., Flores, M. W., Bassey, O., & Le Cook, B. (2022). Racial/ethnic disparity trends in children's mental health care access and expenditures from 2010 to 2017: Disparities remain despite sweeping policy reform. *Journal of the American Academy of Child and Adolescent Psychiatry, 61*(7), 915–925. https://doi.org/10.1016/j.jaac.2021.09.420

Ros-Demarize, R., Orengo-Aguayo, R., & Stewart, R. W. (2022). Telesalud mental con niños y adolecentes [telehealth with children and adolescents]. In J. J. Martí Noguera (Ed.), *Manual de Telesalud Mental: Tecnologías Digitales en la Práctica Clínica* (Telemental health manual: Digital technologies in clinical practice). Pirámide.

Shore, J. H., Yellowlees, P., Caudill, R., Johnston, B., Turvey, C., Mishkind, M., Krupinski, E., Myers, K., Shore, P., Kaftarian, E., & Hilty, D. (2018). *Best practices in videoconferencecing-based telemental health*. American Psychiatric Association & American Telemedicine Association. https://www.psychiatry.org/File%20Library/Psychiatrists/Practice/Telepsychiatry/APA-ATA-Best-Practices-in-Videoconferencing-Based-Telemental-Health.pdf

Stewart, R. W., Orengo-Aguayo, R., Gilmore, A. K., & de Arellano, M. (2017). Addressing barriers to care among Hispanic youth: Telehealth delivery of trauma-focused cognitive-behavioral therapy (TF-CBT). *The Behavior Therapist, 40*, 112–118. 28670047

Stewart, R., Orengo-Aguayo, R., Young, J., Wallace, M. M., Cohen, J. A., Mannarino, A. P., & de Arellano, M. A. (2020). Feasibility and effectiveness of a telehealth service delivery model for treating childhood posttraumatic stress: A community-based, open pilot trial of trauma-focused cognitive-behavioral therapy. *Journal of Psychotherapy Integration, 30*(2), 274–289. https://doi.org/10.1037/int0000225

Stewart, R. W., Orengo-Aguayo, R., Villalobos, B. T., Nicasio, A. V., Dueweke, A., Alto, M., Cohen, J. A., Mannarino, A. P., & de Arellano, M. A. (2020). Implementation of an evidence-based psychotherapy for trauma-exposed children in a lower-middle income country: The use of trauma-focused cognitive behavioral therapy in El Salvador. *Journal of Child & Adolescent Trauma*. https://doi.org/10.1007/s40653-020-00327-9

Stewart, R. W., Orengo-Aguayo, R., Wallace, M., Metzger, I. W., & Rheingold, A. (2021). Leveraging technology and cultural adaptations to increase access and engagement among trauma-exposed African American youth: Exploratory study of school-based telehealth delivery of trauma-focused cognitive behavioral therapy. *Journal of Interpersonal Violence, 36*(15–16), 7090–7109. https://doi.org/10.1177/0886260519831380

Whitney, D. G., & Peterson, M. D. (2019). US national and state-level prevalence of mental health disorders and disparities of mental health care use in children. *JAMA Pediatrics, 173*(4), 389–391. https://doi.org/10.1001/jamapediatrics.2018.5399

Xiong, J., Lipsitz, O., Nasri, F., Lui, L. M. W., Gill, H., Phan, L., Chen-Li, D., Lacobucci, M., Ho, R., Majeed, A., & McIntyre, R. S. (2020). Impact of COVID-19 pandemic on mental health in the general population: A systematic review. *Journal of Affective Disorders, 277*, 55–64. https://doi.org/10.1016/j.jad.2020.08.001

Chapter 5
Telemental Health Delivery of ABA Services

Matthew J. O'Brien

Telemental Health Delivery of ABA Services

Applied behavior analysis (ABA) is the science and practice of studying and modifying observable human behaviors (Miltenberger et al., 2015). ABA is based on the operant learning model, which at its most basic level explains the occurrence of a specific behavior as the product of the environmental events that evoke that behavior (called *antecedents*) and the environmental events that reinforce that behavior (*consequences*). This model also accounts for the reduction or elimination of behaviors when the consequences that follow those behaviors do not include reinforcement (called *extinction*) and/or include an aversive environmental event (called *punishment*). Thus, in this model behaviors recur or fail to recur based on the consequences that follow them.

The principles upon which ABA are based have been employed across many different fields, including education (e.g., Horner & Sugai, 2015), medicine and public health (e.g., Normand et al., 2021), sports and fitness (e.g., Batchelder et al., 2023), language development (e.g., Frazier et al., 2021), and organizational management (e.g., Nastasi et al., 2023). However, as a practice, ABA is best known as the most studied and effective approach in the development of skills and reduction of a challenging behavior for individuals with neurodevelopmental disabilities (Virues-Ortega et al., 2022). Various ABA procedures are considered evidence-based interventions according to several large reviews of interventions for individuals with autism spectrum disorder (ASD; National Autism Center, 2015; Steinbrenner et al.,

M. J. O'Brien (✉)
University of Iowa Carver College of Medicine, Iowa City, IA, USA

University of Iowa Stead Family Children's Hospital, Iowa City, IA, USA
e-mail: matthew-j-obrien@uiowa.edu

L. N. Niec, C. E. Schoonover (eds.), *Telemental Health Care for Children and Families*,
https://doi.org/10.1007/978-3-031-69264-2_5

2020), and the core principles and procedures used in ABA therapy have been integrated into other highly effective intervention approaches.

Although ABA therapy encompasses a broad range of approaches and procedures, in the most basic way, it can be divided into practices dedicated to increasing behaviors or skills, called *skill acquisition*, and practices focused on the reduction of unwanted or challenging behaviors. Skill acquisition models include a variety of techniques that range from structured to naturalistic methods. On the structured side, discrete trial training (DTT) procedures involve breaking down target skills into smaller components, which are taught in trials where correct responses result in access to reinforcers such as praise or edibles. DTT procedures, which were commonly used in the earliest forms of ABA therapy, are often conducted one on one between a child and a therapist in a clinic setting. Naturalistic methods, such as incidental teaching (McGee, 2022), pivotal response training (Koegel & Koegel, 2019), and naturalistic teaching strategies (Bruinsma et al., 2020), are often conducted in the child's natural environments (e.g., the home or school), during natural routines (e.g., playtime or mealtime), and using natural consequences (e.g., a child says "apple" during mealtime, and the therapist delivers an apple slice). These approaches have gained in popularity due to growing empirical support (Schreibman et al., 2015), their flexibility and individualization, and greater parental involvement.

ABA practices focused on the reduction of challenging behaviors (e.g., aggression, destruction, self-injury, refusal) often employ functional behavioral assessment methods to determine the functional relationship between the challenging behavior and environmental variables. More specifically, these methods are used to determine the function or the benefit that a particular challenging behavior serves. Challenging behaviors may function for social positive reinforcement (e.g., toys, activities, attention), social negative reinforcement (e.g., to escape an academic task), automatic reinforcement (e.g., dumping a box of marbles on the ground because it is visually stimulating), or a combination of these forms of reinforcement. For example, a child whose parent is on the phone and momentarily unavailable may cry because crying increases the likelihood that the parent will end the phone call and provide attention (i.e., positive reinforcement). By establishing a functional relationship between a challenging behavior and environmental variables, treatments can be developed that disrupt that relationship in several ways. Common function-based treatments combine differential reinforcement procedures, whereby a more appropriate alternative behavior (e.g., communication) is reinforced, with extinction, whereby reinforcement is withheld for the target challenging behavior.

A Move to Telehealth

With the growing popularity of ABA therapy over the past several decades, the demand for services has outpaced the supply of service providers (BACB, 2023). This is especially true in large rural states where it is common for families to drive long distances to reach the nearest ABA provider (Mello et al., 2016). To address the shortage of providers and reach children and families living in geographically remote areas, researchers in the 1990s began exploring the use of telehealth-delivered ABA services. The earliest study demonstrating the feasibility of telehealth-delivered ABA was published by Barretto et al., 2006. This study described the methods that were used to conduct telehealth-based behavioral evaluations for children exhibiting a challenging behavior in Iowa. Over the course of a 4-year period beginning in 1997, more than 75 evaluations were successfully completed. For these evaluations, parents and school personnel located at school and community sites across the state were coached to conduct assessment procedures by behavioral therapists at a remote site (The University of Iowa). Although this initial demonstration of telehealth-delivered ABA showed promise, the research team noted several challenges associated with communication between the coaching and assessment sites (Wacker et al., 2016).

Despite the successful demonstrations reported by Barretto et al. (2006), in the 15 years that followed, only a limited number of studies incorporating telehealth into ABA practices were published. Like the Barretto et al. study, most of these studies were concerned with assessment and/or treatment of a challenging behavior exhibited by individuals with disabilities, and the majority proved telehealth to be a feasible and effective delivery method (Tomlinson et al., 2018). Even after numerous successful demonstrations, telehealth failed to gain traction as an ABA delivery modality due to the fact that most states did not have legislation that allowed for telehealth services and few public and private insurance plans covered telehealth-based ABA.

Following the US government's issuance of a state of emergency due to the COVID-19 pandemic, states moved quickly to relax rules regarding telehealth-based services, and public and private insurance plans made exceptions for telehealth services. As a result, the provision of ABA services via telehealth surged during the pandemic. With limited research and few experienced telehealth providers, guidelines for transitioning from in-person to telehealth ABA services (CASP, 2020) and ABA telehealth practice recommendations (e.g., Bergmann et al., 2021; Araiba & Čolić, 2022) were rapidly developed to support providers in the transition. As the COVID-19 pandemic waned, many service providers returned to in-person service provision, but the option of telehealth-delivered ABA appears to be here to stay.

Research on Telehealth-Delivered ABA: What Have We Learned?

Research on telehealth-delivered ABA has evolved over time and has moved from studies evaluating its feasibility to studies establishing its effectiveness. Most early studies employed an indirect service model (i.e., caregiver, teacher, or assistant on-site with the client receiving coaching remotely from a therapist) and were largely focused on demonstrating the feasibility of telehealth services across implementers, settings, and behavior analytic procedures for a challenging behavior. These studies showed that telehealth could be used successfully to coach caregivers (Barretto et al., 2006; Wacker et al., 2013a, b), school personnel (Barretto et al., 2006; Frieder et al., 2009; Gibson et al., 2010), non-ABA therapists (Barretto et al., 2006; Frieder et al., 2009), and graduate students (Machalicek et al., 2009a), who were located at schools (Barretto et al., 2006; Gibson et al., 2010; Frieder et al., 2009; Machalicek et al., 2009a, b), human service agencies (Barretto et al., 2006), and medical clinics (Wacker et al., 2013a, b). Early feasibility studies proved successful in conducting preference assessments (Machalicek et al., 2009a), functional analyses (FAs; Barretto et al., 2006; Frieder et al., 2009; Machalicek et al., 2009a; Wacker et al., 2013b), and function-based treatments (e.g., functional communication training or FCT; Gibson et al., 2010; Wacker et al., 2013a).

Recent ABA research has continued to demonstrate the feasibility and effectiveness of telehealth for a challenging behavior but has also extended its use to novel behaviors and procedures. For example, recent studies have successfully evaluated and treated challenging feeding behaviors in young children (Alaimo et al., 2023; Andersen et al., 2021; Bloomfield et al., 2019; Patel et al., 2023; Peterson et al., 2021; Volkert et al., 2014), taught children and adults to wear facemasks (Halbur et al., 2021; Lillie et al., 2021; McHugh et al., 2022; Sivaraman et al., 2021), and coached parents to conduct toilet training (Dabney et al., 2023).

Research establishing the feasibility of telehealth-delivered ABA targeting skill acquisition was slow to develop until recently. Within the past 5 years, studies have begun to evaluate the feasibility of various types of direct and indirect telehealth services. The most common approach studied has included caregiver- or technician-assisted direct ABA telehealth delivery, whereby a caregiver or assistant who is on-site with the client is coached to deliver instruction by a remote therapist. Witt et al. (2018) provided one of the earliest studies on skill acquisition using this model. In this study, a therapist provided remote coaching to the parent of a young boy with traumatic brain injury with the goal of teaching the boy to brush his teeth, write his name, and tie his shoes independently. Caregiver use of behavior analytic teaching methods and child independence with the targeted tasks improved as a result. Caregiver- and technician-assisted telehealth has also been used successfully to teach adults with intellectual disability skills related to their personal interests (Pellegrino & DiGennaro Reed, 2020), help adolescents and young adults with disabilities learn to use speech-generating devices (Carnett et al., 2021), and teach children with ASD daily living skills (Boutain et al., 2020; Craig et al., 2021; Gerow et al., 2021), verbal and nonverbal communication skills (Barkaia et al., 2017; Gevarter et al., 2022; Pollard et al., 2021), and play skills (Pollard et al., 2021).

It is perhaps not a surprise that only a limited number of studies have evaluated the feasibility of direct ABA services via telehealth. Direct service requires that the client exhibit several prerequisite skills to demonstrate that caregiver or technician assistance is not needed. Studies have demonstrated the feasibility of direct ABA services exclusively with individuals with ASD. For instance, Nohelty et al. (2022)

demonstrated successful applications of direct ABA for children and adolescents, using either DTT or naturalistic teaching methods, with and without caregiver support. In another example, Ferguson et al. (2020) demonstrated a more efficient model of direct DTT via telehealth by delivering instruction to child dyads who received services simultaneously but from different locations.

A few comparative studies have been conducted to determine if telehealth-delivered ABA is as effective as in-person ABA. With regard to a challenging behavior, Lindgren et al. (2016) compared the effectiveness of three delivery models—in-person within the home, clinic-to-clinic telehealth, and clinic-to-home telehealth—on challenging behaviors of more than 100 young children with ASD and other disabilities. All ABA procedures (i.e., FA and FCT) were implemented by caregivers with therapist coaching. Treatment was effective in reducing a challenging behavior for all three groups, and no statistically significant group differences were noted. Additionally, caregivers across all three groups rated treatment as highly acceptable. There was, however, one outcome where a statistically significant difference was observed. Based on cost calculations, the two telehealth models were found to cost significantly less to implement than the in-person model.

With regard to skill acquisition, two recent studies directly compared telehealth-delivered instruction versus in-person instruction for young children with disabilities. Peysin et al. (2023) taught six preschool-aged children labeling and sight words using in-person and telehealth modalities. Although all children demonstrated growth via both delivery modalities, for three of the six participants, in-person learning produced more rapid acquisition of the learning materials than telehealth-delivered instruction. Knopp et al. (2023) compared direct DTT instruction delivered in-person and via telehealth for three children with ASD. All children demonstrated mastery of the learning targets at high levels across both modalities and skills was maintained for up to 66 days following intervention. Additionally, child accuracy on daily probes and speed of mastery were nearly indistinguishable between the two modalities. Thus, telehealth appears to offer an effective method of delivering skill acquisition ABA, but whether it matches the outcomes of in-person service delivery warrants additional research.

The Benefits and Limitations of Telehealth-Delivered ABA

The Benefits: When Does a Telehealth Model Make Sense?

Telehealth-delivered ABA holds several advantages over in-person services. The most obvious advantage is the reach that telehealth affords families living in geographically remote and underserved areas. Recent estimates show that more than half of all counties in the USA do not have a Board Certified Behavior Analyst® (BCBA) providing ABA services (Yingling et al., 2021) and those that do tend to be more affluent and urban (Mello et al., 2016; Yingling et al., 2022). Fortunately, the reach of telehealth-delivered ABA services is primarily limited only by interstate practice rules and regulations and the quality of a family's Internet connectivity. Aside from the rules and regulations of practice, telehealth has the potential to reach families across the globe, with the potential to benefit families living in places where there are no practicing behavior analysts. For example, in studies led by Tsami and colleagues (Schieltz et al., 2022; Tsami et al., 2019), ABA services have been successfully delivered via telehealth from US locations to families living in countries without a single practicing BCBA, including Algeria, Cameroon, Nepal, and Venezuela, among many others.

ABA services are expensive (Cooper, 2022); however, one benefit of telehealth-based ABA that may be appealing to the provider and the client is the reduced time and cost associated with telehealth. Several studies have demonstrated substantial cost savings with telehealth-delivered ABA over in-person services (Coon et al., 2022; Lindgren et al., 2016). For the provider, telehealth limits the need for clinic space and materials, as well as time to prep and clean a clinic room before and after an appointment. In turn, this increases the number of clients that a provider can serve and ostensibly increase revenue. For the client and client's family, telehealth reduces the travel time to and from appointments, as well as the costs of travel (e.g., gas and wear and tear on car) and lost wages associated with the additional travel time. To illustrate this point, O'Brien et al. (2021) published a case study involving telehealth-delivered ABA therapy for a young child with ASD and reported that by using telehealth the family saved nearly 3000 miles and 50 h of driving that they would have incurred using in-person services. In addition to the time and cost savings for the provider and client, telehealth may also offer substantial cost savings to Medicaid and other select payers who offer non-emergency medical transportation for specialty care, which sometimes includes reimbursement for lodging, meals, and mileage.

In the initial stages of the COVID-19 pandemic, many providers were able to pivot from in-person to telehealth ABA service quickly and successfully (Crockett et al., 2020; Pollard et al., 2021). Such demonstrations confer another benefit of telehealth-delivered ABA, which is the continuity of care when in-person services are impractical. Although another pandemic may be unlikely soon, it is not uncommon for poor weather, sicknesses, and transportation challenges to arise, which can result in disruptions to in-person services. For families who frequently relocate due to work or military service, recurrent breaks in services may substantially attenuate any positive gains made previously. Additionally, in-person services are often constrained by standard business hours of operation (e.g., 9 a.m.–5 p.m.), which makes client observation and therapy outside of those hours (e.g., dinnertime, bedtime) impractical. In the face of such challenges, the option to move to telehealth, even if temporarily, and maintain services makes the flexibility of telehealth services invaluable.

Individuals with ASD, the primary recipients of ABA therapy, may be more likely than their non-ASD peers to demonstrate weaker treatment generalization (de Marchena et al., 2015; Wass & Porayska-Pomsta, 2014). However, there is a reason to believe that treatment conducted within the home setting via telehealth may lead to better generalization and maintenance of treatment effects. Treatment conducted within the home, where salient physical and social stimuli exist, may lead to greater success in transferring skills to other activities within the home (Stokes & Baer, 1977). Indeed, research has shown that when treatment is conducted in natural contexts (e.g., home, school), with natural implementers (e.g., caregivers), and natural tasks (e.g., picking up toys), generalization is more likely (e.g., Durand & Carr, 1992; Zwaigenbaum et al., 2015). O'Brien et al. (2022) provided a demonstration of successful generalization via telehealth-delivered ABA. In their study, O'Brien and colleagues coached 30 caregivers to conduct FCT in their homes with their young children with ASD who exhibited a challenging behavior. Although generalization was not specifically programmed for in this study, children showed statistically significant improvement on several measures of generalization for targeted and nontargeted behaviors, both within and outside of the training context.

The Limitations: When Does an In-Person Model Make Sense?

Telehealth may be a feasible and effective model for delivering ABA services, but there are important limitations to its use and a variety of barriers to overcome. Some of the barriers are obvious and may be impossible to overcome. For example, lack of necessary equipment or internet connectivity for the provider or client, restrictions due to state or federal laws and regulations governing telehealth practices (e.g., cross-border healthcare), lack of insurance coverage for telehealth, and therapist or client discomfort with telehealth would all preclude the use of telehealth to deliver ABA services. However, there are several less obvious reasons to choose in-person services over telehealth that are based on the type of service to be provided and the characteristics of the client, caregiver, and therapist.

Providers of services targeting a challenging behavior and skill acquisition must consider whether the client being served is appropriate for telehealth. Across many research studies, caregiver-assisted telehealth has been an effective ABA delivery modality for children and adolescents with challenging behavior maintained by social reinforcers (e.g., adult attention, escape from demands); however, with few exceptions (see Gregori et al., 2023, and Shawler et al., 2021), research has failed to evaluate the feasibility and effectiveness of telehealth-delivered ABA for adults with a challenging behavior and for individuals with automatically maintained challenging behavior. There may be a good reason for the lack of studies on adults, as children and adolescents are naturally smaller, which increases the likelihood that a caregiver can safely intervene should challenging behaviors, such as physical aggression or self-injury, require it. With adults, who are bigger and stronger, physical intervention increases the likelihood of client and caregiver injury, and without a therapist's presence to physically support a caregiver, there is greater liability for the provider. With regard to automatically maintained behavior, assessment and treatment present several challenges for telehealth. The standard assessment approach when a challenging behavior is hypothesized to serve an automatic function is to conduct an alone or ignore test condition to determine if the behavior occurs in the absence of social reinforcement (i.e., toys and attention); however, this could present a dangerous situation if physical intervention was needed to maintain safety and the only person available to intervene was purposely removed from the setting. Further, automatically maintained behaviors are particularly difficult to treat and often require approaches that are more intense than can be delivered by a single person (Rooker et al., 2018).

ABA services focused on skill acquisition are most often delivered in a direct (i.e., one-on-one) format. When delivered in-person, a therapist is expected to deliver instructions, various prompts (e.g., vocal, model, physical), and various forms of reinforcement (e.g., praise, edibles, toys) to the client and when necessary and provide physical guidance (e.g., to a work area, to a correct response, to block from elopement). Providing instructions, prompts, and praise vocally is feasible via telehealth, but nonvocal prompts, delivery of tangible reinforcers, and physical guidance are not. Thus, successful telehealth-delivered ABA may depend heavily on the characteristics of the client. A client suitable for telehealth likely possesses several prerequisite skills and/or will require caregiver assistance. The Council of Autism Service Providers (2021) has developed practice parameters for telehealth-delivered ABA services that include a list of required skills for clients considering telehealth. Among the prerequisite skills identified are basic joint attention, discrimination, and motor imitation skills, as well as the ability to follow one-step directions, sit independently at a computer for 8–10 min, and exhibit little safety concerns or challenging behavior.

Even when some of the above barriers are encountered, there may still be a place for telehealth service. Schieltz et al. (2022) identified numerous critical preservice and clinical service considerations for utilizing telehealth for ABA practice and offered suggestions to mitigate many of the challenges when possible. For example, when a client is older or larger, or if the client displays behaviors that risk health and safety, simply adding additional support at the originating (i.e., service) site might make telehealth feasible. However, in some situations, such as when a caregiver is uncomfortable with telehealth or has a limiting disability (e.g., hearing impairment), the only practical and ethical solution is to provide in-person services.

Developing Competence in Telehealth-Delivered ABA

ABA Training and Credentials

Successful delivery of ABA services using telehealth is dependent upon a therapist who is competent in (a) the ABA procedures to be used and (b) the delivery of those procedures via telehealth. ABA principles and practices may be used by virtually anyone (e.g., parents, teachers, therapists), but most fee-for-service ABA practitioners have been credentialed by the Behavior Analysis Certification Board (BACB) or are psychologists licensed in the state in which they practice. BCBAs have a master's or doctoral degree (BCBA-Doctoral or BCBA-D) in psychology, applied behavior analysis, social work, or a related field and have completed the required coursework and experience in applied behavior analysis that makes them eligible to take the BCBA credentialing exam. Although the required coursework for the BCBA credential generally covers the principles and practices of ABA, including skill acquisition and intervention for a challenging behavior, the prospective practitioner's training experiences may vary considerably. Thus, a therapist's scope of competence is determined by a combination of their coursework and knowledge of the research literature, practical experiences, and on-going professional development (Brodhead et al., 2018). Moreover, therapists are likely to vary in their competence across specific behavior analytic procedures, populations, and settings (Brodhead et al., 2018).

Developing Competence in Telehealth-Delivered ABA

No specific credentials are required or have been developed to signify competence in telehealth-delivered ABA; however, ethical codes for BCBAs (BACB, 2020) and licensed psychologists (American Psychological Association, 2017) require behavior analysts and psychologists, respectively, to only practice within the boundaries of their training and education. While many of the skills required to be a competent therapist in a clinic setting are also required for delivering those services via telehealth, they are not sufficient (Neely et al., 2022). Delivering ABA via telehealth requires a therapist who is skilled in providing instruction, knowledgeable about technology, and is comfortable troubleshooting a variety of therapy challenges from afar.

In addition to the requisite experience and skills in delivering behavior analytic procedures, therapists delivering ABA via telehealth must be proficient in "coaching" others, especially when using caregiver- or technician-assisted telehealth models. Successful coaching requires strong verbal skills and the deftness to know when to provide directives, when to provide feedback and praise, and when to fade support. Larsen et al. (2023) examined therapists' coaching behavior during successful telehealth-delivered ABA therapy for young children with ASD exhibiting a challenging behavior. Across seven cases where caregivers were coached to conduct FA and FCT procedures, therapists shifted their behavior from predominately antecedent-based directives and procedural comments (i.e., a description of the procedures and the caregiver's role) during the assessment and the early aspects of treatment to more consequence-based vocal behaviors, such as praise and process comments (i.e., providing insight into the child's behavior or the therapy procedures) in the latter part of treatment. This shift reflected the specific goals of the assessment and treatment phases. More specifically, when the goal was to identify the environmental contexts that evoke a challenging behavior and the variables maintaining such behavior (i.e., the assessment phase), directives were most appropriate. However, when the treatment phase began, the goal shifted from directing to teaching the caregiver procedures that would hopefully continue long term, both inside and outside of therapy sessions, and across contexts not specifically used within the therapy sessions.

Not surprisingly, in the Larsen et al. (2023) study, substantially greater vocal modeling was used than visual modeling. As noted previously, there is a greater emphasis on a therapist's verbal skills in telehealth-delivered ABA. A therapist must be able to describe procedures in a way that a caregiver will understand without the added benefit of visual demonstration. For example, when working with a child who unexpectedly begins head-banging, a therapist coaching a caregiver remotely does not have the benefit of stepping in to demonstrate safe neutral blocking procedures; rather the therapist must quickly explain to the caregiver how to implement neutral blocking such that the caregiver understands safe hand or arm placement and how to maintain a neutral affect and vocal tone while doing so.

A basic understanding of computer technology may not be sufficient for a therapist providing services via telehealth. Lee et al. (2015) provided guidelines on developing a telehealth service, with specific guidance dedicated to the technology aspects of telehealth. In addition to proficiency with a particular teleconferencing platform (e.g., Skype, Zoom, Webex), Lee et al. recommended that a therapist be aware of the minimally acceptable connectivity (e.g., upload and download speeds, latency to transmission), compatible hardware (e.g., computers, tablets, smartphones), and optimal audio (e.g., headphones or bug-in-the ear devices) and visual (e.g., web camera) options. Additionally, fee-for-service therapy requires HIPAA-compliant teleconferencing software and a business associate agreement that protects client privacy (BAA; Bassan, 2020).

Telehealth may present additional unique challenges not likely to be encountered during in-person services. Lerman et al. (2020) identified some of those challenges and offered specific solutions to overcome them. Six types of challenges were noted for caregiver-assisted telehealth with children exhibiting a challenging behavior: (a) technical issues (e.g., poor visibility due to room lighting), (b) challenges with remote viewing (e.g., client difficult to keep in view), (c) disruptions in the client's environment (e.g., other family members disrupt sessions), (d) other issues related to client behavior (e.g., client is reactive to therapist's voice or image), (e) issues related to caregiver behavior (e.g., caregiver insensitive to therapist instruction), and (f) additional issues at the practitioner (host) site (e.g., therapist shares an office with others). Although many of these challenges are easily remedied, in some cases, unique challenges may require termination of telehealth therapy and initiation of in-person services.

Training and Curriculum

Until recently, ABA training programs have not emphasized telehealth delivery models in their curricula. However, a few studies have provided guidance on the training needs for developing competence in telehealth-delivered ABA. Neely et al. (2022) evaluated a curriculum designed to train ABA therapists to deliver caregiver-assisted ABA therapy (i.e., mand training). This curriculum was focused on pre-session preparation (e.g., checking Internet connection, preparing room to ensure confidentiality) and expected behaviors during the session, ranging from the initial greeting of the caregiver to providing descriptive feedback when the caregiver performed a step correctly. The curriculum was taught remotely using videoconferencing to four BCBAs. A 38-item (17 telehealth-specific items) fidelity checklist was used to evaluate therapists' mastery of the skills taught. All four BCBAs mastered the curriculum in a relatively brief time frame, demonstrated maintenance of skills 12 months later, and rated the training as highly acceptable. In an extension of the Neely et al. study, Mac Naul et al. (2022) used the same training curriculum to successfully train seven behavioral technicians (Registered Behavioral Technicians® or RBTs) to conduct caregiver-assisted ABA independently.

A Case Example

The Participant

Our recent federally funded research at the University of Iowa has been focused on scientifically validating behavioral procedures through randomized controlled trials (RCT) using telehealth. The purpose of a recent RCT was to validate the FA and FCT procedures for young children with ASD who exhibited a challenging behavior. It was in this project that we enrolled Akiva and his mother, Annie. Akiva was 6 years old and in the first grade at the time of his enrollment. He is biracial and non-Hispanic. Akiva lived with Annie, who is black, and three younger siblings in rural Iowa, approximately 90 miles from the nearest BCBA and 260 miles from the University of Iowa, where the researchers conducting the study were located. He was diagnosed with ASD and moderate intellectual disability. Akiva was nonverbal and had been prescribed a speech-generating device but had not demonstrated independence with it. Akiva received special education services, including speech and language therapy at school, but no other services were available locally.

Akiva was referred to the study by a psychologist who also provided initial background information. Akiva was reported to exhibit several challenging behaviors, including self-injury (i.e., hand to head hitting, head to surface banging, hand biting), physical aggression (i.e., hitting, biting), and severe refusal. All challenging behaviors were reported to occur multiple times per day at home. Annie identified numerous detrimental outcomes resulting from Akiva's behaviors, including limited community outings, lack of stable employment due to an inability to find care providers for Akiva and her other children, and substantial family stress. Additionally, Akiva experienced numerous recurring injuries (e.g., bruising, lacerations) resulting from self-injury.

Pre-assessment

The author of this chapter was assigned to work with Akiva and Annie on the research grant. At the time, the therapist had more than 3 years of experience delivering ABA therapy via telehealth and more than 10 years of experience conducting behavioral assessments and treatments in-person. The first step for the therapist was to consider whether the child, parent, and setting were appropriate for the procedures in the research project. Following consent, a brief interview was conducted with Annie over the telephone to learn more about Akiva, his behaviors and skills, her skills with technology, and her comfort conducting the procedures via telehealth. Annie confirmed that she had the necessary equipment (laptop with webcam), connectivity, and safe space to conduct the procedures. Although she did not have any previous experiences with telehealth or behavioral therapy, she was comfortable with the procedures and indicated that she could ask a friend for assistance during telehealth visits if Akiva's behavior became too challenging to work with alone. A parent procedural manual was sent via email with step-by-step details on the assessment and treatment procedures so that Annie would be prepared for visits.

Next, a "troubleshooting" visit and parent interview was conducted via telehealth. Akiva was not present during the first half of the visit. We began the visit by testing the audio and video, reviewing the functions of the teleconferencing software (i.e., Vidyo®), exploring laptop placement, and addressing potential safety hazards (e.g., removal of a lamp close to the therapy area). We then conducted a thorough interview regarding Akiva's behaviors, antecedents and consequences of the behaviors, preferred items and activities, and available materials for use in sessions (e.g., work tasks). This was followed by a discussion of several safety procedures should self-injury or physical aggression occur. The purpose of the pre-emptive discussion on safety procedures was to instruct and model how to safely block dangerous behaviors as the therapist would not be available to step in to assist during sessions. Finally, we brought Akiva into the visit, and the therapist conducted a series of brief free play sessions where Akiva and Annie played without any demands. The purpose of the free play sessions was for Akiva and Annie to become acclimated to the audio and video of a therapist (i.e., reduce reactivity). Akiva did fine during these sessions and did not demonstrate any reactivity to the therapist.

Visit Structure

Based on the protocol of this research study, we conducted weekly, 1-h telehealth visits at a time convenient for Annie. Each visit was broken down into three parts: (a) pre-procedure check-in, (b) assessment or treatment procedures, and (c) post-procedure debriefing. During the pre-procedure check-in, we reviewed the previous visit, answered Annie's questions, and discussed the purpose and set goals for the current visit. Study procedures were conducted in 5-min sessions, with approximately four to six sessions completed in each visit. During the post-procedure debriefing, we provided additional feedback to Annie that was not delivered during the sessions, answered any questions, and provided a preview of the next visit. Once we initiated the treatment phase, we also asked Annie to practice treatment between visits.

Assessment

A brief assessment was conducted to determine the likely functions of Akiva's challenging behavior (Call et al., 2013). The therapist coached Annie to conduct a series of sessions that evaluated Akiva's response to free play (i.e., access to toys and attention without demands), restriction of parent attention, restriction of preferred items/activities (i.e., videos on a tablet), and work tasks (i.e., picking up toys and placing them in a toy bin). Annie was asked to safely block self-injury during all assessment sessions. Given that the goal of assessment was not to train Annie to conduct behavioral assessments, coaching mostly included antecedent-based directives and procedural comments. The brief assessment showed that Akiva's challenging behavior likely functioned to escape demands and to access preferred items/activities. Target behaviors were observed at a mean rate of 2.3 responses per minute, and Akiva refused to complete any work tasks without physical guidance.

Treatment

Based on the results of the assessment, and in accordance with the research protocol, the therapist worked with Annie to develop a treatment using FCT. The treatment involved teaching Akiva a two-step process of first completing some work and then touching a picture card to obtain his preferred activity. Challenging behaviors were placed on extinction and when necessary (e.g., self-injury and physical aggression) blocked. Over time and with success, the amount of work Annie presented was slowly increased until the terminal goal (i.e., picking up 40 items and communicating independently with 90% reduction in a challenging behavior) was reached. The shift to treatment resulted in the therapist providing more teaching through praise and process comments. Additionally, Annie reported elevated levels of stress during the early portions of treatment due to increases in the challenging behavior, so the therapist and Annie incorporated a "time-out" system whereby if Annie was frustrated or needed additional guidance, she could signal to the therapist with a time-out gesture. When a time-out was signaled, the therapist would initiate a brief break and address any of Annie's concerns.

The rate of Akiva's challenging behaviors ranged from 0.8 to 5.4 responses per minute ($M = 2.1$) across the initial ten treatment sessions, while communication and task completion were low. However, after the tenth session, Akiva showed a rapid progress including a rapid reduction of challenging behavior to zero and increase in independent communication and task completion to 100%. Low challenging behavior and high independent communication and task completion continued for the duration of treatment. Annie demonstrated high treatment fidelity throughout the study, and no outside assistance was required to conduct sessions in the home.

Overall, Akiva and Annie had 14 telehealth visits. Had they been required to travel for in-person therapy for these visits, they would have totaled 7252 miles and roughly 120 h of driving, which would have prohibited therapy. The audio and video worked well for the therapist and Annie during all visits, but one visit was cancelled early in the treatment phase when a software update began just prior to a visit, preventing Annie from connecting to the appointment. Additionally, there was occasional interference by Akiva's siblings, but it did not seem to affect Akiva's response to the treatment. Annie rated the telehealth approach as "highly acceptable" on the Treatment Acceptability Rating Scale-Revised (TARF-R; Reimers et al., 1992).

Summary and Key Takeaways

ABA is a highly effective approach for developing skills and reducing a challenging behavior, particularly for individuals with neurodevelopmental disabilities. Nearly 20 years of research has demonstrated the feasibility and effectiveness of telehealth-delivered ABA for a challenging behavior, and more recent research has proven telehealth to be an effective delivery modality for ABA targeting skill acquisition as well. When compared to in-person services, several studies have shown that telehealth-delivered ABA is just as effective and similarly acceptable. Additionally, there are several benefits to using telehealth over in-person services, including a greater reach for individuals living in geographically underserved areas, reduced travel time and financial costs for clients and providers, increased continuity of care when in-person services are not feasible or must be discontinued, and greater opportunity for treatment generalization. However, telehealth may not be suitable for all providers and their clients. For example, in situations where a client or provider has inadequate equipment or Internet connectivity, when a client poses a safety risk to themselves or caregivers providing therapy assistance, and when a client receiving direct ABA therapy lacks the ability to follow a provider's directives or sit independently, in-person ABA therapy is likely required. Moreover, telehealth should only be considered when the provider has developed adequate competence in telehealth-delivered ABA, which includes competence in the delivery of ABA procedures, adequate coaching skills, and at least a basic knowledge of the technological aspects of teleconferencing. For a provider interested in developing competence in telehealth-delivered ABA, there is no substitute for training and experience, but training curricula have recently been developed and evaluated within research studies.

References

Alaimo, C. M., Seiverling, L., Weisberg, H. R., Ortsman, J. T., & Jones, E. A. (2023). An evaluation of a telehealth caregiver training package to treat food selectivity. *Behavior Modification, 47*(4), 905–935. https://doi.org/10.1177/01454455221131285

American Psychological Association. (2017). *Ethical principles of psychologists and code of conduct* (2002, amended effective June 1, 2010, and January 1, 2017). https://www.apa.org/ethics/code/.

Andersen, A. S., Hansen, B. A., Hathaway, K. L., & Elson, L. A. (2021). A demonstration of caregiver-implemented functional analysis of inappropriate mealtime behavior via telehealth. *Behavior Analysis in Practice, 14*(4), 1067–1072. https://doi.org/10.1007/s40617-021-00615-2

Araiba, S., & Čolić, M. (2022). Preliminary practice recommendations for telehealth direct applied behavior analysis services with children with autism. *Journal of Behavioral Education, 1–35,* 1. https://doi.org/10.1007/s10864-022-09473-6

Barkaia, A., Stokes, T. F., & Mikiashvili, T. (2017). Intercontinental telehealth coaching of therapists to improve verbalizations by children with autism. *Journal of Applied Behavior Analysis, 50*(3), 582–589. https://doi.org/10.1002/jaba.391

Barretto, A., Wacker, D. P., Harding, J., Lee, J., & Berg, W. K. (2006). Using telemedicine to conduct behavioral assessments. *Journal of Applied Behavior Analysis, 39*(3), 333–340. https://doi.org/10.1901/jaba.2006.173-04

Bassan, S. (2020). Data privacy considerations for telehealth consumers amid COVID-19. *Journal of Law and the Biosciences, 7*(1), lsaa075. https://doi.org/10.1093/jlb/lsaa075

Batchelder, S. R., Van Heukelom, J. T., Proctor, K., & Washington, W. D. (2023). Escalating schedules of incentives increase physical activity with no differences between deposit and no-deposit groups: A systematic replication. *Journal of Applied Behavior Analysis, 56*(1), 201–215. https://doi.org/10.1002/jaba.964

Behavior Analyst Certification Board. (2020). *Ethics code for behavior analysts.* https://bacb.com/wp-content/ethics-code-for-behavior-analysts/.

Behavior Analyst Certification Board. (2023). *US employment demand for behavior analysts: 2010–2022*. Author.

Bergmann, S., Toussaint, K. A., Niland, H., Sansing, E. M., Armshaw, G., & Baltazar, M. (2021). Adapting direct services for telehealth: A practical tutorial. *Behavior Analysis in Practice, 14*(4), 1010–1046. https://doi.org/10.1007/s40617-020-00529-5

Bloomfield, B. S., Fischer, A. J., Clark, R. R., & Dove, M. B. (2019). Treatment of food selectivity in a child with avoidant/restrictive food intake disorder through parent teleconsultation. *Behavior Analysis in Practice, 12*(1), 33–43. https://doi.org/10.1007/s40617-018-0251-y

Boutain, A. R., Sheldon, J. B., & Sherman, J. A. (2020). Evaluation of a telehealth parent training program in teaching self-care skills to children with autism. *Journal of Applied Behavior Analysis, 53*(3), 1259–1275. https://doi.org/10.1002/jaba.743

Brodhead, M. T., Quigley, S. P., & Wilczynski, S. M. (2018). A call for discussion about scope of competence in behavior analysis. *Behavior Analysis in Practice, 11*(4), 424–435. https://doi.org/10.1007/s40617-018-00303-8

Bruinsma, Y. E., Minjarez, M. B., Schreibman, L., & Stahmer, A. C. (2020). *Naturalistic developmental behavioral interventions for autism spectrum sisorder*. Brookes Publishing.

Call, N. A., Zangrillo, A. N., Delfs, C. H., & Findley, A. J. (2013). A comparison of brief functional analyses with and without consequences. *Behavioral Interventions, 28*, 22–39. https://doi.org/10.1002/bin.1353

Carnett, A., Hansen, S., Tullis, C., & Machalicek, W. (2021). Using behavioural skills training via telehealth to increase teachers use of communication interventions and increase student use of speech-generating devices in a high school functional skills classroom. *Journal of Intellectual Disability Research: JIDR, 65*(2), 133–148. https://doi.org/10.1111/jir.12794

Coon, J. C., Bush, H., & Rapp, J. T. (2022). Eight months of telehealth for a state-funded project in foster care and related services: Progress made and lessons learned. *Behavior Analysis in Practice, 15*(4), 1348–1360. https://doi.org/10.1007/s40617-022-00682-z

Cooper, M. (2022). Reducing special education costs by providing early intervention for autistic children. *Behavioral Interventions, 37*(2), 397–414. https://doi.org/10.1002/bin.1839

Council of Autism Service Providers. (2020). *Practice parameters for telehealth-implementation of applied behavior analysis: Continuity of care during COVID-19 pandemic*. Council of Autism Service Providers.

Council of Autism Service Providers. (2021). *Practice parameters for telehealth-implementation of applied behavior analysis* (2nd ed.). Author.

Craig, E. A., Dounavi, K., & Ferguson, J. (2021). Telehealth to train interventionists teaching functional living skills to children with autism spectrum disorder. *Journal of Applied Behavior Analysis, 54*(2), 511–529. https://doi.org/10.1002/jaba.834

Crockett, J. L., Becraft, J. L., Phillips, S. T., Wakeman, M., & Cataldo, M. F. (2020). Rapid conversion from clinic to telehealth behavioral services during the COVID-19 pandemic. *Behavior Analysis in Practice, 13*(4), 725–735. https://doi.org/10.1007/s40617-020-00499-8

Dabney, H. A., DeVries, J., & Jimenez-Gomez, C. (2023). Caregiver-implemented toilet training procedures for children with autism spectrum disorder. *Behavioral Interventions, 38*(3), 804–821. https://doi.org/10.1002/bin.1940

de Marchena, A. B., Eigsti, I.-M., & Yerys, B. E. (2015). Brief report: Generalization weaknesses in verbally fluent children and adolescents with autism spectrum disorder. *Journal of Autism and Developmental Disorders, 45*(10), 3370–3376. https://doi.org/10.1007/s10803-015-2478-6

Durand, V. M., & Carr, E. G. (1992). An analysis of maintenance following functional communication training. *Journal of Applied Behavior Analysis, 25*(4), 777–794. https://doi.org/10.1901/jaba.1992.25-777

Ferguson, J. L., Majeski, M. J., McEachin, J., Leaf, R., Cihon, J. H., & Leaf, J. B. (2020). Evaluating discrete trial teaching with instructive feedback delivered in a dyad arrangement via telehealth. *Journal of Applied Behavior Analysis, 53*(4), 1876–1888. https://doi.org/10.1002/jaba.773

Frazier, T. W., Klingemier, E. W., Anderson, C. J., Gengoux, G. W., Youngstrom, E. A., & Hardan, A. Y. (2021). A longitudinal study of language trajectories and treatment outcomes of early intensive behavioral intervention for autism. *Journal of Autism and Developmental Disorders, 51*(12), 4534–4550. https://doi.org/10.1007/s10803-021-04900-5

Frieder, J. E., Peterson, S. M., Woodward, J., Crane, J., & Garner, M. (2009). Teleconsultation in school settings: Linking classroom teachers and behavior analysts through web-based technology. *Behavior Analysis in Practice, 2*(2), 32–39. https://doi.org/10.1007/BF03391746

Gerow, S., Radhakrishnan, S., Akers, J. S., McGinnis, K., & Swensson, R. (2021). Telehealth parent coaching to improve daily living skills for children with ASD. *Journal of Applied Behavior Analysis, 54*(2), 566–581. https://doi.org/10.1002/jaba.813

Gevarter, C., Najar, A. M., Flake, J., Tapia-Alvidrez, F., & Lucero, A. (2022). Naturalistic communication training for early intervention providers and latinx parents of children with signs of autism. *Journal of Developmental and Physical Disabilities, 34*(1), 147–169. https://doi.org/10.1007/s10882-021-09794-w

Gibson, J. L., Pennington, R. C., Stenhoff, D. M., & Hopper, J. S. (2010). Using desktop videoconferencing to deliver interventions to a preschool student with autism. *Topics in Early Childhood Special Education, 29*(4), 214–225. https://doi.org/10.1177/0271121409352873

Gregori, E., Drew, C., Lory, C., & Kim, N. (2023). Grandparent-implemented interventions to reduce challenging behavior of an adult with autism: A pilot telehealth case study. *Clinical Case Studies, 15346501231159140*, 439. https://doi.org/10.1177/15346501231159140

Halbur, M., Kodak, T., McKee, M., Carroll, R., Preas, E., Reidy, J., & Cordeiro, M. C. (2021). Tolerance of face coverings for children with autism spectrum disorder. *Journal of Applied Behavior Analysis, 54*(2), 600–617. https://doi.org/10.1002/jaba.833

Horner, R. H., & Sugai, G. (2015). School-wide PBIS: An example of applied behavior analysis implemented at a scale of social importance. *Behavior Analysis in Practice, 8*(1), 80–85. https://doi.org/10.1007/s40617-015-0045-4

Knopp, K., Ferguson, J. L., Piazza, J., Weiss, M. J., Lee, M., Cihon, J. H., & Leaf, J. B. (2023). A comparison between direct telehealth and in-person methods of teaching expressive labels to children diagnosed with autism spectrum disorder. *Behavior Modification, 47*(2), 432–453. https://doi.org/10.1177/01454455221130000

Koegel, R. L., & Koegel, L. (2019). *Pivotal response treatment for autism spectrum disorders*. Brookes Publishing.

Larsen, A., Schieltz, K. M., Barrett, A., & O'Brien, M. J. (2023). A retrospective analysis of therapists' coaching behavior when directing parents to conduct behavioral assessments and treatments via telehealth. *Behavior Modification, 47*(1), 154–184. https://doi.org/10.1177/01454455221106127

Lee, J. F., Schieltz, K. M., Suess, A. N., Wacker, D. P., Romani, P. W., Lindgren, S. D., Kopelman, T. G., & Dalmau, Y. C. P. (2015). Guidelines for developing telehealth services and troubleshooting problems with telehealth technology when coaching parents to conduct functional analyses and functional communication training in their homes. *Behavior Analysis in Practice, 8*(2), 190–200. https://doi.org/10.1007/s40617-014-0031-2

Lerman, D. C., O'Brien, M. J., Neely, L., Call, N. A., Tsami, L., Schieltz, K. M., Berg, W. K., Graber, J., Huang, P., Kopelman, T., & Cooper-Brown, L. J. (2020). Remote coaching of caregivers via telehealth: Challenges and potential solutions. *Journal of Behavioral Education, 29*(2), 195–221. https://doi.org/10.1007/s10864-020-09378-2

Lillie, M. A., Harman, M. J., Hurd, M., & Smalley, M. R. (2021). Increasing passive compliance to wearing a facemask in children with autism spectrum disorder. *Journal of Applied Behavior Analysis, 54*(2), 582–599. https://doi.org/10.1002/jaba.829

Lindgren, S., Wacker, D., Suess, A., Schieltz, K., Pelzel, K., Kopelman, T., Lee, J., Romani, P., & Waldron, D. (2016). Telehealth and autism: Treating challenging behavior at lower cost. *Pediatrics, 137*(Suppl 2), S167–S175. https://doi.org/10.1542/peds.2015-2851O

Mac Naul, H., Wimberley, J., Labay, A., Neely, L., Novotny, M., & Morgan, B. (2022). Effects of an adapted telehealth training curriculum for registered behavior technicians®. *Advances in Neurodevelopmental Disorders.*, 1. https://doi.org/10.1007/s41252-022-00285-3

Machalicek, W., O'Reilly, M., Chan, J. M., Lang, R., Rispoli, M., Davis, T., Shogren, K., Sigafoos, J., Lancioni, G., Antonucci, M., Langthorne, P., Andrews, A., & Didden, R. (2009a). Using videoconferencing to conduct functional analysis of challenging behavior and develop classroom behavioral support plans for students with autism. *Education and Training in Developmental Disabilities, 44*(2), 207–217.

Machalicek, W., O'Reilly, M., Chan, J. M., Rispoli, M., Lang, R., Davis, T., Shogren, K., Sorrells, A., Lancioni, G., Sigafoos, J., Green, V., & Langthorne, P. (2009b). Using videoconferencing to support teachers to conduct preference assessments with students with autism and developmental disabilities. *Research in Autism Spectrum Disorders, 3*(1), 32–41. https://doi.org/10.1016/j.rasd.2008.03.004

McGee, G. G. (2022). Incidental teaching research: Early beginnings through recent innovations. In J. B. Leaf, J. H. Cihon, J. L. Ferguson, & M. J. Weiss (Eds.), *Handbook of applied behavior analysis interventions for autism. Autism and child psychopathology series* (pp. 185–206). Springer. https://doi.org/10.1007/978-3-030-96478-8_11

McHugh, C. L., Dozier, C. L., Diaz de Villegas, S. C., & Kanaman, N. A. (2022). Using synchronous reinforcement to increase mask wearing in adults with intellectual and developmental disabilities. *Journal of Applied Behavior Analysis, 55*(4), 1157–1171. https://doi.org/10.1002/jaba.950

Mello, M. P., Goldman, S. E., Urbano, R. C., & Hodapp, R. M. (2016). Services for children with autism spectrum disorder: Comparing rural and non-rural communities. *Education and Training in Autism and Developmental Disabilities, 51*(4), 355–365.

Miltenberger, R., Miller, B. G., & Zerger, H. M. (2015). Applied behavior analysis. In C. M. Nezu & A. M. Nezu (Eds.), *The Oxford handbook of cognitive and behavioral therapies* (pp. 79–95). Oxford University Press. https://doi.org/10.1093/oxfordhb/9780199733255.013.17

Nastasi, J. A., Tassistro, I. B., & Gravina, N. E. (2023). Breaks and productivity: An exploratory analysis. *Journal of Applied Behavior Analysis, 56*(3), 539–548. https://doi.org/10.1002/jaba.995

National Autism Center. (2015). *Findings and conclusions: National Standards Project, phase 2*. National Autism Center.

Neely, L., Tsami, L., Graber, J., & Lerman, D. C. (2022). Towards the development of a curriculum to train behavior analysts to provide services via telehealth. *Journal of Applied Behavior Analysis, 55*(2), 395–411. https://doi.org/10.1002/jaba.904

Nohelty, K., Bradford, C. B., Hirschfeld, L., Miyake, C., & Novack, M. N. (2022). Effectiveness of telehealth direct therapy for individuals with autism spectrum disorder. *Behavior Analysis in Practice, 15*(3), 643–658. https://doi.org/10.1007/s40617-021-00603-6

Normand, M. P., Dallery, J., & Slanzi, C. M. (2021). Leveraging applied behavior analysis research and practice in the service of public health. *Journal of Applied Behavior Analysis, 54*(2), 457–483. https://doi.org/10.1002/jaba.832

O'Brien, M. J., Schieltz, K. M., Berg, W. K., McComas, J. J., & Wacker, D. P. (2021). Delivering interventions via telehealth: Functional communication training with a child with autism as a case example. *Research and Practice for Persons with Severe Disabilities, 46*(1), 53–60. https://doi.org/10.1177/1540796920980452

O'Brien, M. J., Pelzel, K. E., Hendrix, N. M., Schieltz, K. M., Miller, K., Call, N. A., Tsami, L., Lerman, D. C., Berg, W. K., Kopelman, T. G., Wacker, D. P., & Lindgren, S. D. (2022). Parent ratings of generalized and indirect effects of functional communication training for children with autism spectrum disorder. *Behavior Modification, 46*(5), 971–1001. https://doi.org/10.1177/01454455211018815

Patel, M. R., Rosenlund, K., Miller, S. E., Andersen, A. S., & Miles, A. (2023). Using an intensive interdisciplinary telehealth model to treat pediatric feeding disorders. *Journal of Applied Behavior Analysis, 56*(2), 400–415. https://doi.org/10.1002/jaba.976

Pellegrino, A. J., & DiGennaro Reed, F. D. (2020). Using telehealth to teach valued skills to adults with intellectual and developmental disabilities. *Journal of Applied Behavior Analysis, 53*(3), 1276–1289. https://doi.org/10.1002/jaba.734

Peterson, K. M., Ibañez, V. F., Volkert, V. M., Zeleny, J. R., Engler, C. W., & Piazza, C. C. (2021). Using telehealth to provide outpatient follow-up to children with avoidant/restrictive food intake disorder. *Journal of Applied Behavior Analysis, 54*(1), 6–24. https://doi.org/10.1002/jaba.794

Peysin, J., Fienup, D., & Romas, S. (2023). An experimental comparison of in-person and remote instruction for preschoolers with disabilities. *Behavior Analysis in Practice, 16*(2), 558–572. https://doi.org/10.1007/s40617-022-00737-1

Pollard, J. S., LeBlanc, L. A., Griffin, C. A., & Baker, J. M. (2021). The effects of transition to technician-delivered telehealth ABA treatment during the COVID-19 crisis: A preliminary analysis. *Journal of Applied Behavior Analysis, 54*(1), 87–102. https://doi.org/10.1002/jaba.803

Reimers, T. M., Wacker, D. P., Cooper, L. J., & DeRaad, A. O. (1992). Clinical evaluation of the variables associated with treatment acceptability and their relation to compliance. *Behavioral Disorders, 18*(1), 67–76. http://www.jstor.org/stable/23887101

Rooker, G. W., Bonner, A. C., Dillon, C. M., & Zarcone, J. R. (2018). Behavioral treatment of automatically reinforced SIB: 1982–2015. *Journal of Applied Behavior Analysis, 51*(4), 974–997. https://doi.org/10.1002/jaba.492

Schieltz, K. M., O'Brien, M. J., Tsami, L., Call, N. A., & Lerman, D. C. (2022). Behavioral assessment and treatment via telehealth for children with autism: From local to global clinical applications. *International Journal of Environmental Research and Public Health, 19*(4), 2190. https://doi.org/10.3390/ijerph19042190

Schreibman, L., Dawson, G., Stahmer, A. C., Landa, R., Rogers, S. J., McGee, G. G., Kasari, C., Ingersoll, B., Kaiser, A. P., Bruinsma, Y., McNerney, E., Wetherby, A., & Halladay, A. (2015). Naturalistic developmental behavioral interventions: Empirically validated treatments for autism spectrum disorder. *Journal of Autism and Developmental Disorders, 45*(8), 2411–2428. https://doi.org/10.1007/s10803-015-2407-8

Shawler, L. A., Clayborne, J. C., Nasca, B., & O'Connor, J. T. (2021). An intensive telehealth assessment and treatment model for an adult with developmental disabilities. *Research in Developmental Disabilities, 111*, 103876. https://doi.org/10.1016/j.ridd.2021.103876

Sivaraman, M., Virues-Ortega, J., & Roeyers, H. (2021). Telehealth mask wearing training for children with autism during the COVID-19 pandemic. *Journal of Applied Behavior Analysis, 54*(1), 70–86. https://doi.org/10.1002/jaba.802

Steinbrenner, J. R., Hume, K., Odom, S. L., Morin, K. L., Nowell, S. W., Tomaszewski, B., Szendrey, S., McIntyre, N. S., Yücesoy-Özkan, Ş., & Savage, M. N. (2020). *Children, youth, and young adults with autism*. National Clearinghouse on Autism Evidence and Practice.

Stokes, T. F., & Baer, D. M. (1977). An implicit technology of generalization 1. *Journal of Applied Behavior Analysis, 10*(2), 349–367. https://doi.org/10.1901/jaba.1977.10-349

Tomlinson, S. R. L., Gore, N., & McGill, P. (2018). Training individuals to implement applied behavior analytic procedures via telehealth: A systematic review of the literature. *Journal of Behavioral Education, 27*(2), 172–222. https://doi.org/10.1007/s10864-018-9292-0

Tsami, L., Lerman, D., & Toper-Korkmaz, O. (2019). Effectiveness and acceptability of parent training via telehealth among families around the world. *Journal of Applied Behavior Analysis, 52*(4), 1113–1129. https://doi.org/10.1002/jaba.645

Virues-Ortega, J., Pérez-Bustamante, A., & Tarifa-Rodriguez, A. (2022). Evidence-based applied behavior analysis (aba) autism treatments: An overview of comprehensive and focused meta-analyses. In J. L. Matson & P. Sturmey (Eds.), *Handbook of autism and pervasive developmental disorder: Assessment, diagnosis, and treatment* (pp. 631–659). Springer International Publishing. https://doi.org/10.1007/978-3-030-88538-0_27

Volkert, V. M., Peterson, K. M., Zeleny, J. R., & Piazza, C. C. (2014). A clinical protocol to increase chewing and assess mastication in children with feeding disorders. *Behavior Modification, 38*(5), 705–729. https://doi.org/10.1177/0145445514536575

Wacker, D. P., Lee, J. F., Padilla Dalmau, Y. C., Kopelman, T. G., Lindgren, S. D., Kuhle, J., Pelzel, K. E., Dyson, S., Schieltz, K. M., & Waldron, D. B. (2013a). Conducting functional communication training via telehealth to reduce the problem behavior of young children with autism. *Journal of Developmental and Physical Disabilities, 25*(1), 35–48. https://doi.org/10.1007/s10882-012-9314-0

Wacker, D. P., Lee, J. F., Dalmau, Y. C. P., Kopelman, T. G., Lindgren, S. D., Kuhle, J., Pelzel, K. E., & Waldron, D. B. (2013b). Conducting functional analyses of problem behavior via telehealth. *Journal of Applied Behavior Analysis, 46*(1), 31–46. https://doi.org/10.1002/jaba.29

Wacker, D. P., Schieltz, K. M., Suess, A. N., Romani, P. W., Dalmau, Y. C. P., Kopelman, T. G., Lee, J. F., & Lindgren, S. D. (2016). Telehealth. In N. N. Singh (Ed.), *Handbook of evidence-based practices in intellectual and developmental disabilities* (pp. 585–613). Springer International Publishing. https://doi.org/10.1007/978-3-319-26583-4_22

Wass, S. V., & Porayska-Pomsta, K. (2014). The uses of cognitive training technologies in the treatment of autism spectrum disorders. *Autism, 18*(8), 851–871. https://doi.org/10.1177/1362361313499827

Witt, M. R., Stokes, T. F., Parsonson, B. S., & Dudding, C. C. (2018). Effect of distance caregiver coaching on functional skills of a child with traumatic brain injury. *Brain Injury, 32*(7), 894–899. https://doi.org/10.1080/02699052.2018.1466365

Yingling, M. E., Ruther, M. H., Dubuque, E. M., & Mandell, D. S. (2021). County-level variation in geographic access to Board certified behavior analysts among children with autism Spectrum disorder in the United States. *Autism, 25*(6), 1734–1745. https://doi.org/10.1177/13623613211002051

Yingling, M. E., Ruther, M. H., & Dubuque, E. M. (2022). Trends in geographic access to board certified behavior analysts among children with autism spectrum disorder, 2018–2021. *Journal of Autism and Developmental Disorders, 52*(12), 5483–5490. https://doi.org/10.1007/s10803-021-05402-0

Zwaigenbaum, L., Bauman, M. L., Choueiri, R., Kasari, C., Carter, A., Granpeesheh, D., Mailloux, Z., Smith Roley, S., Wagner, S., Fein, D., Pierce, K., Buie, T., Davis, P. A., Newschaffer, C., Robins, D., Wetherby, A., Stone, W. L., Yirmiya, N., Estes, A., et al. (2015). Early intervention for children with autism spectrum disorder under 3 years of age: Recommendations for practice and research. *Pediatrics, 136*(Suppl 1), S60–S81. https://doi.org/10.1542/peds.2014-3667E

Part IV
Parenting Interventions

Chapter 6
Telemental Health Parent Training and Support for Children with Autism Spectrum Disorder: COMPASS for Hope (C-HOPE)

Robert J. Reese, Lisa A. Ruble, and Alyssa L. Clements-Hickman

Parenting interventions are designed to increase parent knowledge and skills through collaboration and coaching support from practitioners. For children with autism, parent-implemented interventions are 1 of 28 evidence-based practices (Amsbary & AFIRM Team, 2017). Access to these specialized interventions is challenging for many families due to geographical (e.g., living in a rural, remote location) and financial (e.g., reliable transportation, childcare, insurance) barriers and simply the limited availability and access to trained clinicians (Antezana et al., 2017). Telemental health (TMH), the use of telecommunication and other technologies to facilitate service delivery of mental and behavioral health services, offers the potential to reduce treatment barriers and improve access to specialized services. The COVID-19 pandemic has changed how TMH services are considered. Historically underutilized (Glueckauf et al., 2018), the pandemic forced the mental health profession, educational settings, third-party reimbursement entities, and those in need of services to pivot to these services. We anticipate that this increased use will continue and believe this is an exciting and needed development. At the same time, the use of technology platforms must be carefully considered to ensure that the quality of care is not compromised.

The purpose of this chapter is to provide an overview of a TMH-based parent training program, called COMPASS for Hope (C-HOPE). C-HOPE is a program

R. J. Reese (✉)
Department of Special Education, Rehabilitation, and Counseling, Auburn University, Auburn, AL, USA
e-mail: rjr0028@auburn.edu

L. A. Ruble
Department of Special Education, Ball State University, Muncie, IN, USA

A. L. Clements-Hickman
Department of Psychological Science and Counseling, Austin Peay State University, Clarksville, TN, USA

L. N. Niec, C. E. Schoonover (eds.), *Telemental Health Care for Children and Families*,
https://doi.org/10.1007/978-3-031-69264-2_6

that was designed to provide both parental/caregiver support and practical behavioral strategies that are tailored to the unique context and challenges of families that have a child with autism spectrum disorder (ASD) with special attention to parents and caregivers from rural areas. Before providing the details of the program, we discuss the advantages and challenges of providing services and the evidence of empirical support for TMH interventions for parent training including C-HOPE. We also offer practice considerations for providing services that are delivered with a technology platform. We conclude with a case study that highlights implementation of C-HOPE that includes participant and clinician perspectives.

Advantages and Challenges of Using TMH

Providing access for individuals and families who live in a remote rural area is an obvious advantage of TMH, but this advantage seems to extend to addressing issues of time, effort, and other resources needed to travel and receive services (Langarizadeh et al., 2017). Comparing three different service models (home TMH, in-home therapy, and clinic TMH), Lindgren and colleagues (2016) found that home TMH services were cheaper to implement than clinic-based TMH services and in-home, direct therapy services. Behavioral health services for children with ASD are typically offered in community- or clinic-based settings (Ingersoll et al., 2016) and are rarely found in rural areas. Yet, caregivers of children with ASD residing in rural areas report behavior management services as one of their highest unmet needs (Drahota et al., 2020; Kuravackel et al., 2018), and the majority of rural counties have no access to a psychiatrist (Andrilla et al., 2018). Beyond geographical limitations, other barriers include financial resources, transportation, childcare, and social disparities (Khetani et al., 2018; Meadan et al., 2013).

In our experiences, both the rural and urban families we have worked with indicated that TMH (both videoconferencing and telephone) helped overcome significant barriers, with convenience and access to specialized services subjectively noted most frequently. Although rural families often acknowledge the obvious benefit of not having to travel a longer distance for services, they more often expressed gratitude for simply having access to specialized services that might benefit their child. Their urban counterparts did not seem much different in this regard but often added that transportation and childcare were issues of concern that were mitigated because of TMH. This feedback is consistent with the feedback reported by others. Ashburner and colleagues (2016) examined parent's views on telehealth versus in-person training on interventions for their children with autism. All caregivers reported benefiting from the feasibility of online training, with time flexibility, lack of issues with travel and location, and reduced financial cost being perceived as advantages.

Although there are multiple potential advantages for TMH to address access barriers, clinicians have not always been willing to embrace technology-mediated services (Glueckauf et al., 2018). Reasons have included concerns about technology reliability, technology know-how, technology costs and maintenance, an assumption that in-person services are better particularly for developing a therapeutic alliance, concerns about privacy and confidentiality, and an inability to observe client nonverbal cues and body language (Connolly et al., 2020). Lack of third-party reimbursement has also been a detractor for the use of TMH. Things have shifted in a short time, however. Technology has become more reliable, affordable, and easier to use, and the COVID-19 pandemic has influenced attitudes toward its use along with third-party reimbursement being modified to better accommodate TMH services.

The TMH delivery format also influences attitudes and use. For example, texting offers no visual or auditory information, the phone has no visual information, and videoconferencing offers both, but visual information can still be limited with all offering limited control of the client environment (unless clients go to a designated location, such as a regional medical center). Interestingly, each of these formats has evidence of being effective, but each format has little evidence of how these limitations influence treatment outcome.

When considering client attitudes toward TMH, clients have generally preferred in-person services (March et al., 2018; Renn et al., 2019; Wallin et al., 2018). Yet, similar to our informal feedback from caregivers who received C-HOPE, research indicates that clients generally hold positive views about TMH services (Apolinário-Hagen et al., 2018). Acceptability of TMH services also seems to improve with exposure, with past users reporting significantly higher acceptability compared to first-time users (e.g., Gun et al., 2011).

Another practical consideration is broadband Internet access for the populations you wish to serve, although access has continually increased in the United States. Roughly 90% of Americans use the Internet (73% having home access), and 81% have a smart phone (Pew Research Center, 2021). Although families may have access, connectivity quality and the number and quality of devices in the home can influence experience. For example, in our experience, when conducting individual sessions with parents, technology issues were a concern with a few that lengthened sessions and were disruptive to the flow of the sessions. The quality of the camera, the monitor, the overall setting, and general user savviness of the clients were all factors that seemed to impact the smoothness and overall productivity of the sessions. Although we did not find differences between in-person and videoconference treatment conditions in a comparison study with C-HOPE (Kuravackel et al., 2018), subjectively it seemed that these factors mattered. Perhaps the perceived advantages outweighed these concerns.

Evidence Base for TMH and TMH Parent Training Interventions

Recent years have seen an increase in empirical studies focused on the effectiveness of TMH. Effectiveness can be measured in multiple ways, including symptom reduction and level of satisfaction. Reviews comparing in-person therapy to TMH in terms of symptom reduction typically yield results comparable to in-person therapy (e.g., Backhaus et al., 2012; Varker et al., 2019). This includes both those delivered via videoconferencing and telephone. Notably, Lin et al. (2021) recently reviewed 20 randomized controlled trials comparing TMH to in-person therapy. Although the reported effect sizes slightly favored in-person therapy, these differences were non-significant.

Previous authors have noted that symptom reduction should not be the only metric for comparing TMH and in-person therapy, noting that the client level of satisfaction is another potential important measure of the effectiveness of telepsychology (Aafjes-van Doorn, 2022). Consistently, research has noted that clients' level of satisfaction is an indicator of the effectiveness of services (Fortin et al., 2018). Some studies comparing in-person and TMH formats that have included a measure of client satisfaction have generally found that clients are equally satisfied with both modalities (Backhaus et al., 2012). With COMPASS in schools, no differences in caregiver and teacher satisfaction were observed between the web-based coaching group and the face-to-face group (Ruble et al., 2013). However, it is important to note that variables such as treatment approach may influence clients' level of satisfaction with TMH (Weintraub et al., 2023).

The majority of TMH research has focused on psychotherapy (Aafjes-van Doorn, 2022). However, research on other interventions such as parent training is increasing. Parent training interventions are where the parent receives training for the benefit of the child. Thus, the parent is viewed as the vehicle for change in the child (Bearss et al., 2015). There is a substantial empirical literature over the past several decades that shows the benefit of parent training programs for reducing challenging child behaviors (e.g., Lundahl et al., 2006; Zisser & Eyberg, 2010), including children with ASD (e.g., Bearss et al., 2015; Hardan et al., 2015). More recently, there are numerous studies that have been published focused on the delivery of parent training interventions via TMH for the treatment of ASD. These studies have typically found that parent training interventions for ASD conducted via TMH are comparable to in-person services across a range treatment targets (e.g., social communication, functional communication training, behavior management; Ellison et al., 2021).

The program we are focused on, C-HOPE, also has empirical evidence to support its use. Using an iterative pre-post randomized control group design that compared in-person (n = 13), videoconferencing (n = 20), and waitlist control (n = 10, who ultimately received the treatment via videoconferencing) conditions, participants in the treatment conditions reported statistically significant decreases in stress, increases in perceived competence, and reduced problem child behaviors

(Kuravackel et al., 2018). There were no significant differences between treatment conditions with effect sizes being comparable to studies targeting similar treatment outcomes, ranging from $d = 0.24$ to 0.73. There were also no differences in the group alliance measures when comparing in-person and videoconferencing formats. Parents/caregivers also rated C-HOPE high in both intervention conditions. In a follow-up study, Dahiya et al. (2021) compared treatment outcomes for rural ($n = 12$) and urban ($n = 8$) parents of children with ASD. Interestingly, urban participants reported larger increases on a measure of parent knowledge but also had significantly lower scores at pre-test. Overall, medium to large effect sizes were noted in both conditions ($d = 0.36$ to 2.12) for parent knowledge, parent activation, and child behavior. The exception is that there was a negligible effect on child behavior for rural participants ($d = 0.01$). There was a strong negative correlation between increased perceived parent competence and pre-post decreases in child problem behaviors. Overall, the evidence for C-HOPE could be categorized as promising, with effect sizes being comparable to parent training interventions provided in person but warrants more research given the sample sizes.

C-HOPE

C-HOPE comes from COMPASS (the Collaborative Model for Promoting Competence and Success; Ruble et al., 2013; Ruble & McGrew, 2023), an intervention originally developed for delivery in schools. COMPASS has been verified in three randomized controlled studies, including its delivery via web-based coaching (Ruble et al., 2010, 2013, 2018) and electronic feedback (Ogle et al., 2023). For standard COMPASS, a trained consultant brings together the child's educational team (primarily caregiver and teacher) for creating a shared understanding of the child at home, in school, and in the community. Prior to the consultation, the caregiver and teacher complete the COMPASS profile, a survey of developmental skills that discern areas of strength and challenge. The profile is aggregated and used to guide the discussion with the team for supporting shared decision-making. Once the team gathers a holistic understanding of the child, goals related to self-determination in the areas of social skills, communication, and self-management skills are identified, and intervention plans are written. Based on evidence-based practice in psychology (EBPP, McGrew et al., 2016), each intervention plan considers the child's personal and environmental challenges and supports, resulting in highly personalized evidence-based intervention plans adapted to the needs of the child and their environment.

COMPASS was extended from the school setting to an outpatient setting with the adaptation of COMPASS for HOPE (C-HOPE). Based on the same philosophical framework that competence results from the balance between challenges and supports, C-HOPE is highly individualized to the child and the developmental skills that children with autism are often missing that can lead to problematic behavior and must be understood as such. When the personal and environmental supports of children outweigh their personal and environmental challenges, competence can be achieved (Ruble & Dalrymple, 2002). We saw more children obtaining an autism diagnosis and recognized there was a need for evidence-based parent-implemented interventions that addressed behavior that was understood from an autism perspective as much as possible. Rather than using another behavior intervention program, we decided to adapt COMPASS to create C-HOPE because of the success of COMPASS for improving child outcomes based on mutually supported opportunities for parents and practitioners to collaborate. The program can be implemented by autism specialists; school, clinical, and counseling psychologists; behavior specialists; and other clinicians with training in autism and behavior.

C-HOPE combines psychoeducational instruction, information on autism and child development, resources for help, consideration of the impact of autism on the family, and instruction on learning theory and behavior in terminology accessible to caregivers. C-HOPE has three desired outcomes: decreased child problem behavior and caregiver stress and increased caregiver competency. As an 8-week program, C-HOPE can be delivered in person or via TMH. Half of the sessions conducted once a week are individual and last about 60–90 min; the other half are group sessions with other caregivers that last about 2 hours. Comparative effectiveness studies show that outcomes are similar independent of treatment delivery modality (described further in the research section). C-HOPE has been expanded and tested using TMH (Kuravackel et al., 2018) and as an asynchronous intervention where caregivers accessed online learning videos and discussion boards with other parents while obtaining individual support via teleconferencing (Rodgers 2018).

Clinical Considerations for C-HOPE

C-HOPE is a behaviorally based parenting program that provides information designed to empower parents and caregivers to best help and care for their child. A unique dimension of this program, one that we believe separates it from other parent-implemented programs, is the emphasis we place on a collaborative, strength-based approach in working with families. We intend for our group approach to be therapeutic as well as educational. This approach requires that the clinician(s) draw upon basic counseling skills that promote active listening and empathy. Clinician(s) also must be aware of group process for the purpose of promoting cohesion among members and to ensure that the goals and needs of the group are met.

One challenge to note when working through a session agenda is easy to be "agenda driven" and place less emphasis on checking in with parents and caregivers and evaluating how they are responding to the information that is delivered. Throughout the program sessions, we build in "check-ins" and other prompts to facilitate a collaborative relationship and strong therapeutic alliance.

Why such concern for a strong therapeutic alliance? It is well known that a strong alliance is foundational to a good helping relationship (Norcross & Lambert, 2018). One type of therapeutic alliance, called the working alliance, is an agreement on *what* is discussed in a session (goals), *how* it is discussed (tasks), and the relationship between the counselor/therapist and client (bond; Bordin, 1979). These dimensions are necessary for good work to occur whether it is a group or individual session. In group sessions, you also must ensure that the parents/caregivers are "rowing in the same direction" and working well together. Cohesiveness in group therapy is a form of alliance and is also critical to group members' success (Yalom & Leszcz, 2020).

Given the additional challenges of a group format, why go to the trouble? A group format offers multiple advantages that we believe are well worth it for families who have a child with autism. Although efficiency could be viewed as an advantage (multiple families served at once), we believe that a group format is particularly powerful given that families who have a child with special needs have a unique understanding of the emotions and challenges that accompany such a role. Collectively, these families can offer great information for one another that typically transcends the knowledge base of any one clinician. In other words, many families have a "lay of the land" for resources in the area and have ideas of how to work with and access local services. Beyond sharing information, they can offer one another support. Research tells us that many families who have a child with autism experience high levels of distress (Krakovich et al., 2016) and, compounding the issue, often feel isolated (Baumgardner, 2019). A group format draws upon the concept of universality ("I am not the only one struggling"; Yalom & Leszcz, 2020) and offers the opportunity for families to also offer emotional support and to feel less isolation.

Building Alliance C-HOPE is proactive in building a strong working alliance. Our activities and the structure of our sessions are designed to promote family engagement by having clinicians check in for understanding and for process. Although a psychoeducational program, C-HOPE is also designed to offer support. Below we outline some key therapist behaviors and our protocol for promoting alliance. This is far from an exhaustive list but is intended to be a reminder for professionals who have clinical training as they begin using C-HOPE.

Behaviors We all build relationships in different ways, and there is no magical step-by-step manual for developing therapeutic relationships with our clients. There are commonalities, however, that are based on research (Norcross & Lambert, 2018) and our clinical experience. We share these below:

1. *Be personable*—This seems obvious, and yet, when trying to implement an agenda-driven program, we can become agenda-driven and forget to check in with families, to be flexible, and most importantly to be ourselves. Building relationships is key—be curious about families' lives and work from the mindset that they will teach you as much or more than you will teach them.
2. *Use Your Basic Counseling Skills*—Mental health professionals sometimes get enamored with the latest, greatest intervention. Learning new approaches is wonderful, but not at the expense of the basics. The use of basic counseling skills with an emphasis on empathy and active listening is core to any intervention being effective.

3. *Don't Try To Be "The Expert"*—We often feel pressured to help families who are in great distress and are looking for answers and often have difficult questions. It is impossible to know it all, and families will "see through" someone who tries to play the expert. We have expertise, yes, but none of us have the market cornered on the best way to help a variety of families who have a variety of complexities (e.g., sociocultural variables, access to resources, child's behaviors, family relationships). Speak confidently when indeed confident, and be humble and honest when less certain. Families don't expect us to know everything, but they do expect us to try and be helpful. Work with families, rather than direct them.
4. *Confidentiality*—Do not forget to stress confidentiality. Covered at the beginning of treatment, it is important to highlight early that what is shared will remain confidential. Although you cannot guarantee confidentiality since group members are not professionally obligated, this should be strongly encouraged for the purpose of promoting safety and trust in the group.
5. *Have a Multicultural Orientation*—Families are deeply embedded within a cultural framework that influences the values and decision-making of families. Being a multiculturally responsive clinician is imperative for being helpful to families who are different in composition, race, religion, class, education, and multiple other identities that will shape how they receive the information presented and in their work with you. Again, our perspective is that C-HOPE is to be tailored to the unique needs of the family. One large consideration in this is tailoring interventions that consider the sociocultural context of each family/caregiver member at the individual and family level.
6. *Seek Feedback*—Clinicians are not good at identifying their clients who get worse in treatment (Hannan et al., 2005). Moreover, clinicians tend to overestimate their effectiveness with clients (Parker & Waller, 2015). Given these findings coupled with the importance of developing a strong working relationship with parents/caregivers, C-HOPE proactively monitors both outcome and alliance using measures from the formal feedback system called the Partners for Change Outcome Management System (PCOMS; Duncan & Reese, 2015; betteroutcomesnow.com). C-HOPE uses the Outcome Rating Scale (ORS; Miller & Duncan, 2000) and the Group Session Rating Scale (GSRS; Duncan & Miller, 2007) measures to monitor the distress levels of group members (ORS) and the group therapeutic alliance (SRS). These measures can be provided in person or via TMH.

Using the ORS/GSRS with C-HOPE The ORS is a brief four-item measure used to frame the discussion regarding parent distress during the individual sessions and to serve as means for monitoring distress throughout both the individual and group sessions. For the sake of time, ORS scores are not discussed individually, but if a score drops dramatically (more than the standard error of measure of 6 points or more), it is important for the clinician to check in with the parent/caregiver in a manner that respects the privacy of the individual. The ORS provides the opportunity to make changes in the group process or individual sessions to meet the needs of the individual. This may also mean attempting to identify additional resources or to recommend mental health treatment to benefit the family member.

The GSRS is also a brief four-item measure used to check in on the working alliance to ensure that the parent/caregiver is feeling heard and that he or she likes the content and process of the program. Again, time does not permit full discussion in group sessions, but follow-up is warranted when scores go below 36 (based on a 0–40 total scale score) for an individual. This can be done with a follow-up call or at the next individual session, depending on the severity of the concerns.

PCOMS is an evidence-based intervention designed not only to monitor treatment outcome but also to promote a collaborative working relationship that privileges the client's voice in treatment. It is important to note that we adopted a briefer, modified version of the PCOMS process that fits within our psychoeducational program. Even though C-HOPE is more than a therapy program, we do intend it to have a therapeutic benefit and that it contains dimensions of therapy. We believed that rather than leave the relationship to chance, using the ORS and GSRS would help clinicians engage families in a discussion of how they think things are going. Such feedback allows the clinician to adjust individual or group sessions as needed for families.

Being Aware of the Process

A good clinician uses a "third eye" to view the bigger picture, both in individual and group sessions. The process-oriented clinician is able to discern the "temperature" in the room, to understand not only what is occurring in the room but also *how* it is occurring, the process. For example, what typically happens in a group where a member monopolizes time in the group? Or when a member seems withdrawn and contributes little? Or when the members talk to one another and exclude the clinician? What do these actions say about the individual, the group, and how do these behaviors influence the group? The recognition of process can help ensure that the group goes smoother and everyone is involved. Participation is an important dimension to treatment outcome (Pisetsy et al., 2015). We want parents to engage. Recognition of process and being responsive are important for creating a good and supportive learning environment.

How individuals respond in group sessions can serve as a microcosm for how individuals engage and respond to others in their everyday lives (Yalom & Leszcz, 2020). Being able to recognize these processes could also be potentially important for giving interpersonal feedback to members or collectively to the group. Rearing a child with autism requires having interactions with a variety of individuals: medical staff, school officials, partners and family members, and other individuals in the community in order to advocate on behalf of his or her child. If a clinician develops a keen awareness of the interpersonal style of a member that may inhibit or impede this advocacy, such feedback may be appropriate. Of course, such feedback should be done with compassion and with empathy.

Process observations should also be treated differently depending on the nature of the observation. If the group seems disinterested in a session, it may be worth noting this sooner rather than later and taking action. This could be done with a process comment such as "I am noting that the energy is low in the room right now. I wanted to check in and see what was going on. I am worried maybe you are already familiar with this information." On the other hand, when noting an observation of an individual group member, it is generally better to be tentative and approach with caution. For example, a group member who is quiet for one session may mean something (e.g., they are scared to speak up) or may mean nothing (e.g., they are tired from work). For something to be noted as a process worth pursuing either at the group level (e.g., group members seem disinterested) or individually (e.g., a caregiver seems depressed), clinical judgment and timing are important for when and whether the clinician should intervene.

Different processes for the clinician(s) to be aware of in the group sessions include how each member responds to the clinician(s) and program, how each member behaves and responds within the group and to the other group member, how the group responds to each member, and collectively how the members respond to one another and the program (e.g., its overall cohesiveness). Recognition of these interrelated processes offers the opportunity to learn how the group members function individually and also how the group is functioning:

1. First is to recognize how the group member is responding to the clinician(s) and the program. Although not exhaustive, we offer some examples of things to consider. Is the member following the information presented? Is the member engaged, bored, or otherwise? How does the member communicate and relate to you? How does this information fit with your understanding of the person's individual situation? Imagine a parent who is compliant and agrees with everything the clinician says. Such a member can feel nice (we often love those who readily agree with us), but how might this parent advocate for their child with a physician who recommends a medication that they are unsure of? Will they be able to assert themselves to advocate for their child?
2. Second is to recognize how the group member responds to the other members in the group and within the group. Is the member participating in the group too little/too much? How do members respond when this occurs? How do group members respond to other behaviors and statements of the member? For example, how might a parent who is quick to disagree with other group members or appears cynical respond to a teacher who is struggling to manage her son's behavior in class?
3. Third is to recognize how the other group members respond to the member. What are the reactions members have to the group member? Again, the question is how these reactions may be relevant for the parent/caregiver being able to effectively advocate and work collaboratively with others to get the needs of their child met?
4. Fourth is to recognize how the overall group cohesiveness and receptiveness to the program. What does it mean if people are bored or frustrated? Is the pace too fast or slow? It is easy to become agenda-driven with our protocol, but it is incumbent on the clinician(s) to adapt how the content is delivered in such a way

that meets the needs of the group and, ultimately, each parent/caregiver. If you sense boredom, lack of understanding, or another process at the group level, the clinician should be checking in with the group about the observation.

Telehealth Considerations

C-HOPE was designed to be delivered in person or using a telehealth format. Specifically, the TMH format uses a videoconferencing format for the group sessions and the telephone or videoconferencing for the individual sessions. Although the research suggests TMH and in-person formats have similar outcomes, we offer some considerations that can help promote the working relationship with families:

1. Determine Appropriateness for Services Modality—Meet in person with families/caregivers (including the child) to determine if they are appropriate for such services, if possible. This also helps develop rapport and mitigates the feeling of interacting with a "stranger" who is in a different location. Culturally this may be critical as well.
2. Informed Consent—Relatedly, parents/caregivers should be informed about the advantages/disadvantages of using a telehealth format (Stoll et al., 2020). Clinician(s) can help determine if families have access to a telephone and are comfortable with the program being delivered in this format. Orienting families to the experience and helping them know what to anticipate can again help build relationships and allay any concerns about the technology format.
3. Technology Matters—Our experience is that lower-end technology is critical—such as disruptions due to Internet connections will certainly impact the quality of delivery. Also, make sure you have adequate cameras and monitors because grainy, small pictures may influence the experience for both clinician and parents/caregivers. Select a videoconference format that is HIPAA compliant. There are now several options available.
4. Group Videoconference Format—"Don't forget about me!" If group members meet in person at a clinic while the clinician(s) is present via the videoconference format, this can create an unusual dynamic and lend itself to group members talking with one another and "leaving out" the clinician(s). Our recommendation is simply to be aware of the potential of this, and there may be a need to be more verbal to direct the group since their ability to pick up on nonverbal cues of the clinician is limited in this format. If everyone is using videoconferencing, verbally checking in more often and stopping to ask for input can be useful to ensure participants are engaged and not distracted by their surroundings or other things on their computer (e.g., e-mail or Internet).
5. Beware of Subtlety—As the clinician is getting to know the families, we have found it helpful to be mindful of less subtle interaction styles. For example, we have found that humor can translate differently when in a video or phone format. With limited access to nonverbal information (even videoconferencing typically

offers limited visual information), some communication such as using sarcasm as a form of humor may not be understood as well. We have found it helpful to be more explicit about humor and describing things, particularly initially until you have a better understanding of the interaction between technology and the exchanges that are occurring.

TMH Practice Recommendations

The COVID-19 pandemic has accelerated not only leading to changes in the amount of TMH services delivered but also where and how these services are delivered. For example, before the pandemic, Medicare reimbursement required that services were rendered in a sanctioned facility, such as a virtual clinic or other secure spaces (e.g., regional medical center). Now, however, people can receive reimbursable services for home-based care. Although we believe that providing services in the client/patient home maximizes the potential benefit of TMH (e.g., convenience, transportation issues, comfort, childcare), this is an issue that must be carefully navigated. We already mentioned some of the disadvantages, including finding space with minimal distractions in the home and technology, connectivity challenges. As we continue to develop TMH interventions that are delivered more flexibly, it is important to remain vigilant about how these changes impact competent and ethical practice. We offer four recommendations (Clements-Hickman et al., 2021):

1. Stay updated with state laws and practice ethics codes—Remain current with TMH regulations and laws in state(s) where you practice, guidelines and ethics specific to your practice discipline, and insurance coverage. Things continue to evolve, and there are exciting opportunities for interstate practice in different disciplines (e.g., PSYPACT), but diligence is needed for compliance as state laws and regulations differ and changes tend to occur for these different dimensions. The Center for Connected Health Policy (https://www.cchpca.org) is a good resource for staying current with state laws, regulations, and policies specific to TMH.
2. Consult the best practice and practice guidelines—Multiple resources are available that can inform TMH practice. We mention a few that we have found helpful. Maheu et al. (2018) have developed a set of TMH competencies. The American Psychological Association offers practice guidelines (https://www.apa.org/practice/guidelines/telepsychology). Lastly, the American Telemedicine Association (ATA) offers a *Best Practices in Videoconferencing-Based Telemental Health* (https://www.psychiatry.org/getmedia/05b9b9cb-dbb5-4df8-8948-e2b9bd659b55/APA-ATA-Best-Practices-in-Videoconferencing-Based-Telemental-Health.pdf.
3. Consultation—Seek professional input from trusted colleagues who are already engaging in TMH practice. Other possibilities include consulting with your discipline's ethics board, your state licensure board, or an attorney experienced with mental health law.

4. General practice considerations—There are multiple considerations when providing TMH services. These include assessing the appropriateness of services for a client, having an emergency plan, and multiple other logistical considerations (e.g., positioning the camera, modifications due to limited visual information). Although not exhaustive, we briefly address a couple of considerations when starting a TMH practice (see Maheu and Donald (2020) for a more detailed review):
   (a) Assessing appropriateness for service—As you would for providing any treatment, formal assessment to determine if a client/family is appropriate for services should be conducted. This should include a risk modifications assessment and having a clear understanding of where services will be received. Related to this, clinicians should be aware of who else will be in the home and proactively ensure that an appropriate setting is available for the client. This should be monitored throughout treatment and is appropriate both for privacy purposes but also emergency situations (e.g., psychiatric emergency or crisis situation) where another person may be needed.
   (b) Emergency plan—An emergency plan in response to a mental health situation (suicide, self-harm, or other behavior of concern) should be discussed and presented in writing to clients, with relevant referrals and resources pertinent to emergency situations provided. The clinician should know the location of where the client is, the contact information for the closest medical and psychiatric facilities, and an emergency contact person.

A Case Example

To better understand the delivery of C-HOPE in a TMH format, we provide a brief case example of a parent training group, highlighting both the group and individual processes (see Table 1 for C-HOPE intervention overview). We use the example of one parent (whose name and details have been altered, but the experiences she had and the resulting outcomes are unchanged) in order to better illustrate the program experience and details of the interventions and processes.

Louise was a White, cisgender woman age of 41 years, who was divorced and had one 10-year-old son (Jake). Her son was diagnosed with ASD and received specialized individual services (applied behavior analysis, sensory integration treatment, and occupational therapy) that were provided both within the school setting and within a local university center. Louise and Jake lived in an urban setting, were from a low socioeconomic background, and had little social support. She sought out the parenting training group at the center where her son received ABA and sensory integration treatment. She was attracted to the idea of meeting other parents who might share some of the same struggles as her and to get ideas of how to better address her son's behavioral issues at home. More recently, her son seemed to function better at school with more structure but was now struggling with a variety of

Table 1 Overview of C-HOPE session content

Session	Session type	Session focus
1	Individual	Overview of C-HOPE and its goals, assessment and initial goal identification using the COMPASS profile
2	Group	Introduction of parents and their child to the group based on an assessment of social, communication, and other behaviors. Discussion of unique and common characteristics of each child. Overview of cognitive theories of autism (central coherence, theory of mind, executive function) and how these relate to behavior and local autism services and resources. The session is concluded with an introduction of a relaxation strategy
3	Group	Direct education on principles of behavior and learning as well as proactive and reactive strategies
4	Individual	Development of the child's personalized behavior plan using the COMPASS framework. Once the disruptive behavior is identified (behavior to decrease), the replacement skill(s) is generated (behavior to increase)
5	Group	Discussion of teaching strategies and positive behavior approaches to prevent disruptive behaviors, teach new skills, and respond effectively
6	Group	Discussion of parents and caregivers as essential "environmental supports" for the child and the emotions associated with the diagnosis, parenting expectations, and transitions. A "wellness" package of activities designed to identify strategies for self-care and relaxation is reviewed
7	Individual	Review of the individual behavior plan and how well it is working. Modifications to the plan may occur based on data tracking the child's problem behavior and new skills
8	Individual Progress	Pertinent skills from previous sessions are reviewed. Toward the goals is examined, and any modifications needed are implemented. Anticipated barriers that might arise related to the implementation of the behavior plan are discussed as well as possible proactive strategies to overcome these issues following the intervention

Note. From "COMPASS for Hope: Evaluating the effectiveness of a parent training and support program for children with ASD," by G. M. Kuravackel et al., 2018, *Journal of Autism and Developmental Disorders, 48*(2), p. 410. Copyright 2018 by Springer Link

behavioral issues at home, including not doing homework, refusing requests, playing alone rather than engaging with siblings socially, and exhibiting some aggressive behavior when asked to discontinue using his computer (moving from a preferred to unpreferred activity).

Session 1 (Individual—60 Minutes) Before attending session 1, Louise was asked to complete the COMPASS profile (available online at compassforautism.org) via e-mail before the first session. The COMPASS profile is an interview guide to gather information from different people's points of view (the parent in this case). The profile is not a measure for diagnosis or measure of behavior but is used to better understand the functioning of the child. She completed the profile a week before the first session.

Louise met with her clinician via Zoom (using a HIPAA-compliant format). After introducing C-HOPE and providing an overview, the clinician and Louise began to collaboratively identify goals using the COMPASS profile. Louise was eager to talk about her stressors as a parent with a child with ASD and her journey to educate herself and advocate for services for her son. She was highly motivated for the parent training group and was engaged. Most of the session was spent discussing her responses to the COMPASS profile for her son's self-management skills, communication, social and sensory issues, and preferences. She also shared information on behavioral issues at home and what strategies have worked/not worked. Discussion of these items all informed potential goals. Initial goals were focused on how to increase communication for requesting more time with the desired activities, social play with peers, and reductions in disruptive behaviors when transitioning from preferred activities, especially being on his computer.

From a clinician perspective, individual sessions using a videoconferencing platform felt similar to meeting in person. The clinician was able to develop rapport in this format with the client, although there were some subtle differences. Access to body language was limited although Louise's presentation was enthusiastic and positive. She also had questions regarding confidentiality and whether the sessions were being recorded. They appeared to be questions of curiosity rather than concern, but it is easy to imagine how the introduction of technology may create concern around the issues of privacy and access.

Session 2 (Group—2 Hours) A group of seven parents met. The group was comprised of five individual parents (four mothers and one father) and a couple (father and mother). The session focused on introducing the parents and their child (although the child was not present) to the group using a general framework of social, communication, and other behaviors. An introduction of central coherence (Happe et al., 2001), executive dysfunction (Pennington & Ozonoff, 1996), and theory of mind (Baron-Cohen et al., 2000) was provided using PowerPoint slides with invitations to provide examples of how this applied to their child. Louise shared that Jake had a great difficulty taking the perspective of others (theory of mind) and having an inability to see the bigger picture when he obsesses on often irrelevant details that detract from the task at hand (central coherence). Information for local resources and services for ASD were included. Louise learned from a couple of new possibilities, and parents also shared their experiences, both positive and negative, with the resources in the community. Given that a purpose of C-HOPE is to provide support and encourage self-care for parents/caregivers, the session concluded with the introduction of a mindfulness strategy to promote relaxation. At the end of the session, everyone completed the GSRS which indicated high scores regarding feeling heard/understood, the goals and topics discussed, the approach used, and the overall session. All of the participants had high scores above 36 (which is the cut-score, indicated that scores below 36 suggest alliance concerns that should be discussed). The measures were scored in the session, and all of the parents had scores over 36 except Louise. We followed up with her privately, and she indicated that the mindfulness strategy was anxiety provoking and unhelpful. She indicated having a trauma history and that the intervention left space for intrusive, uncomfortable thoughts and memories. We agreed to try a different relaxation strategy, and she reported that she enjoys looking at clouds and drawing them. We agreed for her to use this strategy but to check in with her to evaluate if it was helpful or not while we pursued additional strategies that she could implement immediately and when not outside.

Session 3 (Group—2 Hours) This session has a significant didactic component where behavior and learning principles are presented. Examples of evidence-based approaches for problem behaviors were provided, including functional behavior assessment along with antecedent manipulation, differential reinforcement, and self-management strategies (e.g., Braithwaite & Richdale, 2000; Frea et al., 2001; Keeling et al., 2003). We then focused on connecting these principles to behavioral management concerns that the parents were currently facing. Louise offered that she didn't realize it until the session that the antecedents for Jake complying to requests (such as completing chores) were critical. For him, he was more likely to respond when getting home and pairing them with a snack. She reasoned that Jake was still in a "school mindset" upon arrival than when he was in a different area of the house later where his computer, toys, and the TV were located. The session concluded with a progressive muscle relaxation strategy rather than a strategy more cognitive focused such as mindfulness or guided imagery. The GSRS was again administered, and all scores, including Louise's, were above 36.

Session 4 (Individual—1 Hour) This session is used to individualize what was learned in the group sessions to each family/child. Using the COMPASS framework, a personalized behavior plan was identified with a focus on behaviors to decrease and subsequent replacement behaviors and the skills needed to do so. Louise started by noting how much she enjoyed the group and that it had already helped with Jake getting his chores done when he got home from school. The association of a snack (sometimes healthy!) with responding to requests seemed to be effective for Jake. On days that she had to work until 6 p.m., however, completing chores remained an issue. Louise and the clinician identified an alternate strategy that would simultaneously help with transitioning from an activity such as his computer to doing chores, eating dinner, or getting ready for bed.

Session 5 (Group—2 Hours) This session builds upon what has been learned to this point with an emphasis on having a mutual common language and understanding of the concepts being shared, including antecedents, consequences, and joint attention. There is a focus on positive parenting skills that encourage positive child behaviors with rationale. Examples and updates on how things are going within the group to promote group cohesion are part of the group. Parents shared what was working and where they were feeling stuck. Louise admitted that, while things had improved overall, it has been challenging to not slide back into previous habits, and she worries about maintaining the changes when the group ends. A couple of other parents echoed these comments and said they would start an "accountability group" where they would check in with each other once a week. Louise loved this idea and admitted that having some social and emotional support was one of the things she needed. GSRS scores were all high at the end of the group session.

Session 6 (Group—2 Hours) The focus of the final group session is to consolidate what has been learned and to focus on eventual environmental supports for the child and the emotions associated with the diagnosis, challenging parenting expectations, and the transition of dealing with an ASD diagnosis. It permits participants to share in their struggles and the adjustments that they had to make to their hopes and aspirations as parents. We intentionally do this later in the intervention when group cohesion is likely to be higher, and it feels safer to be honest and vulnerable. The session revealed a mixture of parents sharing that they were still processing how to adjust and others saying they had come out on the other side. A couple also disclosed having to deal with depression and feelings of grief. These feelings were normalized by both the clinician and group members who had similar feelings. Following this, the group focused on putting together a "wellness package" that they could take with them including the relaxation strategies used in previous sessions. Group members were able to say goodbye to one another with some exchanging contact information to stay in touch. GSRS scores were all above 36. Louise expressed gratitude and that the emotional support of the group was the most meaningful part as well as feeling a sense of clarity about strategies that would help Jake.

Session 7 (Individual—1 Hour) The focus of this session is to check in with each group member/couple and see how the individualized behavior plans are working. Part of Louise's plan was to track behaviors focused on Jake completing his chores and transitioning behaviors that are recreational- or computer-based. She also used a sticker reward system that was displayed on the refrigerator that came with rewards of more recreational/computer time. Louise said that the emotional support she has received in the group and the weekly accountability check-ins with two other parents in the group have been motivational for her. She has recognized that being consistent is key but that she also needed to be self-compassionate when there is a slip. One thing that was tweaked was beginning to fade a reward strategy that was put in place to reinforce positive behaviors. It had been effective, but Louise said that Jake had become too focused on the reward system and did not seem to be internalizing the consequences of positive behaviors beyond the extrinsic rewards. Louise and the clinician both agreed that using more positive verbal reinforcers and beginning to fade the reward system (reducing external rewards) were good next steps.

Session 8 (Individual—1 Hour) The last intervention session is to review skills from the previous sessions to further consolidate knowledge and skills acquired. Progress toward goals is again reviewed, and any modifications are discussed. There is also a focus on the future and anticipated barriers and challenges that might arise related to the implementation of the behavior plan. Louise and the clinician spent the majority of the session focused on discussion of what she had learned and anticipating challenges in the future. She indicated that the fading strategy has had some bumps, Jake wanted to keep the reward system, but Louise's proactive strategy of using more verbal rewards and focusing on the intrinsic aspects of meeting the behavior goals (affirming how appreciate she is of his help and that she can count on him that they are a team) have had some benefit. Overall, she said Jake's grades have gone up a little and his problem behaviors have reduced.

Summary

TMH has an impressive research evidence base that indicates it can be implemented for multiple mental health issues across the lifespan. There is also evidence that technology-mediated interventions can be of benefit to children with ASD and their families. We are excited about the potential of TMH to help children and families, especially those who have significant barriers to receiving specialized mental health services. C-HOPE was specifically designed for this purpose. We are excited about the research and the possibility of using technology to increase access to treatment and the increase in use resulting from the COVID-19 pandemic, and at the same time we are concerned about ensuring that practitioners are being trained to ethically and competently provide TMH services. More effort is needed to ensure that the research is translational to clinical practice and also culturally responsive.

Based on our experiences with TMH delivery of C-HOPE, we are confident that the feasibility and the program structure are well-suited to delivery either in person or via videoconferencing. We know that other interventions designed to help children with ASD and their families by similarly can be adapted to be delivered effectively in a TMH format. For us, we adapted an evidence-based intervention, COMPASS, to a TMH format. We spent a significant amount of time focused on what would or would not be appropriate for a videoconferencing format, considering both content, process, and how to deliver the service in a reliable and secure way. There is preliminary evidence to support its use with both rural and urban families—although more work remains to establish it as an evidence-based practice.

Our experience is that families and caregivers were grateful and found the content, tools, and resources provided and the support to all be useful and meaningful. The technology did not detract from building a therapeutic alliance with the clinician or building cohesion with other parents participating in the training. C-HOPE affords the ability to provide services to multiple families at once and a means for families to share community resources and have a feeling of universality—I am not alone in my challenges and struggles. Our hope is that we can continue to move forward with culturally responsive and effective TMH interventions that can be utilized to reach more families, more readily.

References

Aafjes-van Doorn, K. (2022). The complexity of teletherapy: Not better or worse, but different. *Clinical Psychology: Science and Practice, 29*(2), 182–184. https://doi.org/10.1037/cps0000073

Amsbary, J., & AFIRM Team. (2017). *Parent implemented intervention (PII) . EBP Brief Packet.* National Professional Development Center on Autism Spectrum Disorders.

Andrilla, C. H. A., Patterson, D. G., Garberson, L. A., Coulthard, C., & Larson, E. H. (2018). Geographic variation in the supply of selected behavioral health providers. *American Journal of Preventive Medicine, 54*(6), S199–S207. https://doi.org/10.1016/j.amepre.2018.01.0047

Antezana, L., Scarpa, A., Valdespino, A., Albright, J., & Richey, J. A. (2017). Rural trends in diagnosis and services for autism Spectrum disorder. *Frontiers in Psychology, 8*, 590. https://doi.org/10.3389/fpsyg.2017.00590

Apolinário-Hagen, J., Harrer, M., Kählke, F., Fritsche, L., Salewski, C., & Ebert, D. D. (2018). Public attitudes toward guided internet-based therapies: Web-based survey study. *JMIR Mental Health, 5*(2), e10735. https://doi.org/10.2196/10735

Ashburner, J., Vickerstaff, S., Beetge, J., & Copley, J. (2016). Remote versus face-to-face delivery of early intervention programs for children with autism spectrum disorders: Perceptions of rural families and service providers. *Research in Autism Spectrum Disorders, 23*, 1–14. https://doi.org/10.1016/j.rasd.2015.11.011

Backhaus, A., Agha, Z., Maglione, M. L., Repp, A., Ross, B., Zuest, D., et al. (2012). Videoconferencing psychotherapy: A systematic review. *Psychological Services, 9*(2), 111–131. https://doi.org/10.1037/a0027924

Baron-Cohen, S., Tager-Flusberg, H., & Cohen, D. J. (2000). *Understanding other minds: Perspectives from developmental cognitive neuroscience* (2nd ed.). Oxford University Press.

Baumgardner, D. J. (2019). Social isolation among families caring for children with disabilities. *Journal of Patient-Centered Research and Reviews, 6*(4), 229–232. https://doi.org/10.17294/2330-0698.1726

Bearss, K., Johnson, C., Smith, T., Lecavalier, L., Swiezy, N., Aman, M., et al. (2015). Effect of parent training vs parent education on behavioral problems in children with autism spectrum disorder: A randomized clinical trial. *JAMA: Journal of the American Medical Association, 313*(15), 1524–1533.

Bordin, E. S. (1979). The generalizability of the psychoanalytic concept of the working alliance. *Psychotherapy: Theory, Research and Practice, 16*, 252–260.

Braithwaite, K., & Richdale, A. (2000). Functional communication training to replace challenging behaviors across two behavioral outcomes. *Behavioral Interventions, 15*(1), 21–36.

Clements-Hickman, A. L., Hollan, J., Drew, C. M., Hinton, V., & Reese, R. J. (2021). The use of telehealth in behavioral health and educational contexts during COVID-19 and beyond. In H. D. O'Hair & M. J. O'Hair (Eds.), *Communicating science in times of crisis: Coronavirus* (pp. 189–214). Wiley.

Connolly, S. L., Miller, C. J., Lindsay, J. A., & Bauer, M. S. (2020). A systematic review of providers' attitudes toward telemental health via videoconferencing. *Clinical Psychology: Science and Practice, 27*(2), e12311. https://doi.org/10.1111/cpsp.12311

Dahiya, A. V., Ruble, L., Kuravackel, G., & Scarpa, A. (2021). Efficacy of a telehealth parent training intervention for children with autism spectrum disorder: Rural versus urban areas. *Evidence-Based Practice in Child and Adolescent Mental Health, 7*(1), 41–55. https://doi.org/10.1080/23794925.2021.1941431

Drahota, A., Sadler, R., Hippensteel, C., Ingersoll, B., & Bishop, L. (2020). Service deserts and service oases: Utilizing geographic information systems to evaluate service availability for individuals with autism spectrum disorder. *Autism, 24*(8), 2008–2020. https://doi.org/10.1177/1362361320931265

Duncan, B. L., & Miller, S. D. (2007). *The group session rating scale.* Author.

Duncan, B. L., & Reese, R. J. (2015). The Partners for Change Outcome Management System (PCOMS) revisiting the client's frame of reference. *Psychotherapy, 52*(4), 391–401. https://doi.org/10.1037/pst0000026

Ellison, K. S., Guidry, J., Picou, P., Adenuga, P., & Davis, T. E., III. (2021). Telehealth and autism prior to and in the age of COVID-19: A systematic and critical review of the last decade. *Clinical Child and Family Psychology Review, 24*(3), 599–630. https://doi.org/10.1007/s10567-021-00358-0

Fortin, M., Bamvita, J. M., & Fleury, M. J. (2018). Patient satisfaction with mental health services based on Andersen's behavioral model. *The Canadian Journal of Psychiatry, 63*(2), 103–114. https://doi.org/10.1177/0706743717737030

Frea, W., Arnold, C., & Vittimberga, G. (2001). A demonstration of the effects of augmentative communication on the extreme aggressive behavior of a child with autism within an integrated preschool setting. *Journal of Positive Behavior Interventions, 3*(4), 194–198.

Glueckauf, R. L., Maheu, M. M., Drude, K. P., Wells, B. A., Wang, Y., Gustafson, D. J., & Nelson, E.-L. (2018). Survey of psychologists' telebehavioral health practices: Technology use, ethical issues, and training needs. *Professional Psychology: Research and Practice, 49*(3), 205–219. https://doi.org/10.1037/pro0000188

Gun, S. Y., Titov, N., & Andrews, G. (2011). Acceptability of internet treatment of anxiety and depression. *Australasian Psychiatry, 19*(3), 259–264. https://doi.org/10.3109/10398562.2011.562295

Hannan, C., Lambert, M. J., Harmon, C., Nielsen, S. L., Smart, D. W., Shimokawa, K., & Sutton, S. W. (2005). A lab test and algorithms for identifying clients at risk for treatment failure. *Journal of Clinical Psychology, 61*(2), 155–163.

Happe, F., Briskman, J., & Frith, U. (2001). Exploring the cognitive phenotype of autism: Weak "central coherence" in parents and siblings of children with autism: I. Experimental tests. *Journal of Child Psychology and Psychiatry, 42*(3), 299–307.

Hardan, A. Y., Gengoux, G. W., Berquist, K. L., Libove, R. A., Ardel, C. M., Phillips, J., & Minjarez, M. B. (2015). A randomized controlled trial of pivotal response treatment group for parents of children with autism. *Journal of Child Psychology and Psychiatry, 56*(8), 884–892. https://doi.org/10.1111/jcpp.12354

Ingersoll, B., Wainer, A. L., Berger, N. I., Pickard, K. E., & Bonter, N. (2016). Comparison of a self-directed and therapist-assisted telehealth parent-mediated intervention for children with ASD: A pilot RCT. *Journal of Autism and Developmental Disorders, 46*(7), 2275–2284. https://doi.org/10.1007/s10803-016-2755-z

Keeling, K., Myles, S. B., Gagnon, E., & Simpson, R. (2003). Using the power card strategy to teach sportsmanship skills to a child with autism. *Focus on Autism and Other Developmental Disabilities, 18*(2), 103–109.

Khetani, M. A., Richardson, Z., & McManus, B. M. (2018). Social disparities in early intervention service use and provider-reported outcomes. *Journal of Developmental Behavioral Pediatrics, 38*(7), 501–509. https://doi.org/10.1097/DBP.0000000000000047

Krakovich, T. M., McGrew, J. H., Yu, Y., & Ruble, L. A. (2016). Stress in parents of children with autism spectrum disorder: An exploration of demands and resources. *Journal of Autism and Developmental Disorders, 46*, 2042–2053.

Kuravackel, G. M., Ruble, L. A., Reese, R. J., Ables, A. P., Rodgers, A. D., & Toland, M. D. (2018). COMPASS for Hope: Evaluating the effectiveness of a parent training and support program for children with ASD. *Journal of Autism and Developmental Disorders, 48*(2), 404–416. https://doi.org/10.1007/s10803-017-3333-8

Langarizadeh, M., Tabatabaei, M. S., Tavakol, K., Naghipour, M., Rostami, A., & Moghbeli, F. (2017). Telemental health care, an effective alternative to conventional mental care: A systematic review. *Acta informatica medica: AIM: Journal of the Society for Medical Informatics of Bosnia & Herzegovina: Casopis Drustva za medicinsku informatiku BiH, 25*, 240–246. https://doi.org/10.5455/aim.2017.25.240-246

Lin, T., Stone, S. J., Heckman, T. G., & Anderson, T. (2021). Zoom-in to zone-out: Therapists report less therapeutic skill in telepsychology versus face-to-face therapy during the COVID-19 pandemic. *Psychotherapy, 58*(4), 449–459. https://doi.org/10.1037/pst0000398

Lindgren, S., Wacker, D., Suess, A., Schieltz, K., Pelzel, K., Kopelman, T., Lee, J., Romani, P., & Waldron, D. (2016). Telehealth and autism: Treating challenging behavior at lower cost. *Pediatrics, 137*(2), 167–175. https://doi.org/10.1542/peds.2015-2851O

Lundahl, B. W., Nimer, J., & Parsons, B. (2006). Preventing child abuse: A meta-analysis of parent training programs. *Research on Social Work Practice, 16*(3), 251–262.

Maheu, C., Hilty, J. E., & Donald, M. (2020). *Telebehavioral health: Foundations in theory and practice for graduate learners*. Cognella.

Maheu, M. M., Drude, K. P., Hertlein, K. M., & Hilty, D. M. (2018). A framework of interprofessional telebehavioral health competencies: Implementation and challenges moving forward. *Academic Psychiatry, 42*(6), 825–833. https://doi.org/10.1007/s40596-018-0988-1

March, S., Day, J., Ritchie, G., Rowe, A., Gough, J., Hall, T., et al. (2018). Attitudes toward e-mental health services in a community sample of adults: Online survey. *Journal of Medical Internet Research, 20*(2), e59. https://doi.org/10.2196/jmir.9109

McGrew, J. H., Ruble, L. A., & Smith, I. M. (2016). Autism spectrum disorder and evidence-based practice in psychology. *Clinical Psychology: Science and Practice, 23*(3), 239.

Meadan, H., Meyer, L. E., Snodgrass, M. R., & Halle, J. W. (2013). Coaching parents of young children in rural areas using internet-based technologies: A pilot program. *Rural Special Education Quarterly, 32*(3), 3–10. https://doi.org/10.1177/875687051303200302

Miller, S. D., & Duncan, B. L. (2000). *The outcome rating scale*. Authors.

Norcross, J. C., & Lambert, M. J. (2018). Psychotherapy relationships that work III. *Psychotherapy, 55*(4), 303–315. https://doi.org/10.1037/pst0000193

Ogle, L. N., Ruble, L. A., Toland, M. D., & McGrew, J. H. (2023). Type and dosage of performance feedback following COMPASS consultation on teacher and student outcomes. *Remedial and Special Education*, Advance online publication, *45*, 30. https://doi.org/10.1177/07419325231164755

Parker, Z. J., & Waller, G. (2015). Factors related to psychotherapists' self-assessment when treating anxiety and other disorders. *Behaviour Research and Therapy, 66*, 1–7. https://doi.org/10.1016/j.brat.2014.12.010

Pennington, B. F., & Ozonoff, S. (1996). Executive functions and developmental psychopathology. *Journal of Child Psychology and Psychiatry, 37*(1), 51–87.

Pew Research Center. (2021, April 7). *Demographics of internet and home broadband usage in the United States*. https://www.pewresearch.org/internet/fact-sheet/internet-broadband/.

Pisetsy, E., Durkin, N., Crosby, R., Berg, K., Mitchell, J., Crow, S., Wonderlich, S., & Peterson, C. (2015). Examination of early group dynamics and treatment outcome in a randomized controlled trial of group cognitive behavioral therapy for binge eating disorder. *Behavior Research and Therapy, 73*, 74–78. https://doi.org/10.1016/j.brat.2015.07.013

Renn, B. N., Hoeft, T. J., Lee, H. S., Bauer, A. M., & Areán, P. A. (2019). Preference for in-person psychotherapy versus digital psychotherapy options for depression: Survey of adults in the US. *npj Digital Medicine, 2*(1), 1–7. https://doi.org/10.1038/s41746-019-0077-1

Rodgers, A. D. (2018). *Examining an asynchronous group discussion board adaptation of a parent-mediated behavior intervention for children with autism Spectrum disorders*. Doctoral dissertation. University of Kentucky.

Ruble, L. A., & Dalrymple, N. J. (2002). Compass: A parent—Teacher collaborative model for students with autism. *Focus on Autism and Other Developmental Disabilities, 17*(2), 76–83.

Ruble, L., & McGrew, J. (Eds.). (2023). *COMPASS and innovative education for students with autism*. Springer.

Ruble, L., Dalrymple, N., & McGrew, J. (2010). The effects of consultation on individualized education program outcomes for young children with autism: The collaborative model for promoting competence and success. *Journal of Early Intervention, 32*(4), 286–301.

Ruble, L. A., McGrew, J. H., Toland, M. D., Dalrymple, N. J., & Jung, L. A. (2013). A randomized controlled trial of COMPASS web-based and face-to-face teacher coaching in autism. *Journal of Consulting and Clinical Psychology., 81*(3), 566–572. https://doi.org/10.1037/a0032003

Ruble, L. A., McGrew, J. H., Toland, M., Dalrymple, N., Adams, M., & Snell-Rood, C. (2018). Randomized control trial of COMPASS for improving transition outcomes of students with autism Spectrum disorder. *Journal of Autism and Developmental Disorders, 48*(10), 3586–3595.

Stoll, J., Müller, J. A., & Trachsel, M. (2020). Ethical issues in online psychotherapy: A narrative review. *Frontiers in Psychiatry, 10*, 993. https://doi.org/10.3389/fpsyt.2019.00993

Varker, T., Brand, R. M., Ward, J., Terhaag, S., & Phelps, A. (2019). Efficacy of synchronous telepsychology interventions for people with anxiety, depression, posttraumatic stress disorder, and adjustment disorder: A rapid evidence assessment. *Psychological Services, 16*(4), 621–635. https://doi.org/10.1037/ser0000239

Wallin, E., Maathz, P., Parling, T., & Hursti, T. (2018). Self-stigma and the intention to seek psychological help online compared to face-to-face. *Journal of Clinical Psychology, 74*(7), 1207–1218. https://doi.org/10.1002/jclp.22583

Weintraub, M. J., Denenny, D., Ichinose, M. C., Zinberg, J., Morgan-Fleming, G., Done, M., Brown, R. D., Bearden, C. E., & Miklowitz, D. J. (2023). A randomized trial of telehealth mindfulness-based cognitive therapy and cognitive behavioral therapy groups for adolescents with mood or attenuated psychosis symptoms. *Journal of Consulting and Clinical Psychology, 91*(4), 234–241. https://doi.org/10.1037/ccp0000782

Yalom, I. D., & Leszcz, M. (2020). *The theory and practice of group psychotherapy* (6th ed.). Basic Books.

Zisser, A., & Eyberg, S. (2010). Parent-child interaction therapy and the treatment of disruptive behavior disorders. In J. R. Weisz & A. E. Kazdin (Eds.), *Evidence-based psychotherapies for children and adolescents* (2nd ed., pp. 179–193). Guilford Press.

Chapter 7
Mom Power via Telemental Health

Diana Morelen, Sarah Gray, Jamie Lawler, Kelly Daniel, Hilary Skov, Sanshawanna Jones, Renee Lamoreau, Sarah Freeman, and Katherine Rosenblum

Background and Overview of Mom Power

Safe, stable, and nurturing relationships are essential to healthy development in early childhood and beyond (Schofield et al., 2013). Conversely, adverse childhood experiences (ACEs; e.g., maltreatment, family dysfunction, parental incarceration, poverty, bullying) and trauma exposures (e.g., actual or threatened death, serious injury, or sexual violence) have substantial and deleterious consequences for health, well-being, and overall functioning (Felitti et al., 1998). There is a dose-response relationship between adversity and poorer outcomes such that the greater frequency

Funding: Families Free (PI: Morelen), Ballad Health Community Health Initiative (PI: Morelen), ETSU RDC Major Grant (PI: Morelen); K23MH119047 (PI: Grey), Michigan Health Endowment Fund (PI: Lawler), Flinn Foundation (PI: Lawler).

D. Morelen (✉) · K. Daniel
Department of Psychology, East Tennessee State University, Johnson City, TN, USA
e-mail: morelen@etsu.edu

S. Gray
Department of Psychological Sciences, University of Connecticut, Storrs, CT, USA

J. Lawler · S. Freeman
Department of Psychology, Eastern Michigan University, Ypsilanti, MI, USA

H. Skov
Department of Psychological Sciences, University of Connecticut, Storrs, CT, USA

Department of Psychology, Tulane University, New Orleans, LA, USA

S. Jones · R. Lamoreau
Department of Psychology, Tulane University, New Orleans, LA, USA

K. Rosenblum
Department of Psychiatry; Zero to Thrive, Michigan Medicine, Ann Arbor, MI, USA

L. N. Niec, C. E. Schoonover (eds.), *Telemental Health Care for Children and Families*,
https://doi.org/10.1007/978-3-031-69264-2_7

and duration of ACEs and the higher risk for deleterious physical, psychological, and relational health outcomes (Masten et al., 2021; Miller et al., 2011; Nelson et al., 2020). Trauma, adversity, and mental health symptoms also affect how one responds to and engages in interpersonal relationships (Edwards et al., 2003). This is particularly relevant for parents as these experiences and symptoms significantly interfere with effective parenting and the parent-child relationship (Goodman et al., 2011). Specifically, symptoms of withdrawal, anhedonia, fatigue, affective lability, and anxiety interfere with the development of the parent-child relationship (Feldman et al., 2009). Disruptions in the mother-child relationship are related to negative outcomes for children (e.g., impaired cognitive functioning, emotional and behavioral problems) and represent one pathway for understanding the intergenerational transmission of risk from parent to child (Kujawa et al., 2020).

Parent-child relationships, also referred to as attachment relationships, are paramount for optimal child development and to build the framework (i.e., internal working models) for how children will experience themselves, others, and their environment (Bowlby, 1969). Of note, all caregivers, regardless of gender or gender identity, are essential for healthy child development; however, the majority of parenting research has been conducted with mothers, and this chapter focuses specifically on mothers. As such, we will switch our language to focus on mothers from here on out. The quality of the attachment relationship differs between mother and child dyads and is affected by both a mother's behavioral responsivity and sensitivity to her child as well as the internal working models about her child and her relationship with her child (i.e., maternal mental representations; Goodman & Gotlib, 1999; Rosenblum et al., 2017a). Maternal representations encompass the meanings a mother ascribes to the relationship with her child as well as her expectations for herself as a mother. Maternal representations shape the attachment relationship and have implications for sensitive caregiving behaviors (Rosenblum et al., 2017a). Certain factors (e.g., mental illness, history of trauma/ACEs) heighten the risk for mothers to have unbalanced maternal representations (i.e., confused/conflicted about their relationship with child, overwhelmed by the child's emotional state or needs) which are associated with more insecure attachment relationships (Rosenblum et al., 2017a). In turn, insecure attachment relationships are predictive of less optimal development in infancy, disruptions in emotion regulation, and poorer functioning later in life (IJzendoorn et al., 1995). Thus, the attachment relationship serves as a crucial target for intervention to promote more adaptive functioning and development for children and mitigate the transmission of risk from mother to child (Rosenblum et al., 2017a; Rosenblum et al., 2017b).

Mom Power

Mom Power is an evidence-based, trauma-informed, and attachment-based parenting skills intervention specifically designed for mothers with high psychosocial stress and their young children (ages 0–6), which promotes positive outcomes for

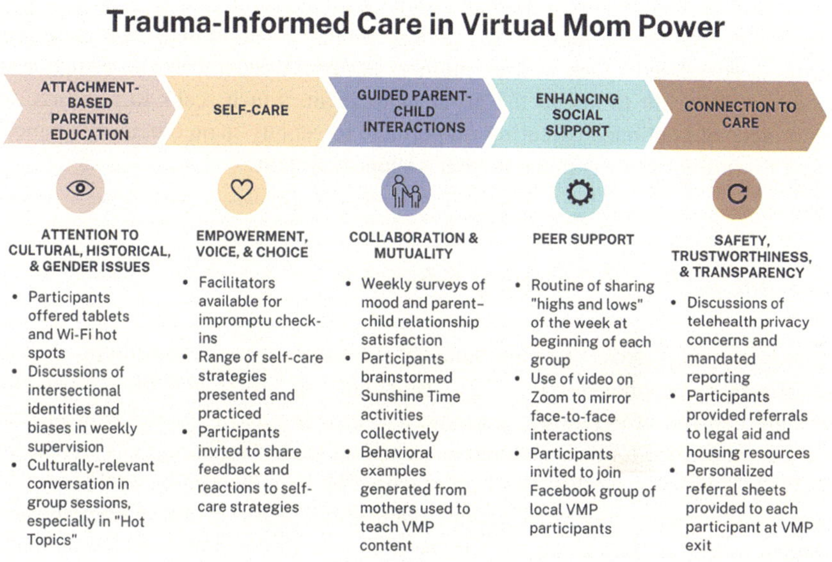

Fig. 7.1 Connecting the six tenets of trauma-informed care with the five pillars of Mom Power

children by improving the mother-child relationship (Rosenblum et al., 2017a; Rosenblum et al., 2017b). More specifically, the core components of Mom Power are connected to the Strengthening Families evidence-based protective factors curriculum (Center for the Study of Social Policy, 2023) and seek to strengthen protective factors and reduce risk factors for children by increasing sensitive caregiving, decreasing maternal mental health symptoms, and promoting balanced maternal representations (Rosenblum et al., 2017b; Lawler et al., 2018). These aims are highlighted through the five main components of the Mom Power intervention: (1) enhancing social and peer support, (2) attachment-based parenting education, (3) mental health and self-care practice, (4) guided parent-child interactions, and (5) connecting to care. Of note, Mom Power is grounded in trauma-informed practice principles across all facets of intervention (see Fig. 7.1; SAMHSA, 2014).

Enhancing Social and Peer Support

Mom Power is held in a group format, which provides an opportunity for mothers to develop relationships with other mothers in a safe and nurturing environment as well as to build supportive networks in their community. The Mom Power intervention team members are intentional to engage in relationship-based practice that models strategies to cultivate safe, stable, and nurturing relationships with the mothers in the hope that this experiential learning of what it feels like to be "held" in a healthy relationship will help scaffold the mothers' skills in cultivating safe, stable, and nurturing relationships with their child(ren). This is referred to as *parallel process*: Doing unto to the mothers as we hope mothers will do unto their child(ren). During a scheduled "guest week," mothers are encouraged to invite a supportive person in their life to attend the group with them, which seeks to reinforce the importance of continued parenting support and to get buy-in on crucial attachment-based parenting concepts in the mother's support system.

Attachment-Based Parenting Education

Mom Power emphasizes the importance of the attachment relationship through the use of a Tree metaphor (see Fig. 7.2). "Branching out" represents times when children are capable of exploring, learning, and growing and is paired with mothers being a secure base for their children to branch off from. "Building roots" represents times when children are distressed and is paired with mothers being a safe haven for their children who may need greater connection in these times. Regardless of whether a child is "branching out" or "building roots," the mother acts as the metaphorical sun in their child's life: the warmth, joy, and support that all children need to thrive. Throughout Mom Power, weekly structured activities and reflective exercises help mothers learn to recognize moments of "branching out" or "building roots" for their children and work to identify how to act as a secure base or safe haven in these moments. Experiential learning activities are used to promote maternal efficacy in what we can do (i.e., behavior) or say (i.e., words chosen to convey intentional meaning) to meet a child's need for connection (roots) or exploration (branches).

Mental Health and Self-Care Practice

Each week, mothers learn a new self-care skill in the group and are invited to practice outside of the group, which helps mothers build a "toolkit" for future self-care and mental wellness practice. Evidence-based techniques from empirically supported mental health treatments are taught each week to help promote maternal emotion regulation and resources for coping with stress. Stress reduction, mindfulness, and emotion regulation skills are taught through the use of guided meditation and breathing, visualization exercises, and positive coping thoughts. The central aim of these Mom Power self-care practices is to help mothers build coping skills to reduce stress, particularly related to parenting. The curriculum emphasizes the importance of being able to "calm ourselves before we can calm our children." And that in order for a mother to be "bigger, stronger, wiser, kinder, and calmer" with her child, she needs tools to manage stress and distressing emotions.

Fig. 7.2 Mom power tree graphic and script

Guided Parent-Child Interactions

Mothers learn to create and sustain predictable routines for their children, especially related to separation and reunion. Separations (i.e., mother leaves for group) and reunions (i.e., mother returns from group) are built into the curriculum which enable mothers to practice the attachment-based skills learned in the group. Group leaders support mothers as they practice noticing their child's behavior, wondering about their child's needs and feelings, and sensitively responding to their child. Of note, in vivo practice is an essential part of the in-person Mom Power groups. Adaptations to virtual Mom Power will be discussed below.

Connecting to Care

Throughout the intervention, group leaders monitor each family to assess for ongoing family needs and provide "warm handoffs" or referrals to community resources, interventions, or providers as needed. These are considered "warm" handoffs as group leaders work to ensure a referral is relational prior to suggesting it to a mother. This could look like calling ahead, calling with, or going with a mother to connect to a needed service. Mom Power also prioritizes individual and private check-ins with mothers about current emotional or physical needs by group leaders throughout the intervention. Connections to care provided during these sessions range from, but are not limited to, referrals to individual psychotherapy or early intervention programs to safe housing programs and high-quality childcare.

Structure of Mom Power

Mom Power is a time-limited and manualized group intervention. The curriculum includes ten consecutive group sessions and three individual sessions offered throughout the group. Individual sessions typically occur prior to week 1, at midpoint (week 5), and following the conclusion of the group (after week 10). Individual sessions serve to provide opportunities to increase therapeutic alliance and to assess for ongoing needs for the mother-child dyad throughout the intervention. When held in person, mothers and their children (aged 0–6) attend a group together each week. Each session lasts approximately 3 h and begins with a shared meal between all intervention team members, mothers, and children, which aims to build shared community and supportive relationships. During the meal, mothers engage in discussions of their "highs" and "lows" from the week as well as reflect on content reviewed during the previous week. Following the meal, mothers, supported by group leaders, engage in mindful and sensitive separations from their children and then children transition to a child group. While mothers attend a group focused on the attachment-based education and self-care skills practice discussed previously, children attend a group facilitated by the "Child Team" where they receive one-on-one care from an adult caregiver who provides individualized attention and safe opportunities for developmentally appropriate, child-led play. Group ends with reunion, and mothers and their children engage in shared group time "Circle Time" which models developmentally appropriate play, song, and games as well as provides mothers an opportunity to share positive affect with and delight in their children (please see Table 7.1 for adaptations to this structure when implementing the virtual format).

In-person Mom Power works to combat barriers to treatment and increase treatment retention by providing transportation to group, offering a shared meal before group, and ensuring access to safe and high-quality childcare during group.

Essential components of Mom Power also include weekly team debrief meetings and reflective supervision with a Mom Power reflective supervisor. Debrief meetings, held immediately following group, allow group leaders an opportunity to process aspects of the group, provide peer support, and discuss observations of children from Child Team. Reflective supervision provides group leaders with weekly consultation with a Mom Power supervisor to process the group session, reflect on their experiences and emotions in group, and identify ways for continuing to hold and support each family. Reflective supervision also attends to the parallel process, allowing the Mom Power supervisor to hold and support group leaders in the same way that group leaders hold and support the mothers who, in turn, hold and support their children.

Table 7.1 Comparisons of mom power implementations (in person v. virtual)

Attachment-based parenting education	
In person	*Virtual*
Mom Power curriculum. Use of visuals, handouts, group activities.	Mom Power curriculum. Use of visuals, handouts, group activities.
Enhancing social and peer support	
In person	*Virtual*
Shared meal between families and leaders. Opportunities for informal relationship building between mothers and group leaders during meals, before/after group. Check-ins from group leaders between sessions. Guest week.	Meal not provided. More reliance on online chat interactions. Increased use of social media for communication and sharing content relevant to curriculum. Socially distanced community-based shared experiences offered for some groups (e.g., park meetings). Home visits and check-ins from group leaders between sessions. Guest week (virtual).
Mental health and self-care practice	
In person	*Virtual*
Self-care skill education and practice. Self-care kits provided at group.	Self-care skill education and practice. Self-care kits delivered to homes. Some groups offered post bedtime to allow for mothers' undivided attention.
Guided parent-child interactions	
In person	*Virtual*
Supported in vivo separations and reunions between mother and child(ren). "Circle Time" Developmentally appropriate activities.	Virtual "Circle Time" for groups with little ones present. Discussion of separations and reunions. Community-based "Circle Time" offered in some groups (e.g., park meetings). Developmentally appropriate activities provided (e.g., craft materials, toys that promote serve and return).
Connections to care	
In person	*Virtual*
Individual sessions and needs assessments. Targeted referrals/"warm hand-offs".	Individual sessions and needs assessments. Targeted referrals/"warm hand-offs".
Reduced treatment burden/accessibility	
In person	*Virtual*
Transportation provided. Meals provided. Childcare provided.	Technology access provided (e.g., tablets, Wi-Fi hotspots). In-home childcare offered for some groups. Grocery support provided for some groups.

Virtual Implementation of Mom Power

During the COVID-19 pandemic, Mom Power shifted in-person implementation to online virtual implementation, providing continued support for mothers throughout the challenges of isolation and social distancing. Four groups in different regions of the United States (Southern United States, middle Appalachia, east coast, Midwest United States) implemented virtual Mom Power. The virtual implementation of Mom Power used the same manualized Mom Power curriculum including attachment-based parenting education and self-care skills. The length of group was shortened from 3–3.5 h to 1.5–2 h, reflective of some of the changes necessitated by the pandemic (e.g., no shared meal before group). While many aspects of the group changed to accommodate virtual attendance, leaders worked to ensure fidelity to the overall model and to center the importance of accessibility, reduction of treatment burden, and importance of community support. These efforts included providing Internet access to all participants if needed (e.g., tablets, Wi-Fi hotspots), delivering group materials and goods (e.g., printed handouts, diapers/wipes, self-care kits) to mothers' homes, offering in-home childcare (for some groups, not all), and offering virtual "Circle Time" for children. A full comparison of the components of in-person Mom Power versus virtual Mom Power is provided in Table 7.1.

Strengths of Virtual Mom Power

Virtual implementation of Mom Power appeared to provide greater flexibility and accessibility to the intervention. Most importantly, online implementation provided continued services, with virtually no gap in treatment, in the context of an unpredictable global pandemic. Virtual Mom Power provided mothers with essential support and community at a time when parents faced new and scary challenges daily (e.g., virtual schooling, job losses, food/essentials shortages). More logistically, the online implementation created more flexibility in the delivery of Mom Power. For example, with provided tablets, the use of online video conferencing enabled mothers to access group from anywhere. The accessibility of the virtual group also made it easier to accommodate late arrivals or mothers who needed to leave group early. This convenience and flexibility also extended to group leaders who experienced greater flexibility in their schedules during the virtual group and reported greater ability to communicate with co-leaders during group (e.g., Zoom chat, text messages) to adapt the content in the moment as needed. These same features also allowed mothers to discretely communicate with group leaders via private chat messaging during the group without disrupting the group process.

The virtual format was also set up nicely to allow for easy screen sharing of group materials and eliminated the need for mothers to manage and keep track of paper handouts. The use of online breakout rooms also provided an innovative method for conducting group activities and providing more individualized check-ins as indicated. Several virtual groups also saw an increase in attendance for guest week as guests were easily able to join a video conference call for 2 h as opposed to traveling to/from an in-person group and staying for 3 h. Additionally, since mothers attended group most often from their home environment, many of their partners or family members had greater exposure to the group and curriculum, something typically reserved only for "guest week." Other online features, like muting/unmuting or raising virtual hands, contributed to a more cohesive group dynamic at times.

Challenges of Virtual Mom Power

While some aspects of the virtual implementation of Mom Power created greater flexibility and accessibility for mothers and leaders, the impact of socially distanced and virtual communication created challenges for group members and leaders. At its core, Mom Power strives to provide opportunities for healthy, secure, and safe relationship-building opportunities between mothers and team members. These relationships typically develop informally through one-on-one interactions before and after group, during the shared meal, and during in vivo "Circle Time." The virtual implementation of Mom Power reduced the number of these more informal moments (Gray et al., 2022). In addition, the use of online video conferencing resulted in some group members attending group with their cameras off or while engaging in other activities (e.g., driving), creating another challenge for building social support and relationships throughout group. Group leaders prioritized creating a sense of community throughout the online group and practiced flexibility to adapt content to create more moments for connection. For example, choosing to share fewer visual aids during virtual group allows for more face-to-face time online between mothers and group leaders (Gray et al., 2022). Further, as with any online communication, technological difficulties added additional challenges to the implementation (e.g., loss of service, audio problems, and small screens on tablets/phones make viewing screen sharing hard). Overall, practicing flexibility and openness, often cultivated through reflective supervision, enabled group leaders to adapt to the current needs of the group and pivot appropriately when virtual challenges arose.

Some, but not all, virtual Mom Power groups offered in-home childcare support in the form of a Child Team member volunteer who could come to their home to play with the children during group time (while following relevant pandemic precautions). However, no mothers expressed a desire for that option. Of note, the group that was offered in-home childcare was the group in the Appalachian Highlands where we engaged families with high rates of poverty, systems involvement, and other psychosocial stressors. Though all individuals are unique, broad Appalachian culture tends to value familial ties, emphasize kinship, and hold a wariness of outsiders (Owens et al., 2007), and the Appalachian Highlands Mom Power team wondered if mothers declined the in-home childcare option out of a desire to protect the privacy of their homes and families. Thus, across all virtual groups, mothers did not have Mom Power provided childcare and often had to divide their attention between the groups and caring for their children. This was challenging given that the Mom Power program emphasizes "holding the baby in mind" and considering the child's needs through a developmental and relational lens. Thus, group leaders knew that it was unfair and unrealistic to expect young children to tolerate their mother's attention being distracted (by Mom Power class) for 2 h. To navigate this challenge, group leaders were intentional to encourage childcare options during group time and to offer encouragement for mothers to step away from the electronic device during group time to care for child needs. This allowed for in vivo practice of attuned parenting and allowed for group discussion around the challenges of balancing attention. Mothers also commonly navigated other distractions in their environment (e.g., family interruptions) or attended group from unconventional locations (e.g., doctors' appointments, grocery stores) which increased distractions for others and limited the privacy and confidentiality provided in group. Group rules and expectations were discussed during the first session (and throughout future sessions, as needed) to help mitigate distracted group participation and confidentiality issues.

Another core component of Mom Power, guided parent-child interactions, was also affected by virtual implementation. Without the traditional separation and reunions built in to Mom Power before and after group, group leaders had significantly reduced opportunities to observe these sensitive moments and were limited in their ability to scaffold mothers in their interactions with their children. Some groups worked to offer these moments within the virtual setting, including virtual "Circle Time" implementation as well as efforts to engage with mothers and children outside of group with scheduled outdoor group activities at local parks. Group facilitators were also intentional to take advantage of in vivo opportunities to scaffold parenting via telehealth. For example, if children expressed needs while mothers were attending virtual class, facilitators viewed these interruptions as opportunities to practice attuned parenting rather than disruptions to covering the curriculum.

Review and Critique of the Evidence Base for Mom Power

Since its inception, Mom Power has been empirically derived, incorporating evidence-based strategies from other empirically supported treatments (e.g., cognitive behavior therapy (CBT), dialectical behavior therapy (DBT)). With a foundation in attachment theory and trauma-informed care, it was co-designed with community members through an iterative, culturally responsive process (Muzik et al., 2009) and with attention to client engagement (Muzik et al., 2014). Mom Power was developed with the intention to engage high-need families who are often faced with significant risk factors, including trauma exposure, mental health challenges, economic oppression, and navigating single parenting or parenthood without high levels of social support, and the research projects around Mom Power have intentionally recruited for families with high psychosocial needs through working with community partners who serve families impacted by poverty, addiction, trauma, mental illness, and/or other adversities (LePlatte et al., 2012; Muzik et al., 2015). These types of challenges can often make it more difficult to engage families in services or programs due to both practical and psychological barriers, yet despite serving this often hard-to-engage population, the program has proved to be acceptable and engaging to parents with >65% retention. Participants reported that they received helpful parenting information from the intervention, that they felt welcomed by the friendly facilitators, and that they felt more supported and made connections with other women in the group as a result of the intervention (Muzik et al., 2016). The effects of the original (in-person) Mom Power program in improving parenting and mental health have been evaluated in several empirical studies. First, in an "open" trial (i.e., no control group) with 99 mothers completing Mom Power, researchers found that the program decreased mothers' depression, PTSD, and caregiving helplessness and improved parenting confidence, social support, and connection to care (Muzik et al., 2015, 2016). Adolescent mothers participating in the intervention demonstrated improvements in depression and post-traumatic stress disorder symptoms post-intervention and also reported feeling less guilty and shameful regarding their parenting skills after program completion (LePlatte et al., 2012).

A randomized controlled trial (NCT01554215) of 75 mothers demonstrated that mothers who participated in Mom Power (n = 42) showed improvements in mental health symptoms and parenting stress and an increase in "balanced" maternal representations and in maternal reflective capacity, that is, insights regarding their parenting qualities and their children's thoughts, feelings, and needs (Rosenblum et al., 2017a; Rosenblum et al., 2017b). There were no significant changes in the control group (n = 33), despite having received weekly informational mailings that covered the same topical content that was shared in the in-person parent group. The differential results of the Mom Power versus control condition on maternal mental health and parenting were even more accentuated for mothers with a history of interpersonal trauma, demonstrating that the intervention successfully reached those mothers with the highest need (Rosenblum et al., 2017a, b). Additionally, a neuroimaging pilot study (N = 29) revealed that mothers who received the Mom Power intervention demonstrated changes to their "parental social brain" indicative of greater reflective capacity and empathic attunement toward their children compared to those mothers in the control group (Swain et al. 2017). Further neuroimaging findings demonstrated support for the notion that Mom Power reduces parenting stress via changing neural activities related to empathic attunement in parenting "under-coupling" (Ho et al., 2020).

In a separate open trial (the first conducted by researchers outside of the intervention developers), Huth-Bocks and colleagues found evidence for reduced anxiety, depression, PTSD symptoms, and parenting stress, as well as improved emotional and concrete social support, and increased total "protective factors" from pre- to post-intervention in a study with 72 women who experienced significant stressors including economic oppression and mental health challenges (Amin et al., 2019; Huth-Bocks et al., under review; Lytle et al., 2018).

While empirical support for the original, in-person Mom Power is solid, the evidence base for the telehealth version of Mom Power is still in its infancy. The only published study examining virtual Mom Power reports on a pilot telehealth adaptation (Gray et al., 2022). With a sample of nine mothers from New Orleans who completed the virtual Mom Power program during a winter surge in early COVID-19, Gray et al. (2022) described the adaptation process and reported on feasibility, acceptability, and preliminary efficacy of the telehealth intervention. Maternal reports of maternal and child functioning from pre- to post-intervention were consistent with improvements in maternal depressive and post-traumatic stress symptoms and child competence, compared to outcomes from in-person trials. The authors highlight the benefits of telehealth delivery, including decreasing barriers to treatment engagement (Gray et al., 2022).

Two federally funded randomized controlled trials of virtual Mom Power are currently underway. The first (Virtual Mom Power with High-Adversity Mothers and Children; NCT05129397) is an expansion of the pilot study described by Gray et al. (2022), which is looking at the efficacy of Mom Power in a large sample of families with preschool-aged children (ages 3–5). Similar to the pilot study, participants are lower socioeconomic status (eligible for government assistance programs or Head Start) and live in New Orleans. Planned outcomes include maternal social support, psychopathology, sensitive parenting, child psychopathology, two-generational biobehavioral self-regulation targets (respiratory sinus arrhythmia), parent and child emotion and behavior regulation, and dyadic behavioral and physiological synchrony. Assessments will occur before, after, and 6 months following the group.

The second study underway is an examination of virtual Mom Power in mothers with opioid use disorders (Postpartum Intervention for Mothers with Opioid Use Disorders; NCT05614661). This study is delivering virtual Mom Power to mothers with OUD during the first 6 months postpartum. The multisite research team is examining effects on drug use, mood, and brain mechanisms. This study is funded by a two-part grant mechanism (R61/R33) wherein promising results from the pilot will then lead to a larger-scale randomized controlled trial.

Program developers continue to work toward cultural responsiveness and diversity-informed practice, with recent qualitative studies examining areas for improvement through focus groups and key informant interviews (Forer et al., 2023).

In sum, published studies examining the efficacy of Mom Power indicate the intervention is feasible, acceptable to families, and effective at improving important outcomes such as parenting stress, mental health symptoms, representations of the child, reflective functioning of the mother, and connection to resources and other care services. Overall, the evidence base for Mom Power is emerging, meeting the criteria of a "possibly efficacious treatment" (Southam-Gerow & Prinstein, 2014), but results from additional independent randomized controlled trials are needed to meet the threshold of a "probably efficacious" or "well-established treatment" (Southam-Gerow & Prinstein, 2014).

Mom Power Training

To become trained in the Mom Power model, individuals participate in a 25-h synchronous training over 3–5 days and must complete 5–10 h of asynchronous training materials prior to and during the synchronous training. Asynchronous materials serve to help familiarize trainees with Mom Power core concepts and underlying theories, as well as support trainees in engaging with the material at a deeper level through a series of reflection questions that trainees respond to on a discussion board in an online learning management system. The synchronous portion of the training is delivered by a team of individuals from the developers' organization (Zero to Thrive). In terms of credentials needed to run a Mom Power group, at least one facilitator in every group must hold a master's degree in a mental health-related field. However, it is not necessary for all facilitators to have a master's degree, and individuals from a variety of educational backgrounds may deliver Mom Power.

Although the training incorporates didactic elements throughout, the synchronous portion of the training is designed to be highly experiential in nature; throughout training, trainees are guided through many of the same exercises and activities that moms in the group will participate in and are provided with opportunities to practice facilitation through roleplay. In the spirit of Mom Power, trainers model a stance that is simultaneously "strong and in charge" and "warm and kind" to provide a holding space that promotes exploration, learning, connection, and reflection. This way of being is modeled by trainers intentionally and explicitly as a parallel to the dynamics intended between group facilitators and mothers, which is in turn meant to parallel the holding space that Mom Power supports mothers in providing for their children.

Because Mom Power groups may be delivered either virtually or in person, training is designed to prepare facilitators for either possibility. Throughout training, trainers describe ways in which virtual and in-person groups may differ (e.g., in terms of their incorporation of the Child Team component) and offer tips regarding adapting the program for virtual implementation. The learning management system contains modules further outlining differences and important considerations and provides separate materials and curricula for each modality.

After completing all synchronous and asynchronous training requirements, facilitators maintain access to curricula and materials (e.g., PowerPoints, curricula, videos, suggested supplies, and handouts) in the learning management system for a minimum of 6 months, and the Zero to Thrive team remains available for consultation and guidance as needed. To support fidelity to the Mom Power model, reflective consultation for the first two groups that are run by newly trained facilitators is mandatorily provided by a trained Zero to Three reflective supervisor who has expertise in the curriculum and in reflective practice. Facilitators also complete a fidelity survey following each week so that the reflective supervisor may monitor and assist with delivering the intervention with fidelity. Following the first two groups, ongoing reflective consultation remains a requirement but may be provided internally if the organization has the capacity.

Case Study: Gabrielle from New Orleans

The following case study is drawn from a virtual Mom Power group run by the Tulane Child and Family Lab (PI: Gray) in New Orleans, Louisiana, a city with high rates of trauma exposure and a history of endemic structural racism, violence, and poverty. Groups were offered as part of a randomized controlled trial of Mom Power's impacts on biobehavioral self-regulation. The trial launched in 2020, and, given the timing in relation to the COVID-19 pandemic, Mom Power group services were provided virtually (VMP; see Gray et al., 2022). However, in-person intake and exit home visits with mothers and target children were retained. Services were framed as preventive, and mothers of children aged 3–5 years self-referred from local partner service agencies, including Head Starts and WIC clinics. Inclusion criteria were broad, but mothers were required to be at or near the federal poverty level, as assessed through eligibility for services, to be able to participate in assessments and groups in English, and to be biological mothers, given interest in heritable biomarkers. Families were excluded if children had received a diagnosis of autism or global developmental delay. Dyads were randomized to receive (a) the full Mom Power intervention or (b) individual assessment visits, case support, and weekly informational mailers. Randomization was stratified by child age and behavioral concerns, assessed at intake with the Child Behavior Checklist (Achenbach & Rescorla, 2000). As part of the implementation, tablets and hotspots were provided to mothers who did not have Internet access (see Gray et al., 2022). Mothers were compensated for their assessment visits ($50) as well as for group attendance ($15). The following case study is drawn from a mother and child who participated in the trial.

At intake for VMP in 2023, Gabrielle, a mother in her mid-20 s, was excited to connect with other mothers, improve her mental health, and strengthen her relationships with her two children, a 10-year-old Destiny and a 5-year-old James, the target child. She shared the goal of having "better health for [herself] to have better health for [her] kids" but was facing both internal and external barriers to treatment access and engagement. In semi-structured interviews and on self-report measures, she reported a family history of mental health difficulties and interpersonal trauma exposure beginning in her early childhood. Gabrielle wanted to support her children with boundaries, to "have them listen without having to raise [her] voice." However, hypervigilance and difficulty sleeping were making it difficult to stay calm, and she had been exhibiting post-traumatic stress symptoms since she and her children witnessed a shooting in their apartment building 2 months prior to intake. She wanted to move out but was still recovering financially from the loss and disruption related to Hurricane Ida and the COVID-19 pandemic. Gabrielle also possessed several parenting strengths that facilitated her treatment engagement. Gabrielle previously had participated in a voluntary parenting group through another agency and was excited to participate in VMP and continue to grow her parenting skills in the groups. At intake, research staff noted her patience and her son's excellent turn-taking and communication skills.

Intervention

Gabrielle attended eight of the ten scheduled VMP sessions, with each session lasting approximately an hour and a half. Sessions took place on Zoom and incorporated a combination of structured group discussion and facilitator-delivered content. All four participants (including Gabrielle) self-identified as Black/African-American. There were two facilitators, both female-identifying masters-level mental health clinicians enrolled in a doctoral psychology program. One facilitator identified as Black/African-American, was originally from Louisiana, and was the mother of one young child. The other facilitator identified as White, was not from Louisiana, and was not a mother. They were supervised by a White licensed psychologist, originally from Louisiana and the mother of two young children, working out of a predominantly White institution. Reflective consultation took place weekly for 1 h and was used to consider the influence of facilitators' own attachment styles, identities, and biases in the therapeutic process.

In alignment with the tenets of both Mom Power and trauma-informed care, the goal was to honor mothers as the experts of their own experiences. Facilitators used the ten-session VMP manual, making adaptations according to the needs of the group. Implementation was guided by the five core pillars of Mom Power (social support, attachment-based parenting education, self-care, guided parent-child interactions, and connection to care) and the six tenets of trauma-informed care (safety; collaboration and mutuality; peer support; trustworthiness and transparency; empowerment, choice, and voice; cultural/historical/gender issues; Fig. 7.1). Gabrielle's progress over time is outlined below in the context of these overlapping tenets.

Tenets

Social Support At intake, Gabrielle shared her feelings of loneliness and desire to connect with local moms: "It was always me and the kids…I don't have any friends. I don't have any mom friends." The VMP group was intentionally small to allow for relationship building and discussion. To promote safety and establish trust, group guidelines around telehealth privacy and confidentiality were co-constructed by group members and facilitators during the first group session. Similar to mothers who participated in previous rounds of VMP, mothers in this group preferred flexible and transparent telehealth guidelines that prioritized participation over privacy (Gray et al., 2022). Like many VMP participants, Gabrielle often participated on her smartphone while commuting or juggling parenting responsibilities. In her midpoint individual session, she expressed appreciation for this reduced barrier: "I liked how it was virtual. It was easy, it wasn't time consuming, instead of having to go somewhere, it was right there." Although facilitators were guiding from a relative place of power and privilege, they strove to position themselves alongside mothers experiencing the curriculum. To honor mothers as experts of their own experiences, facilitators listened to and used their language during these virtual conversations. Similarly, they balanced using examples from the curriculum with discussing examples mothers provided of their children's challenging behavior. This emphasis on content raised by mothers increased the interactive nature of the group while providing facilitators with meaningful cultural context and insight into mother's most salient parenting concerns. By the last group session, Gabrielle described Mom Power as feeling "like a sisterhood" and expressed gratitude for a space with "lots of moms going through the same thing" where "you can all just help each other." Co-constructing boundaries around privacy honored the trauma-informed tenant of collaboration and mutuality and facilitated opportunities for informal social interaction in a safe and supportive environment. At the end of each group, mothers and facilitators named what they learned from one another to encourage sharing and acknowledge each mother's power, choice, and voice. This sense of safety and empowerment encouraged Gabrielle to "share things that [she] never really shared with other people," "be a little more open with people," and "give people a chance."

Attachment-Based Parenting Education Over the course of 10 weeks, Gabrielle grew immensely in her sensitivity to her children's distress signals, both by her own report and by observation of project staff at intake and exit visits. At intake, she reported feeling ineffective and helpless in response to her children's daily fights: "I feel like I am the bad parent, I am getting looked at funny cause y'all acting this way, when we go somewhere people have to bring y'all back cause you don't know how to control yourselves. Y'all can't even sit next to each other without it being a problem." Through using VMP concepts such as the Tree and the Wondering and Response Wheel (see Figs. 7.2 and 7.3), Gabrielle was quick to embrace the framework of when her children were seeking exploration (i.e., branching out) or connection (i.e., building roots), which strengthened her insightfulness into the *why* behind their behavior: "Sometimes it be hard for me to see the kid's point of view or give them a chance to really express themselves and talk instead of me just hurrying up, getting mad, angry, or fussing at them. This helps me calm down and really try to understand the kids." As Gabrielle grew in her capacity to identify the feelings behind her children's behavior, she grew more confident scaffolding their need to explore through providing a secure base and supporting their need to connect through providing a safe haven. Gabrielle's increased insightfulness enhanced both her sense of self-efficacy and her responsiveness to her children's social and emotional needs.

Self-Care At intake, Gabrielle reported wanting to have a "clear head," which was challenging when she was "mentally battling stuff that [didn't] want to go away." At the midpoint individual session, she expressed gratitude that VMP provided her with "personal me time." Gabrielle reported trying a variety of self-care strategies over the course of VMP, including deep breathing, yoga, and journaling. Like many moms in VMP, the dedicated weekly group sessions provided Gabrielle with structured time to reflect on her own well-being: "Sometimes I'd forget to take a moment out for myself. It would be all about the kids, the move. With the group, it reminds

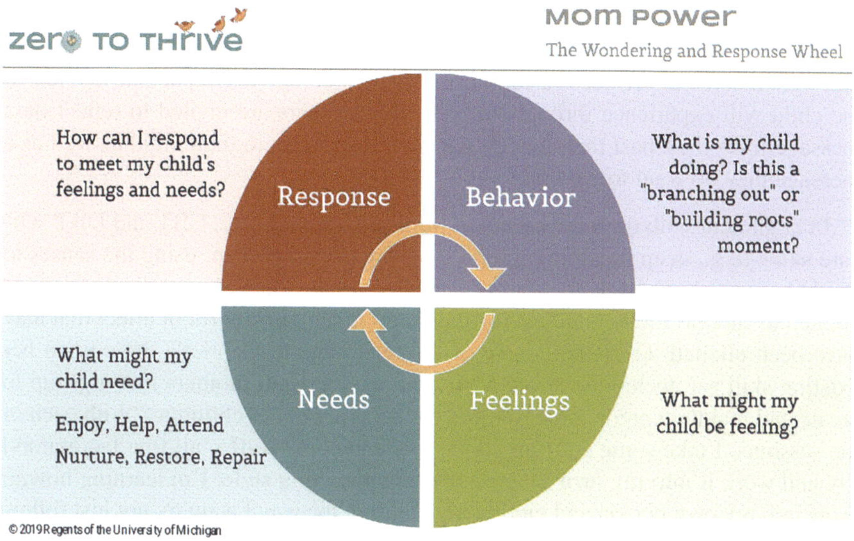

Fig. 7.3 Mom power wondering and response wheel

me that I need to take care of my own self first." In addition to using Mom Power techniques to manage her own stress, Gabrielle bought journals for her children and initiated family journal time at home. She described journaling as part of her practice of the Mom Power concept of "sunshine time." Sunshine time is the MP term used to capture warm, intentional, (mostly) child-led parent-child interactions marked with attention and delight. Journaling together also modeled for her children the self-reflection that Gabrielle was nurturing in VMP sessions and opened up communication channels between the dyads.

Guided Parent-Child Interactions The virtual format presented challenges regarding observing parent-child interactions during separation and reunion. However, both in the group and in individual sessions, facilitators spent time exploring the parent-child relationship across generations with Gabrielle. When discussing her early life experiences, Gabrielle identified intergenerational cycles of unpredictability and stress that she wanted to break: "I wanted to have kids so I can show them the love and support I always wanted." VMP concepts, including background music, helped Gabrielle reflect on her early experiences of separations and reunions and identify if and how they shaped her present parenting behaviors: "I never wanted to be like my mom, but in the end she was the biggest influence on me, and that's what I saw," she reported during session. Of note, background music is a metaphor used in MP to illustrate how the experiences we've had in our past, albeit pleasant or aversive experience, create the metaphorical music through which we subjectively experience our lives. For individuals with high levels of adversity and/or trauma, they may be more prone to "scary background music" that impacts their experience of the world and, most relevant to MP, their experience of parenting.

Background music is one of the intervention tools used to teach about the impact of past adversity and trauma on current thoughts and feelings. It's also used to help highlight that the experiences a child has with their caregivers impact the music that the child will experience throughout their life. Mothers are invited to reflect on a message from their past that they do not want to pass on to their child as well as a message they do want to pass on.

In alignment with the safety tenet of trauma-informed care, CBT and DBT self-care skills (e.g., deep breathing, progressive muscle relaxation, using the senses to soothe) were practiced at the end of group sessions when these reflections were elicited to support mothers in leaving the group feeling in control of affect that may have been elicited. Over the course of the intervention, Gabrielle drew upon her existing skill set, techniques from VMP, and advice from mothers in the group to create and maintain predictable routines for herself and her children: "With each of the sessions, I take some stuff the moms say and some stuff y'all [the facilitators] say and work it into my own lifestyle and my parenting style. I'm learning how to grow into my own person and mother my children the way I want to, not just follow in my mom's footsteps," she reported during one session. While this implementation of VMP did not include a dedicated Child Team, the flexible virtual implementation allowed for intermittent "in vivo" observation of Gabrielle and James's interactions. These interactions were discussed by the facilitators in reflective supervision, and facilitators used these "pop-in" moments to label and reinforce Mom Power concepts. For instance, James joined Zoom to share his Pokémon journal with the group, which provided the opportunity to recognize Gabrielle's scaffolding of their co-regulation and reflection. They delighted in describing their shared joy in journaling together as "sunshine time."

Connection to Care Gabrielle faced structural and interpersonal difficulties as a mother in New Orleans, a city with a long history of structural racism and endemic violence that is still recovering from the collective trauma and structural disenfranchisement of Hurricane Katrina as well as the COVID-19 pandemic. In alignment with tenets of trauma-informed care and the Mom Power pillar of connection to care, facilitators identified and connected Gabrielle to services beyond the VMP preventive intervention. At intake, she was connected with legal services so that she and her children could escape an unsafe living situation. Overlapping with the tenets of peer and social support, another mother connected her with a club for children who are interested in science, technology, engineering, and math. During the time period of the group, Gabrielle made the decision to relocate her family out of state. Subsequently, research staff connected her with a mutual aid group that helped with the high and unexpected cost of moving. Additionally, consistent with the "soft safe entry" framing of Mom Power as a program that is designed to facilitate engagement in more in-depth, targeted, and appropriate mental health services, Gabrielle expressed interest in pursuing individual treatment following VMP, and facilitators connected her with mental and physical health resources in their new state of residence to ensure continuity of care. Establishing a positive experience in a therapeutic environment contributed to Gabrielle's trust and safety and connecting her to a wide but targeted range of family-focused services facilitated empowerment and healing.

Case Study Conclusion

Group facilitators and research staff witnessed tremendous growth in Gabrielle's parental sensitivity, reflective capacities, and self-regulation over the course of the intervention (see Fig. 7.4). Relative to intake, she exhibited a 17-point reduction in her post-traumatic stress symptoms on the PTSD Checklist (PCL-5; Blevins et al., 2015), which surpasses the measure's recommended threshold (10 points) for clinically meaningful improvement; she was also significantly reduced on self-reports of depressive symptoms and difficulties in emotion regulation. Her reports of James's problem behaviors on the CBCL also decreased, and her reports of his social competence increased. Although follow-up over a longer time period is necessary to track if treatment gains persist, Gabrielle's case speaks to VMP's acceptability in improving parenting and mental health outcomes in mothers with exposure to trauma. Specifically, her case demonstrates how attention to social support, attachment-based parenting education, self-care, guided parent-child interactions, and connection to care may positively impact trajectories of both mother and child.

Summary

Mom Power is an evidence-based trauma-informed 10-week group parenting intervention that is rooted in attachment theory and infant and early childhood mental health-based practice. Clinical trials from two sites and two randomized control trials have evidenced MP's efficacy in promoting adaptive maternal and child outcomes and for promoting resilience across generations for families with high psychosocial risk. When the COVID-19 pandemic began, colleagues across the United States began to adapt the curriculum to bring MP into a virtual format (VMP). These colleagues collaborated with community partners, the Zero to Thrive Strong Roots team, and each other to ensure VMP held fidelity to the core components of the original intervention. In MP, it's often said "it takes a village" to raise a child *and* "it takes a village to support a caregiver." We're not meant to do any of it alone—parenting, the pandemic, and running community-based parenting interventions—and the adaptation to virtuality allowed us ways to stay connected during a time of high stress and isolation. Across VMP implementation sites, there was resounding clear feedback about the ease of access of telemental health—from mothers living in urban New Orleans to mothers living in rural southern Appalachia. Mothers across groups also clearly communicated a desire for "more" connection beyond the 10-week virtual groups—for example, many mothers expressed interest in park play dates, communicating on social media, and requests to come back and "do it again," once classes were back on the ground. The pandemic was a time when many of us needed to be nurtured and in connection and yet were expected to branch out (explore) and try many new ways of being. Virtual Mom Power created a safe haven and secure base for the mothers, children, and team members to be held in

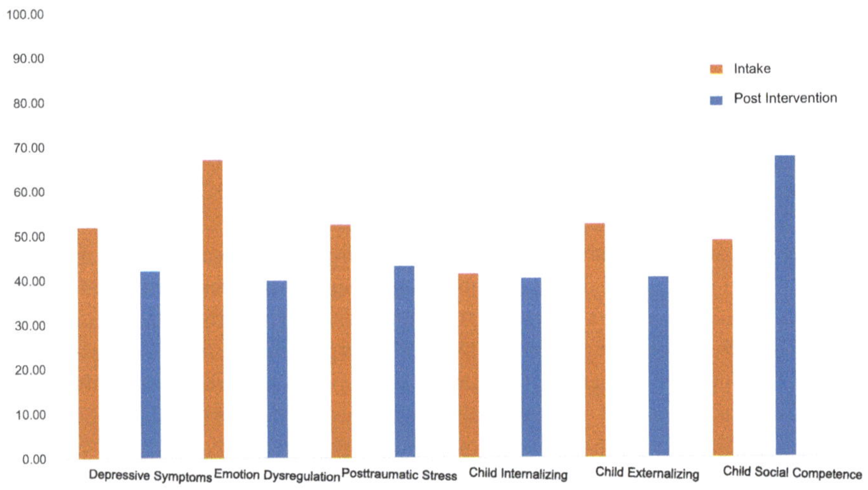

Fig. 7.4 Longitudinal representation of one dyad's standardized symptoms and behaviors across several measures. (Note: Symptoms of depression were measured using the Patient Health Questionnaire, symptoms of emotion dysregulation were measured using the Difficulties in Emotion Regulation Scale, symptoms of post-traumatic stress were measured using the Post-Traumatic Checklist, child internalizing and externalizing symptoms were measured using the Child Behavior Checklist, and child social competence was measured using the Social Competence Scale. Standard scores were calculated in SPSS through creating z-scores and converting these to t-scores)

safe, stable, and nurturing relationships and allowed for learning and growth, in community, during the pandemic, and beyond.

This Tree represents the ways that children learn, grow, and thrive. Parents and caretakers are represented as part of the Tree, the outer rings of the trunk that hold and provide support for the developing child. How do parents do this? By providing two key things that every child needs: a secure base and a safe haven.

When a child feels safe and secure, she feels ready to go outward and explore. When we are in exploration mode, we can branch out, try new things, and enjoy. Exploring includes playing, learning, and trying new things. Yet even at these times a child still needs a secure base, that is, her parent or caretaker to help her, to enjoy with her, and to attend to her to keep her safe.

There are other times when a child feels unsure, vulnerable, hurt, or distressed. At these times, we say that he has a need for connection and that this is a time to build, nurture, and strengthen the roots. To strengthen roots a child needs connection with a parent or caretaker; he needs to be welcomed into his safe haven. Meeting the child's needs for nurturance, restoring his emotional balance, and repairing disruptions help him grow deeper roots and thrive.

A child's sense of self develops through this balancing of exploration and connection-branching out and building deeper roots. Parents or caregivers are part of their inner world that guide and support their secure growth. The child's inner core strength is built up, ring by ring, through daily experiences of having their needs met when branching out and building roots, exploring, and connecting. This process begins in the earliest infancy, when parents hold, nurture,and comfort their child and gradually support their exploration. It continues throughout childhood and adolescence, as parents guide and support their children in exploration and connection.

Notice that the Tree's branches and roots are symmetrical, that is, there is a balance between the size of the branches and the depth of the roots. If the Tree's roots aren't as wide and thick as the branches, the Tree will topple. Notice that during times of stress, for example, during a drought, a Tree will not flower, but focuses on survival by strengthening its roots.

The sun represents the environment for children's growth. Both the branches and the roots need warmth and joy to grow and thrive. Parents provide this warmth and joy by meeting and welcoming their children's needs with a sense of delight and acceptance. When parents or caregivers convey, "I just love supporting your exploration," or "I just love being your safe haven," they provide the sun and warmth that children need not just to grow, but to thrive.

References

Abraham, E., Letkiewicz, A. M., Wickramaratne, P. J., Bunyan, M., Van Dijk, M. T., Gameroff, M. J., Posner, J., Talati, A., & Weissman, M. M. (2022). Major depression, temperament, and social support as psychosocial mechanisms of the intergenerational transmission of parenting styles. *Development and Psychopathology, 34*(5), 1997–2011. https://doi.org/10.1017/S0954579421000420

Achenbach, T. M., & Rescorla, L. A. (2000). *Manual for the ASEBA preschool forms & profiles: An integrated system of multi-informant assessment; Child behavior checklist for ages 1 1/2-5; Language development survey; Caregiver-teacher report form*. University of Vermont.

Amin, J., Nagle-Yang, S., Huth-Bocks, A., Lytle, S., & Gabriel, M. (2019). *Mom power*. Presented at Marce of North America.

Blevins, C. A., Weathers, F. W., Davis, M. T., Witte, T. K., & Domino, J. L. (2015). The Posttraumatic Stress Disorder Checklist for DSM-5 (PCL-5): Development and initial psychometric evaluation. *Journal of Traumatic Stress, 28*, 489–498. https://doi.org/10.1002/jts.22059

Bowlby, J. (1969). *Attachment*. Basic Books.

Center for the Study of Social Policy. (2023). *Protective factors framework*. Retrieved from https://cssp.org/our-work/projects/protective-factors-framework/

Edwards, V. J., Holden, G. W., Felitti, V. J., & Anda, R. F. (2003). Relationship between multiple forms of childhood maltreatment and adult mental health in community respondents: Results from the Adverse Childhood Experiences study. *American Journal of Psychiatry, 160*(8), 1453–1460. https://doi.org/10.1176/appi.ajp.160.8.1453

Feldman, R., Granat, A., Pariente, C., Kanety, H., Kuint, J., & Gilboa-Schechtman, E. (2009). Maternal depression and anxiety across the postpartum year and infant social engagement, fear regulation, and stress reactivity. *Journal of the American Academy of Child & Adolescent Psychiatry, 48*(9), 919–927. https://doi.org/10.1097/CHI.0b013e3181b21651

Felitti, V., Anda, R., Nordenberg, D., Williamson, D., Spitz, A., Edwards, V., Koss, M., & Marks, J. (1998). Relationship of childhood abuse and household dysfunction to many of the leading causes of death in adults: The adverse childhood experiences (ACE) study. *American Journal of Preventative Medicine, 14*(4), 245–258.

Forer, R., Johnson, A., Warburton-Silva, A., Carter, B., Fernandez, C., Novara, S., ... & Muzik, M. (2023). Improving the cultural responsiveness of the Mom Power perinatal mental health intervention via stakeholder input. *General Hospital Psychiatry, 83*, 201–202.

Goodman, S. H., & Gotlib, I. H. (1999). Risk for psychopathology in the children of depressed mothers: A developmental model for understanding mechanisms of transmission. *Psychological Review, 106*(3), 458–490.

Goodman, S. H., Rouse, M. H., Connell, A. M., Broth, M. R., Hall, C. M., & Heyward, D. (2011). Maternal depression and child psychopathology: A meta-analytic review. *Clinical Child and Family Psychology Review, 14*(1), 1–27. https://doi.org/10.1007/s10567-010-0080-1

Gray, S. A. O., Moberg, S. A., Obus, E. A., Parker, V., Rosenblum, K. L., Muzik, M., Zeanah, C. H., & Drury, S. S. (2022). Harnessing virtual Mom Power: Process and outcomes of a pilot telehealth adaptation of a multifamily, attachment-based intervention. *Journal of Infant, Child, and Adolescent Psychotherapy, 21*(1), 6–18. https://doi.org/10.1080/15289168.2022.2045464

Harvard Center on the Developing Child. (2007). The science of early childhood development (InBrief). Retrieved from www.developingchild.harvard.edu.

Ho, S. S., Muzik, M., Rosenblum, K. L., Morelen, D., Nakamura, Y., & Swain, J. E. (2020). Potential neural mediators of mom power parenting intervention effects on maternal intersubjectivity and stress resilience. Frontiers in psychiatry, 11, 568824.

Huth-Bocks, A., Amin, J., Gabriel, M., Lytle, S., Wolfish, E. & Nagle-Yang, S. (under review). Effectiveness of the Mom Power parenting intervention for women with interpersonal violence experiences and their young children.

IJzendoorn, M. H., Juffer, F., & Duyvesteyn, M. G. C. (1995). Breaking the intergenerational cycle of insecure attachment: A review of the effects of attachment-based interventions on maternal sensitivity and infant security. *Journal of Child Psychology and Psychiatry, 36*(2), 225–248. https://doi.org/10.1111/j.1469-7610.1995.tb01822.x

Kujawa, A., Arfer, K. B., Finsaas, M. C., Kessel, E. M., Mumper, E., & Klein, D. N. (2020). Effects of maternal depression and mother–child relationship quality in early childhood on neural reactivity to rejection and peer stress in adolescence: A 9-year longitudinal study. *Clinical Psychological Science, 8*(4), 657–672. https://doi.org/10.1177/2167702620902463

Lawler, J. M., Rosenblum, K. L., Schuster, M., & Muzik, M. (2018). Mom Power: A parenting group intervention for mothers with trauma histories. In M. Muzik & K. L. Rosenblum (Eds.), *Motherhood in the face of trauma* (pp. 165–180). Springer International Publishing. https://doi.org/10.1007/978-3-319-65724-0_11

LePlatte, D., Rosenblum, K. L., Stanton, E., Miller, N., & Muzik, M. (2012). Mental health in primary care for adolescent parents. *Mental Health in Family Medicine, 9*(1), 39.

Lytle, S., Nagle-Yang, S., Wolfish, E., Gabriel, M. T., Amin, J., & Huth-Bocks, A. (2018, October). *Mom power: Promoting parenting and maternal mental health among families with young children*. In 65th Annual Meeting. AACAP.

Masten, A. S., Lucke, C. M., Nelson, K. M., & Stallworthy, I. C. (2021). Resilience in development and psychopathology: Multisystem perspectives. *Annual Review of Clinical Psychology, 17*(1), 521–549. https://doi.org/10.1146/annurev-clinpsy-081219-120307

Miller, G., Chen, E., & Parker, K. (2011). Psychological stress in childhood and susceptibility to the chronic diseases of aging: Moving toward a model of behavioral and biologial mechanisms. *Psychological Bulletin, 137*(6), 959–997. https://doi.org/10.1037/a0024768

Muzik, M., Marcus, S. M., & Flynn, H. A. (2009). Psychotherapeutic treatment options for perinatal depression: emphasis on maternal-infant dyadic outcomes. *The Journal of Clinical Psychiatry, 70*(9), 16274

Muzik, M., Schmicker, M., Alfafara, E., Dayton, C., Schuster, M., & Rosenblum, K. (2014). Predictors of treatment engagement to the parenting intervention mom power among Caucasian and African American mothers. *Journal of Social Service Research, 40*(5), 662–680.

Muzik, M., Rosenblum, K. L., Alfafara, E. A., Schuster, M. M., Miller, N. M., Waddell, R. M., & Kohler, E. S. (2015). Mom Power: preliminary outcomes of a group intervention to improve

mental health and parenting among high-risk mothers. *Archives of Women's Mental Health, 18*(3), 507–521.
Muzik, M., Rosenblum, K., Schuster, M., Kohler, E. S., Alfafara, E., & Miller, N. M. (2016). A mental health and parenting intervention for adolescent and young adult mothers and their infants. *Journal of Depression and Anxiety, 5*(233), 2167–1044.
Nelson, C., Bhutta, Z., Burke Harris, N., Danese, A., & Samara, M. (2020). Adversity in childhood is linked to mental and physical health throughout life. *BMJ: British Medical Journal, 371*. https://doi.org/10.1136/bmj.m3048
Owens, J. S., Richerson, L., Murphy, C. E., Jageleweski, A., & Rossi, L. (2007). The parent perspective: Informing the cultural sensitivity of parenting programs in rural communities. *Child & Youth Care Forum, 36*(5–6), 179–194. https://doi.org/10.1007/s10566-007-9041-3
Patrick, S. W., Henkhaus, L. E., Zickafoose, J. S., Lovell, K., Halvorson, A., Loch, S., Letterie, M., & Davis, M. M. (2020). Well-being of parents and children during the COVID-19 pandemic: A national survey. *Pediatrics, 146*(4), e2020016824. https://doi.org/10.1542/peds.2020-016824
Rosenblum, K., Lawler, J., Alfafara, E., Miller, N., Schuster, M., & Muzik, M. (2017a). Improving maternal representations in high-risk mothers: A randomized, controlled trial of the Mom Power parenting intervention. *Child Psychiatry & Human Development., 49*, 372. https://doi.org/10.1007/s10578-017-0757-5
Rosenblum, K., Muzik, M., Morelen, D. M., Alfafara, E. A., Miller, N. M., Waddell, R. M., Schuster, M. M., & Ribaudo, J. (2017b). A community-based randomized controlled trial of Mom Power parenting intervention for mothers with interpersonal trauma histories and their young children. *Archives of Women's Mental Health, 20*(5), 673–686. https://doi.org/10.1007/s00737-017-0734-9
Schofield, T. J., Lee, R. D., & Merrick, M. T. (2013). Safe, stable, nurturing relationships as a moderator of intergenerational continuity of child maltreatment: A meta-analysis. *Journal of Adolescent Health, 53*(4), S32–S38. https://doi.org/10.1016/j.jadohealth.2013.05.004
Southam-Gerow, M. A., & Prinstein, M. J. (2014). Evidence base updates: The evolution of the evaluation of psychological treatments for children and adolescents. *Journal of Clinical Child & Adolescent Psychology, 43*(1), 1–6. https://doi.org/10.1080/15374416.2013.855128
Substance Abuse and Mental Health Services Administration. (2014). SAMHSA's concept of trauma and guidance for a trauma-informed approach. HHS Publication No. (SMA) 14-4884.
Swain, J. E., Ho, S. S., Rosenblum, K. L., Morelen, D., Dayton, C. J., & Muzik, M. (2017). Parent–child intervention decreases stress and increases maternal brain activity and connectivity during own baby-cry: An exploratory study. *Development and Psychopathology, 29*(2), 535–553.

Chapter 8
Byte-Sized Bonding: The Tech-Savvy Route to Internet-Based Parent-Child Interaction Therapy

Abigail Peskin and Jason F. Jent

Parent-child interaction therapy (PCIT; Eyberg & Funderburk, 2011) is a well-established treatment for disruptive behaviors in young children with decades of evidence backing its efficacy and effectiveness in many different populations (Thomas et al., 2017). Originally developed to treat children with conduct disorder and oppositional defiant disorder (ODD), it was later found to be efficacious for increasing compliance and decreasing disruptive behaviors for children with other diagnoses, including attention-deficit/hyperactivity disorder (ADHD), autism spectrum disorder (ASD; Parlade et al., 2020), and a variety of anxiety and mood disorders (Luby et al., 2020; Matos et al., 2009; Niec, 2018; Parladé et al., 2020; Phillips & Mychailyszyn, 2021). PCIT is historically a live parent-coaching treatment in which a caregiver and child dyad plays together in one room, and a therapist coaches the caregiver through an earpiece from behind a one-way mirror. The treatment is divided into two parts. First, in child-directed interaction (CDI), caregivers are taught and coached to increase the warmth in the caregiver-child relationship by interacting with their children utilizing toys that provide opportunities for creative and collaborative play, providing specific positive verbal feedback to positive and appropriate child behaviors and verbalizations, and allowing the child to lead the play. In the second phase of treatment, parent-directed interaction (PDI), caregivers are taught and coached to give effective, direct commands to children and to follow through with specific praise, timeout warnings, and/or a specific timeout procedure depending upon the child's responses to a command (Eyberg & Funderburk, 2011).

Conceptually, PCIT was developed from both behavioral and attachment research with the simultaneous goals of increasing warmth in the caregiver-child relationship and increasing limit-setting. Caregivers are first taught to use differential attention, decreasing disruptive behaviors by ignoring them, and increasing positive behaviors

A. Peskin (✉) · J. F. Jent
University of Miami Miller School of Medicine, Miami, FL, USA
e-mail: a.pooch@umiami.edu; jjent@med.miami.edu

L. N. Niec, C. E. Schoonover (eds.), *Telemental Health Care for Children and Families*,
https://doi.org/10.1007/978-3-031-69264-2_8

by providing intentional positive attention (McNeil & Hembree-Kigin, 2011). In the second part of treatment, caregivers are taught to use calm, consistent consequences for noncompliance, undoing coercive cycles (Patterson et al., 1982) of interaction with their children.

The majority of each PCIT session takes place without the clinician in the room, instead coaching the caregiver in an adjacent observation room through a one-way mirror. This caregiver-coaching model is powerful for child behavior change during the preschool years, as the goal is to both optimize the amount of time that a child receives consistent behavioral consequences (e.g., the clinician is with them 1 h per week, the primary caregiver much longer) and to reduce coercive cycles of interaction between the caregiver and the child.

Internet-Based PCIT

PCIT is traditionally performed in a clinic setting, but as technology advanced, therapists expanded the utilization of PCIT in a telehealth format to reach families who cannot come into the clinic weekly to receive treatment (Comer et al., 2017). PCIT is uniquely suited for telehealth service delivery (Gurwitch et al., 2020), as clinicians are not in the room with the family during a PCIT session in the clinic, but rather coaching the caregiver through a wireless headset (Eyberg & Funderburk, 2011). During Internet-based PCIT (IPCIT) sessions, families interact with their child at home playing with their toys instead of in the clinic room, and caregivers are coached by therapists via secure video conferencing calls and a wired or wireless headset that allows them to maintain communication with the therapist during sessions.

Effectiveness of IPCIT

Initial outcome studies of IPCIT have demonstrated remarkable promise for this treatment format in promoting significant positive outcomes in child disruptive behavior reductions and growth in caregiver parenting skills. Comer and colleagues (2017) conducted a randomized controlled trial comparing clinic-based and telehealth-delivered IPCIT in a racially and ethnically diverse sample and found that both treatment formats significantly decreased child disruptive behaviors and that in some ways IPCIT produced more robust child behavior changes than clinic-based PCIT. Caregivers who completed IPCIT also perceived fewer barriers to treatment than those whose treatment took place in the clinic. Additional case studies and open trials of IPCIT have demonstrated that IPCIT increases treatment access for families who reside in rural settings (Fleming et al., 2020; Kohlhoff et al., 2019) and for families with children with special healthcare concerns (e.g., brain cancer; Bono, 2022). More recent large trials have continued to demonstrate the positive effects of IPCIT on reducing children's disruptive behaviors and improving parenting skills in racially and ethnically diverse families, families with children with developmental delays, and families in low-income or poverty categories (Garcia et al., 2021; Bagner et al., 2023; Peskin et al., 2023).

However, there may be some differences in caregiver skill outcomes when services are delivered via IPCIT. In a large open trial of almost 400 racially and ethnically diverse families, families who self-selected into IPCIT versus clinic-based PCIT demonstrated similar child behavior outcomes but demonstrated fewer observed gains in positive parenting verbalizations at the end of treatment (Peskin et al., 2023). It is possible that conducting behavior observations in natural home environments relative to controlled clinic settings yields several unique challenges including less control over distractions and resources (e.g., toys, mobile devices, Internet connection, quality of sound) in the natural environment than within clinic settings (Peskin et al., 2023). However, these findings need to be replicated in future trials to understand whether differences in outcomes are environmental in nature or truly treatment format related.

Advantages and Challenges of IPCIT

Implementation of IPCIT provides several unique advantages relative to clinic-based PCIT services that increase the reach of this evidence-based intervention. IPCIT reduces a number of common barriers to behavior parent training including but not limited to transportation, access to childcare, flexibility of appointment scheduling, and geographic restrictions. IPCIT also provides the opportunity for therapists to work with families on child behaviors within their homes where many of the presenting problematic behaviors naturally occur. Within clinic settings, it can be difficult to simulate behaviors that only happen in the home. Whereas IPCIT provides an opportunity to coach caregivers on behaviors that most frequently happen in the home such as transitioning away from screen time, morning and bedtime routines, mealtime, and natural interactions that happen between family members (e.g., sibling interrupting, baby waking up from a nap, sibling arguments).

Despite its unique advantages and increased reach, IPCIT does come with some challenges related to technology problems and the home environment. Within treatment, technology disruptions such as unreliable Internet, dropped video conference calls, noise interference from background noise, depleted batteries for Bluetooth headsets, or mobile devices used for services (e.g., tablet, smartphone) can negatively impact the quality of IPCIT services received. If these issues are not addressed quickly and early in treatment, families can be at increased risk for discontinuing treatment because they feel like they are spending more time addressing technological barriers than receiving services. The home environment is oftentimes far less controlled than clinic-based PCIT playrooms, which are typically stripped down rooms with a table, chairs, a play rug, and special time toys ("special time" is the name given to brief, daily one-on-one play time between caregiver and child in which caregiver practices therapeutic skills). IPCIT therapists have to navigate through more hectic and busy environments within the family's home than clinic settings. There can be multiple children present during the session which can present challenges for coaching dyadic caregiver-child interactions. Environmental distractions can be present in multiple forms such as pets, visitors to the home, family members coming and leaving the home during session, video and audio distractions (e.g., television in another room, kids outside playing, another caregiver preparing dinner). These environmental distractions can result in children and/or caregivers leaving the designated play area that is within the video conference camera field of view multiple times within the session, which can make it more difficult for therapists to provide ongoing coaching when the caregiver or child is out of sight. Through effective IPCIT training and problem-solving approaches, the frequency and intensity of these disadvantages of IPCIT can be mitigated.

IPCIT Training and Implementation Approaches

While the foundation and the evidence for IPCIT were developed before COVID-19, interest and uptake of IPCIT drastically increased at the onset of COVID-19. In a national survey, over 80% of PCIT therapists expressed interest in implementing IPCIT at the start of COVID-19 (Barnett et al., 2021), and over 80% of PCIT therapists transitioned to delivering IPCIT services (Green Rosas et al., 2022) during the pandemic. Therapists perceived unique benefits of delivering services via telehealth including receipt of services in the home setting (e.g., seeing the home environment, generalization of skills) and increased access and engagement (e.g., no transportation or childcare needed, convenience of location, possible increased session attendance; Barnett et al., 2021). However, transition to IPCIT so quickly and on such a large scale was not without its struggles. Therapists in more rural areas described multiple barriers to IPCIT implementation including families lacking access to appropriate equipment for services (e.g., webcam, mobile device with camera), poor Internet connectivity during services, and significant time spent troubleshooting technological issues during scheduled therapy sessions (Druskin et al., 2022). Therapists and families who received IPCIT services within urban settings did not report similar technological barriers but also were implementing IPCIT prior to COVID-19 and had a built-in framework for effectively setting up technology with families and working through structuring the environment prior to service delivery (Garcia et al., 2021).

Despite very promising initial findings related to IPCIT treatment outcomes and significant interest in delivering services via this modality, research on effective training approaches to IPCIT implementation is less developed. In a statewide PCIT dissemination project in Oklahoma, researchers evaluated the effectiveness of two training models (live video conferencing consultation and post hoc phone consultations) on family outcomes for therapists who received initial PCIT training (Funderburk et al., 2015). Live remote secure video conferencing consultation allowed a remote PCIT trainer to directly observe parent-child interactions during a PCIT session, observe the PCIT therapist coaching the parent, and provide live two-way communication and feedback with the therapist during actual coaching sessions. On rare occasions, consultants would remotely lead a session and model coaching skills directly to the family for the therapist in training (Funderburk et al., 2015). The study found that therapists who received approximately 4 months of live video consultation, in addition to the initial training workshop, demonstrated a small but significant benefit in family outcomes, with clinically significant reductions in disruptive behaviors reported by caregivers. However, the phone consultation strategy did not show any effect on family outcomes.

During COVID-19, PCIT therapists had to rapidly transition to the use of telehealth to continue to deliver PCIT services to families. In a national survey of PCIT therapists during COVID-19, therapists with larger existing PCIT caseloads and those that received IPCIT training [e.g., free online video training (Jent et al., 2020) and free online guides (Peskin et al., 2020)] had increased odds of providing IPCIT services to families (Green Rosas et al., 2022). With regard to family treatment outcomes, Garcia et al. (2021) found that specific IPCIT therapist training strategies were associated with a variety of significant improvements in children's behaviors and parenting behaviors. These training strategies included viewing video recordings of local IPCIT trainings, the utilization of a locally developed free PDF guide for practical implementation of IPCIT (Peskin et al., 2020), and participating in IPCIT communities of practice (CoPs) where implementation and troubleshooting were discussed. In these IPCIT CoPs, clinicians met virtually 1 h per week to discuss challenges they encountered transitioning to telehealth services, including novel approaches to technological problems and strategies for difficulties unique to telehealth (e.g., not being able to see or hear the child). These CoPs often did not have a set agenda and followed a group discussion format rather than including any formal didactics.

While initial IPCIT training approaches provide some guidance for the types of training that are helpful for IPCIT therapist uptake of service delivery and treatment outcomes, the specific content within training that is the most effective for IPCIT dissemination has not yet been established. Within the existing research, most PCIT therapists transitioning to IPCIT were already trained in implementing clinic-based PCIT prior to attempting to deliver services via telehealth. Less is known regarding the most effective approaches for training therapists that are new to PCIT delivery in effective implementation of IPCIT. Considering the lack of established guidelines for training therapists new to PCIT delivery in effective implementation of IPCIT, the discussion now turns to exploring strategies and approaches that could facilitate successful telehealth service delivery for these therapists.

IPCIT Training Recommendations for Therapists New to PCIT

When considering getting trained in PCIT with an emphasis on telehealth delivery, therapists need to carefully select a trainer who has experience in delivering IPCIT and building in IPCIT training activities. Specifically, therapists should ask trainers how much they emphasize IPCIT training and skill practice opportunities (e.g., setting up the home environment, technology troubleshooting) within their training and consultation approach. Further, ask the trainer's own successes and challenges in delivering IPCIT to the proposed populations that are the same or similar to whom you will be providing IPCIT services.

The following training recommendations have not been formally evaluated but have been successfully utilized for training approximately 20 new PCIT therapists from 2021 to 2023 to deliver services via telehealth and to meet all therapist training and experience competencies required by PCIT International, the only certification authority recognized by the developer of the intervention. PCIT International provides a number of therapist competencies and experience requirements including reliable behavior observation coding, demonstration of parenting skills that caregivers learn in treatment, delivery of didactic and coach sessions with fidelity, and completion of treatment with two families. To train therapists to demonstrate these competencies and to be able to effectively deliver IPCIT, it is recommended that a significant emphasis should be placed on active telehealth practice of behavior observation coding and coaching within training and follow-up consultation.

Initially, therapists should be trained regarding what telehealth equipment options and secure video conferencing software will be used for service delivery and how to effectively set up family environments for successful implementation of services. Unlike a typical video conference call where the camera field of view is each user's head and shoulders, IPCIT coach sessions will require a much broader camera field of view within a designated play area so that the therapist can see the caregiver and child playing together while being coached. A broader field of view can typically be accomplished by placing the camera up and away from the play area or on the floor away from the play area. Because the caregiver and child are typically not close to the computer or mobile device's microphone while playing, an additional wired or Bluetooth headset is needed during sessions so that the therapist can coach the caregiver and listen to caregiver-child interactions. Depending on the computers and mobile devices available in the family's home, families can connect to sessions using one device (e.g., smartphone with camera for video and a Bluetooth headset connected to the smartphone for audio) or multiple devices (e.g., tablet with webcam for video and smartphone call into video conference with wired headset or Bluetooth headset). During IPCIT training, therapists roleplay by setting up telehealth equipment via video conference with trainers acting as the caregivers receiving services. The trainers acting as the "caregivers" demonstrate difficulties connecting the video and audio for the session and trainees have to work through troubleshooting with the "caregivers." Similarly, trainers teach therapists how to structure the CDI and PDI coaching play environment for success through reviewing pictures of rooms and collaboratively identifying aspects of a space that may assist with success of the session (e.g., room with a closed door, limited breakable items in the room) and aspects of a space that may potentially become problematic (e.g., television, video game consoles, fragile objects, high traffic area within the home). Trainers then simulate structuring the environment via behavioral rehearsal with trainees where they examine a real living space and advise the trainers (roleplaying as the caregiver) to reduce/eliminate potentially problematic aspects of the space. This activity may include the roleplay caregiver being instructed to shift to a front-facing camera on a mobile device and providing a tour of the home to identify the space that will be the most ideal for conducting coach sessions.

During IPCIT session behavioral rehearsals, trainers should advise therapists to always check the size of the family's screen being used to ensure that graphs and text are visible when sharing a screen during video conferencing. Finally, it is preferred that trainers simulate IPCIT coaching practice via a video conference behavioral rehearsal in which a volunteer caregiver and child within their home receive coaching from a trainee. Trainers can provide feedback about therapists' coaching using video conferencing chat functions or a phone call outside of the video conference session where verbal feedback can be provided. Within these behavioral rehearsals, trainers have volunteer families simulate via video conference some of the common following scenarios that are unique to delivering IPCIT including but not limited to the following: child difficulty joining special time because of a tablet or television, child frequently leaving the room during a simulated session, and/or child leaves the timeout chair and leaves the field of view of the video conference. These behavioral simulation training activities have been viewed as very helpful by therapists in training and can enhance the preparation of therapists new to IPCIT.

IPCIT Recommendations for Therapists Already Trained in PCIT

Before a PCIT therapist decides to attempt PCIT via telehealth, it will be important to reflect on their own feelings about the use of telehealth more generally and their initial thoughts or feelings about whether telehealth is an effective modality for conducting therapy more generally and PCIT specifically. Regardless of the published evidence on the matter, many people have strong feelings about the use of telehealth in therapy, and those feelings can impact the outcome of treatment.

Therapists conducting telehealth also need a basic understanding of how to host a video conference meeting on their platform of choice. At a minimum, technologically, from their side of the video conference, the therapist should be able to share the meeting link with the family, join the meeting from their computer, and effectively set up their own audio and video to see and hear the family. From the side of the family, the therapist should be capable of helping the caregiver access the video link and set up their audio and video. For PCIT, the therapist should be able to troubleshoot with the parent reasons why their video is off; their audio is off; their video is frozen or pointing in the wrong direction; their audio is poor (e.g., cutting in and out, muffled, child cannot be heard); they need help setting up Bluetooth or other headset/earphones; and/or the video call is dropped. Specific suggestions for how to troubleshoot these technological challenges are detailed in Peskin and colleagues' freely available IPCIT resource guide (2020).

Before embarking on PCIT via telehealth, therapists also need some awareness and capacity for how to coach parents to set up their home for both CDI and PDI, with an additional need for flexibility to accommodate caregivers' diverse home structures. Keep in mind that even for clinic-based families, many of these discussions should occur to increase caregiver success practicing CDI and PDI within their own homes. The following provides some recommendations for teach and coach sessions within IPCIT.

Teach Session Considerations

Each phase of PCIT is started with a Teach session where caregivers receive a didactic about the parenting skills that they will be coached on during the CDI or PDI phase of treatment. Performing a CDI or PDI Teach session remotely feels very similar to in person, with a few important differences. First, when caregivers hear that it will be a caregiver-only session, some assume that means they can take the call on-the-go (e.g., in the car). To prevent this misassumption, therapists should be prepared ahead of time to emphasize the importance of caregivers being in a location where they can comfortably sit, engage, and fully focus on the content during the Teach session. It is strongly recommended that the therapist reschedule a Teach session if the caregiver signs in to the session but appears to be occupied with another task (e.g., grocery shopping) or at a location that is not the agreed-upon location for telehealth sessions (e.g., a coffee shop). A second consideration for Teach sessions includes the sharing of handouts. In person, handouts are physically reviewed and then given to the caregiver to take home. Virtually, it typically works best if handouts are emailed prior to the appointment so caregivers have a physical copy to review during the session. Therapists can also share their screens during the session to review together, but if a caregiver tends to use their smartphone as their device for video conferencing, then the handout is often too small to read via screen share. The third consideration, and likely the most challenging part of completing a Teach session virtually, is the roleplay, in which the caregiver practices the skills with the therapist pretending to be the child. For CDI, to complete the roleplay most effectively, the clinician should have toys available for them and should prompt the caregiver at the beginning of session to grab a few toys to engage in the play as well (so the therapist can model the positive attention skills). For PDI, with two caregivers the clinician can coach them to take turns acting as the child. With only one caregiver, the therapist can pretend to be the child and have the caregiver practice that way; in that case the therapist must act as both the child and the coach, and importantly, they need to prepare their space to practice being in timeout with the caregiver on camera (e.g., background clear, timeout chair clearly available, toys present).

CDI Coach Considerations

Before a therapist starts each CDI coaching session, they should ensure that the toys available are appropriate for CDI within the family's home. Therapists should not assume that, because they discussed appropriate toys during the CDI Teach, the caregiver will have toys out that are CDI-appropriate. Additionally ensure that other distractions are considered. Is the caregiver anticipating that anyone else in the home will be a distraction? Are there pets that will interrupt the play, and if so, can they be kept anywhere else? The therapist also needs to make sure that the caregiver has a headset they can use so the child will not be able to hear the coaching. In subsequent coaching sessions, it is important not to assume that, since the caregiver had a functioning headset in previous sessions, they will have this headset every time. Many caregivers are using someone else's headset (e.g., an older child, spouse, etc.) or misplace the headset they are using from one session to the next. So be prepared to (1) check in about whether the headset is available and charged, and (2) troubleshoot about finding another headset if the previous one is not available at the beginning of every session. It can also be helpful for caregivers to set a reminder for themselves the day before or morning of the session to charge the headset.

Therapists should consider the following questions to promote a more successful environment for CDI coaching via IPCIT:

- Is the space planned for play too distracting? Is there a TV? Are there too many toys or toys that are not appropriate for special time? Is there a door that leads outside that may be tempting for the child to leave the room and the play?
- Is the space too big? Often playing in an open-plan living space can make it difficult for the child to stay in the area.
- Do other people need to use that space during session or play time? If the bedroom is a shared bedroom, will the other child need to get in before play is over? If it's a living room, will other members of the household be there, and will they be distracting for the child?

PDI Coach Considerations

IPCIT PDI coaching sessions also require much preparation. The more effectively therapists prepare for PDI Coach sessions with caregivers, the smoother the session will typically go. The first PDI Coach session will require a more detailed discussion between the therapist and the caregiver, including a video tour of the room, the placement of the timeout chair, etc. The therapist and caregivers also need to discuss their plan for how they will communicate if/when the child or caregiver goes off camera during the timeout process. They will also need to establish a back-up plan for communication, if the video conference call drops, which can sometimes happen during a chaotic timeout sequence. Because PDI Coach sessions can sometimes last longer than a typical session, therapists will need to revisit the importance of having all devices (e.g., tablets, smartphones, headsets) used for IPCIT fully charged prior to the start of the session. When feasible, caregivers should leave the video conference device (e.g., laptop, tablet, smartphone) plugged in especially for PDI Coach sessions.

Therapists should consider the following questions to promote a more successful environment for PDI coaching via IPCIT:

- Where is the timeout chair located, and what type of chair is the family planning to use? It's a good idea during the PDI Teach session to have the family show you the chair on camera so that if it's not appropriate for PDI (e.g., a couch, a rocking chair, a high stool), you can brainstorm together different ideas for a more appropriate chair or space.
- Which room in the home will be used for the timeout room? What are potential behaviors the family is concerned about occurring in that room, and how can those concerns be mitigated through prevention (e.g., temporary removal of anything dangerous or fun, turning off the water in the bathroom)?
- How close is the timeout chair and the timeout room to one another? The rooms should be as close as possible, so it is easy to transition between the timeout chair and the timeout room. Sometimes this means changing the location where special time play took place during CDI to get closer to the room that will be used for timeout room.
- At times, therapists will not be able to hear the caregiver if the child is yelling/screaming during timeout. How can therapists coach ahead so that caregivers still feel supported during intense moments? How will the therapist and the caregiver communicate about what is happening when the therapists cannot hear or see what the child is doing (e.g., escaping timeout chair)? Establishing and agreeing to forms of communication (e.g., caregiver will provide a narrative of what they see when the therapist cannot see the child) before intense moments happen during treatment can allow the therapist to be more supportive and helpful in coaching caregivers through difficult PDI sequences.

Despite all the provided recommendations and considerations for successful implementation of IPCIT, these strategies will have varying levels of success with individual families. The following case examples not only highlight some of the strengths of utilization of proposed recommendations but also acknowledge the limitations of some strategies based on a number of family-specific factors.

Case Studies

Families receiving IPCIT may need different levels of support to navigate technological challenges. Therapists have worked with caregivers who were IT specialists, who set up their home audio system to work for PCIT sessions, whereas other caregivers have needed their teenage children to help them set up their video conference sessions or lend them their headset for the session. Technological glitches in telehealth are often repetitive; either the family encounters the same or similar difficulties each session, or technological issues are resolved in the first session. The case illustrations presented below highlight multiple problems that families encountered during IPCIT, along with the collaborative solutions developed between therapists and families to overcome challenges.

- **Case 1: Significant Technological Barriers**

Before COVID-19, a family receiving clinic-based PCIT services consisted of a grandmother and her 2-year-old grandson, who exhibited disruptive behaviors and had a diagnosis of autism spectrum disorder (ASD). The family had just completed the CDI phase of PCIT in a clinic setting when the PCIT clinic transitioned to exclusively providing services via telehealth due to COVID-19. During this transition, the grandmother was able to have one clinic-based session where the therapist prepped and planned with the family on how to initiate an IPCIT session for their next visit. Despite the in-person prepping and planning, for the first session, the grandmother did not sign in; when the therapist called her after 5 min, she said she could not get into her email where she had the Zoom link. She had not used email in so long; she could not remember the password. Instead, the therapist texted the Zoom link via secure texting service, and the grandmother joined on her phone. Once connected, the therapist observed how the grandmother set up their play area at home. The living room had openings for the child to access every other room in the house, making it easy for the child to leave or escape the play area. For example, the kitchen was right next to the play area, and the child often went to get a snack during home-based special time. This was one of the advantages to having an IPCIT session with this family. The therapist was able to troubleshoot home-based barriers to consistent practice because the therapist was able to observe the family's environment and make suggestions for structuring the environment for successful special time practice. The grandmother agreed to rearrange the play setup so that a large kitchen playset visually and physically blocked the child's path to leaving the play area and helped him stay focused on special time in the living room. In addition, it was suggested that the child receives a healthy snack prior to starting special time so there was less interest in going to the kitchen. Once it was time to conduct PDI coaching via telehealth, the grandmother said that she did not have any headphones of any kind—neither wireless nor wired. Although for many children, coaching may lose effectiveness if the child can hear the therapist through the phone (on speaker phone), this child did not respond when he could hear the therapist coaching, so the therapist elected to just coach the grandmother through the phone speaker. This technological solution was less successful when the child was crying while sitting in the timeout chair because it was harder for the grandmother to hear the therapist's voice and more difficult for the therapist to hear the grandmother's voice during the Zoom session. However, this challenge was addressed through lots of roleplays with the grandmother and foreshadowing coaching when the child was quieter during the timeout process (e.g., "We're almost 3 min on the chair. If he's quiet after 5 seconds, you're going to say, you're sitting quietly…."). Ultimately, even without the recommended headset for IPCIT service delivery, this family was able to successfully complete IPCIT through ongoing troubleshooting between the therapist and the grandmother. Because the therapist was willing to spend additional time and effort tailoring telehealth services (e.g., phone speaker coaching vs. headset), structuring the environment (e.g., special time set up modifications), and shifting the timing of coaching statements (e.g., coaching when the child was quiet so the grandmother could hear statements), this family experienced the benefits of PCIT during the onset of COVID-19.

- **Case 2: Chaotic Home Environment Due to Multiple Siblings**

One of the barriers to treatment attendance and engagement is a family's access to childcare for other children. Telehealth offers a possible solution to this problem, although often the challenge then becomes how to provide coaching of caregiver-child dyadic interactions with other siblings interrupting or attempting to join the play. This difficulty can be exacerbated by not having a second caregiver within the home to monitor and supervise the other children during coaching. One family decided to institute a weekly movie night for the other siblings so that it would not interfere with PCIT coaching sessions, and the caregiver intermittently checked on the other children throughout the session to ensure appropriate supervision and monitoring. In other instances, development of a solution for reducing sibling interference during sessions requires ongoing problem-solving and troubleshooting. For example, one family with three children, ages 4 and 5 years and 7 months old, had difficulty logistically managing to get one-on-one special time for the 5-year-old boy, the identified participant for IPCIT. The 5-year-old had difficulties with compliance, emotion regulation, and irritability. Unfortunately, this meant that he was sometimes not motivated to engage with his mother in special time. What's more, the 4-year-old frequently attempted to interrupt the special time, causing the 5-year-old to hit him. This resulted in the mother ending special time due to physically aggressive behavior (a rule that is consistent with therapist instructions for special time homework in CDI). This cycle resulted in the mother having very limited opportunities to practice using the PRIDE skills within special time. Subsequently, the 5-year-old boy had difficulty receiving reinforcement from the play or his mother.

In this case, the largest barrier to coaching was the 4-year-old brother interfering with his older brother's special time. The therapist and the mother generated and attempted multiple strategies, all with varying degrees of success:

- **Environmental strategy:** The mother attempted to complete the IPCIT coach session in the boys' bedroom with the door closed to create a closed environment.

The door could not lock from the inside as it was a child's bedroom, so the younger brother often pushed the door open, even after the mother put furniture in front of it to keep it closed. The older brother also continued to leave the bedroom even with a closed environment, and when he did so, the younger brother came into the room to try to play with his mother. This strategy did not result in the intended change for this family but has been successful for other families.
- **Additional caregiver strategy:** The mother elicited the help of a neighbor to watch the baby and the younger brother during IPCIT sessions. However, the mother subsequently decided that she was not comfortable with this arrangement so future sessions were conducted again with all three children present at home.
- **Behavior contingency strategy:** The therapist planned with the mother to tell the younger brother that he could have special time with his mother when his older brother completed special time. Within the IPCIT session, the therapist would initially coach the mother with the older brother for 20–25 min and then would coach the mother and the younger brother for the final 5 min of the coaching before completing the end of session check-out. Outside the session, the mother was instructed to complete special time individually with each of her sons and alternate daily who received special time first. This process reduced the number of interruptions experienced in each session and increased the mother's ability to apply the PRIDE skills with both brothers with an emphasis on praising the children for taking turns, staying patient and calm, and keeping hands to self.

Some therapists might anticipate that a case like this would be more suitable for clinic-based PCIT services. However, the reality is that the mother's challenges represent her everyday life. Offering support and problem-solving in her natural environment via IPCIT may foster skill generalization and allow her to better manage her children's behaviors where and when she needs it most. Other families in similar situations have tried a variety of other strategies in collaboration with their therapist, including:

- Planning session for when other children take their naps.
- Have an infant sibling in a playpen or highchair (within sight) during session to avoid interference with the play. In this situation the caregiver will need to pause special time briefly through the session to check on and attend to the child.
- Reserve a limited-availability activity (e.g., screen time, TV) for session for the other child, so that they look forward to the special thing they get to do when the sibling is in special time. This can be highly effective if caregivers are willing to give the child an hour of caregiver-controlled screen time for each session, and if the child does not already have free access to screens. Therapist may need to consult with the caregivers around how to implement parental controls on screens and/or developmentally appropriate content for the sibling.

Nevertheless, if a therapist and a family attempt multiple strategies to promote child engagement in special time and reduce interruptions with limited success, a hybrid model of service, where some sessions are completed in a clinic setting, may be warranted, when feasible. Completion of even a few sessions in a controlled clinic setting can provide the opportunity for a child to obtain the reinforcement from the caregiver needed for CDI to begin to increase a cycle of adaptive and positive caregiver-child interactions and, in PDI, for timeout behaviors/testing to be somewhat extinguished before introducing to a less controlled home environment.

- **Case 3: Chaotic PDI Timeout**

Coaching a caregiver through PDI in the home via IPCIT for the first time introduces its own unique set of challenges. Sometimes the way that a therapist coaches a caregiver during CDI (e.g., on speaker phone, with a wired headset) becomes difficult if not impossible if the child escapes timeout and runs to another room not visible by the video conference field of view. Additional preparation and structuring of the environment and equipment can reduce struggles that may occur during the discipline phase of IPCIT. For example, "coaching ahead" or "foreshadowing coaching" is a very helpful strategy during virtual PDI, because the therapist at times will not be able to view everything that is happening if the caregiver and child go out of the field of view of the camera. Likewise, the caregiver should be prepared to describe to the therapist what is happening when the therapist cannot see caregiver-child interactions so that the therapist can continue to provide effective coaching. If the caregiver says the child is on the chair, the therapist should coach for what the next two steps will look like based on the PDI timeout sequence. For example, "If your child stays on the chair for 3 min, then… And if your child gets off the chair, you will say…."

The biggest IPCIT PDI coaching challenges come when, despite careful forethought and planning, neither the caregiver nor the experienced IPCIT therapist can foresee the hurdles that will occur in PDI and must respond to them in the moment. A family with a 4-year-old boy was receiving IPCIT with the primary presenting concerns of noncompliance, verbal aggression, and oppositional behaviors. During the PDI Teach, the mother agreed that the best approach to getting her son to the timeout chair was to carry and place her son safely on the timeout chair. She also decided that if he got off the timeout chair prior to being allowed to, she would carry him to the timeout room, which is a back-up procedure for the timeout chair. However, just because a plan is agreed to, it does not mean that an IPCIT session will play out as intended. During the first PDI Coach session, when the mother was coached to carry her son to the timeout chair, the mother repetitively told her son to sit on the timeout chair with no physical support or intervention. The son instead argued and continued to play. The mother continued to verbally prompt the child despite the therapist coaching in her ear to move the child to the chair. After a few minutes of therapist redirection, the mother moved her son to the timeout chair, and he promptly got off the chair twice (e.g., again after the one-time room warning). The therapist then coached the mother to move the child to the timeout room, but the mother again verbally reminded her son to sit on the timeout chair multiple times. The mother then began to give a series of commands for her son to go to the timeout room, and the headset fell out of her ear and she could not hear coaching from the therapist. Eventually, after repeated prompting, the mother was able to get her son into the timeout room. The mother then placed the headset back in her ear so that she could hear the therapist coaching, but her son then escaped from the timeout room. With therapist coaching, the mother was able to return her son to the timeout room and then was coached to hold the door to the room closed. Given the child's escape behaviors and the mother's reluctance to physically move the child to the timeout chair or the timeout room, the therapist and the mother jointly decided on a "swoop and go" procedure where her son would be prompted to sit in a timeout chair that would be placed in the timeout room when the mother opened the door rather than the mother carrying her son back to the timeout chair in a different room, which would likely provide him another chance to escape timeout. However, as the therapist and the mother were deciding on this solution, the child's father and older sister arrived home. The father began to ask the mother questions about what was happening, and the sister started to kick the mother to get her to open the door, behind which her brother was yelling. At this juncture, another family may have abandoned the timeout procedure and may have even terminated PCIT due to the challenges of smoothly completing PDI/timeout. However, the mother had seen the significant benefit of applying CDI skills learned in treatment with her son and, while she was unsure of the timeout procedure, understood the behavioral strategies behind the use of it and why the first timeout might be especially difficult. Because of her increased parenting self-efficacy, the mother calmly explained to the father and her daughter the timeout process while continuing to hold the timeout room door shut, with supportive coaching statements from the IPCIT therapist. The father then took their daughter to another room to not further interfere with the timeout process. The mother with additional coaching was able to successfully complete the timeout procedure. The father was then invited to attend the check-out portion of the session to debrief with the mother about the timeout procedure. While this timeout was chaotic for this family, the mother was able to regularly practice PDI at home following this session and successfully complete treatment. Of note, the goal is always to include all caregivers in as many sessions as possible. However, consistent attendance is sometimes only possible for one caregiver, and in that case the therapist should aim to include other caregivers whenever possible and work with the main caregiver however possible so they feel supported in using the PCIT strategies with their child.

In hindsight, there were lessons learned from this first PDI Coach session that helped with preparing for the remainder of IPCIT sessions with this family and other families. In fact, each first coaching session in PDI is a unique experience for families and therapists to learn new things that will allow for more effective subsequent discipline coaching sessions. In this case, the father and daughter had never been present at home during any of the previous IPCIT sessions, so no conversation occurred in the PDI Teach session about their presence during the first PDI Coach session. As a result, during subsequent PDI coaching sessions, this therapist learned to routinely ask if there is a *chance* of any family members/visitors being in the home during PDI Coach sessions, and what is the caregivers' plan for telling them about PDI (of note, the caregiver in this case was invited to be involved in sessions more regularly but declined. Therefore, the therapeutic goal was shifted to supporting the caregiver in treatment to ensure she felt comfortable using the skills no matter who was home). Second, although the mother expressed comfort carrying her son to the timeout chair and room during the PDI Teach session, in the moment during the session, she was no longer comfortable doing so. It is not uncommon for caregivers to change their minds about how they want to proceed during initial PDI Coach sessions when it is time to place a child in the timeout chair or when the child does not stay in the chair. Review of all timeout chair options (e.g., location of chair, procedure for getting the child to the chair) and back-ups to the timeout chair (e.g., swoop-and-go procedure, separate timeout room) should be thoroughly discussed with caregivers prior to the coaching sessions. Delivery of services in the home via IPCIT provides the therapist the ability to provide guidance on what strategies are likely to be the most viable because the caregiver can show them the physical space they intend to implement the timeout and back-up to timeout (e.g., there is somewhere to sit for a timeout chair in the room that will be used for timeout room or a chair nearby that could be moved in). Review of these options prior to the first PDI Coach session may make it easier to personalize the first coach session if/when a timeout procedure becomes chaotic.

Summary

Parent-child interaction therapy (PCIT) is a well-established treatment for disruptive behaviors in young children. Originally developed for conduct disorder and oppositional defiant disorder, it has also shown efficacy in treating other diagnoses such as ADHD, autism spectrum disorder, and anxiety disorders. PCIT involves live parent-coaching, where a caregiver and child play together while a therapist provides guidance from behind a one-way mirror. The treatment consists of two phases: child-directed interaction (CDI) and parent-directed interaction (PDI). In CDI, caregivers focus on building warmth and positive interaction with their child, while in PDI, they learn to give effective commands and provide consequences for noncompliance.

Recently, PCIT has been adapted for telehealth delivery, allowing families who cannot come to the clinic regularly to receive treatment. Telehealth PCIT or IPCIT utilizes secure video conferencing calls and wireless headsets for coaching sessions. Studies have shown that IPCIT produces significant positive outcomes in reducing child disruptive behaviors and improving parenting skills. Therapists report benefits such as increased treatment access, convenience, and the ability to see the home environment. Benefits of IPCIT include overcoming barriers like transportation and childcare. Challenges include technological issues and distractions in the home environment.

Recommendations are provided for training therapists new to PCIT on delivering IPCIT, such as hands-on practice with equipment setup and troubleshooting. For experienced PCIT therapists transitioning to IPCIT, self-reflection and technological competence are advised. Recommendations for IPCIT CDI and PDI Teach and Coach sessions include additional time and effort related to effectively setting up technology for sessions, structuring the environment in the home for optimal CDI and PDI practice, and shifts in coaching strategies to support not always being able to see or hear caregivers and children during sessions.

Case examples illustrate creative solutions families and therapists developed to manage common IPCIT challenges like sibling interruptions, distracting home environments, and chaotic timeout sequences. Despite obstacles, collaborative problem-solving enables families to complete IPCIT successfully. The case examples reviewed demonstrate the importance of flexibility and ongoing troubleshooting in implementing IPCIT.

In summary, emerging PCIT evidence and practice highlights the effectiveness of IPCIT while acknowledging unique training needs and implementation challenges. Creative collaboration between therapists and families is key to overcoming barriers and achieving positive outcomes with IPCIT. As technology continues to evolve, some technology disruptions will be significantly reduced (e.g., being able to simultaneously hear caregiver and child voices), but they will be replaced with new forms of technology (e.g., VR headsets, artificial intelligence suggestions for caregiver verbalizations) and new obstacles that PCIT trainers, therapists, and families will need to collaborate on to effectively incorporate within IPCIT sessions.

References

Bagner, D., Berkovits, M. D., & Coxe, S. (2023). Telehealth treatment of behavior problems in young children with developmental delay: A randomized clinical trial. *JAMA Pediatrics, 177*(3), 231–239.

Barnett, M., Sigal, M., Rosas, Y. G., Corcoran, F., Rastogi, M., & Jent, J. (2021). Therapist experiences and attitudes about implementing internet-delivered parent-child interaction therapy during COVID-19. *Cognitive and Behavioral Practice, 28*(4), 630–641.

Bono, M. H. (2022). Telehealth provision of parent–child interaction therapy during the COVID-19 pandemic: A case report. *Clinical Practice in Pediatric Psychology, 10*(3), 307–313.

Comer, J. S., Furr, J. M., Miguel, E. M., Cooper-Vince, C. E., Carpenter, A. L., Elkins, R. M., Kerns, C. E., Cornacchio, D., Chou, T., Coxe, S., DeSerisyl, M., Sanchez, A. L., Golik, A., Martin, J., Myers, K. M., & Chase, R. (2017). Remotely delivering real-time parent training to the home: An initial randomized trial of internet-delivered parent-child interaction therapy (I-PCIT). *Journal of Consulting and Clinical Psychology, 85*, 909–917.

Druskin, L. R., Han, R. C., Phillips, S. T., Victory, E. J., Aman, E., Tiano, J., et al. (2022). The dissemination of parent–Child interaction therapy in West Virginia during the Opioid Epidemic and COVID-19 pandemic: A qualitative study. *International Journal of Environmental Research and Public Health, 19*(22), 15085.

Eyberg, S. M., & Funderburk, B. W. (2011). *Parent–child interaction therapy protocol*. PCIT International.

Fleming, G. E., Kohlhoff, J., Morgan, S., Turnell, A., Maiuolo, M., & Kimonis, E. R. (2020). An effectiveness open trial of internet-delivered parent training for young children with conduct problems living in regional rural Australia. *Behavior Therapy*. in press.

Funderburk, B., Chaffin, M., Bard, E., Shanley, J., Bard, D., & Berliner, L. (2015). Comparing client outcomes for two evidence-based treatment consultation strategies. *Journal of Clinical Child & Adolescent Psychology, 44*, 730–741.

Garcia, D., Blizzard, A. M., Peskin, A., Rothenberg, W. A., Schmidt, E., Piscitello, J., et al. (2021). Rapid, full-scale change to virtual PCIT during the COVID-19 pandemic: Implementation and clinical implications. *Prevention Science, 22*, 269–283.

Green Rosas, Y., Sigal, M., Park, A., & Barnett, M. L. (2022). Predicting a rapid transition to telehealth-delivered parent-child interaction therapy amid COVID-19: A mixed methods study. *Global Implementation Research and Applications, 2*, 292–304.

Gurwitch, R. H., Salem, H., Nelson, M. M., & Comer, J. S. (2020). Leveraging parent–child interaction therapy and telehealth capacities to address the unique needs of young children during the COVID-19 public health crisis. Psychological Trauma: *Theory, Research, Practice, and Policy, 12*(S1), S82–S84.

Jent, J. F., Peskin, A., Bernard, D., Sherman, J., Perle, J., & Garcia, D. (2020). Telehealth: The ins and outs of technological proficiency [video]. *YouTube*.. https://youtu.be/AEAlF9UqDfo

Kohlhoff, J., Wallace, N., Morgan, S., Maiuolo, M., & Turnell, A. (2019). Internet-delivered parent-child interaction therapy: Two clinical case reports. *Clinical Psychologist, 23*, 271–282.

Luby, J. L., Gilbert, K., Whalen, D., Tillman, R., & Barch, D. M. (2020). The differential contribution of the components of parent-child interaction therapy emotion development for treatment of preschool depression. *Journal of the American Academy of Child & Adolescent Psychiatry, 59*(7), 868–879.

Matos, M., Bauermeister, J. J., & Bernal, G. (2009). Parent-child interaction therapy for Puerto Rican preschool children with ADHD and behavior problems: A pilot efficacy study. *Family Process, 48*(2), 232–252.

McNeil, C. B., & Hembree-Kigin, T. L. (2011). *Parent-child interaction therapy* (2nd ed.). Springer Science.

Niec, L. N. (2018). *Parent-child interaction therapy: A transdiagnostic intervention to enhance family functioning. Handbook of Parent-Child Interaction Therapy* (pp. 3–15). Springer.

Parladé, M. V., Weinstein, A., Garcia, D., Rowley, A. M., Ginn, N. C., & Jent, J. F. (2020). Parent–Child Interaction Therapy for children with autism spectrum disorder and a matched case-control sample. *Autism, 24*(1), 160–176.

Patterson, G. R., Chamberlain, P., & Retd, J. B. (1982). A comparative evaluation of a parent-training program. *Behavior Therapy, 13*(5), 638–650.

Peskin, A., Sherman, J., Schmidt, E., Parlade, M., Rothenberg, W.A., & Jent, J.F. (2020). *Internet based-PCIT (IPCIT): Recommendations for service delivery prepared in response to COVID-19 version 2*. Technical Manual. From http://www.pcit.org/uploads/6/3/6/1/63612365/ipcit_training_for_providers_during_covid-19_v2__2_.pdf

Peskin, A., Barth, A., Rothenberg, W.A., Turzi, A., Formoso, D., Jent, J., & Garcia, D. (2023). New therapy for a new normal: Comparing telehealth and in-person parent-child interaction therapy. *Behavior Therapy, 55*(1), 106–121. https://doi.org/10.1016/j.beth.2023.05.002

Phillips, S., & Mychailyszyn, M. (2021). A review of Parent-Child Interaction Therapy (PCIT): Applications for youth anxiety. *Children and Youth Services Review, 125*, 105986.

Thomas, R., Abell, B., Webb, H. J., Avdagic, E., & Zimmer-Gembeck, M. J. (2017). Parent-child interaction therapy: A meta-analysis. *Pediatrics, 140*(3).

Part V
Telehealth Through An Equity Lens

Chapter 9
Affirmative Telemental Healthcare with LGBTQ+ Youth

Melissa A. Cyperski

Telehealth Considerations for Affirmative Mental Healthcare with LGBTQ+ Youth

A recent Gallup poll (Jones, 2024) showed that 7.6% of people in the USA identify with one or more LGBTQ+ identities (e.g., lesbian, gay, bisexual, transgender, queer, Two-Spirit); however, this number is likely an underrepresentation due to possible sampling bias and the effect of stigma which prevents authentic identity exploration, expression, or declaration. The prevalence of LGBTQ+ or sexual and gender minority (SGM) individuals has been growing over the past few decades, with increasing numbers of children, adolescents, and young adults self-identifying as LGBTQ+ across the generations. Demographic trends reveal that the prevalence has been growing steadily, particularly among younger generations: 2.3% of Baby Boomers (1946–1964) identify as LGBTQ, 4.5% of Generation X (1965–1980), 9.8% of Millennials (1981–1996), and 22.3% of Generation Z (1997–2012) (Jones, 2024).

In addition to the population census, LGBTQ+ individuals also represent a significant portion of people who are seeking mental health services (Fish et al., 2023; Platt et al., 2018). Despite enrolling in mental health services more often than their non-SGM (i.e., cisgender, heterosexual) counterparts, LGBTQ+ individuals have ongoing, unmet mental health needs that would benefit from further support (Filice & Meyer, 2018).

No known conflicts of interest to disclose.

M. A. Cyperski (✉)
Department of Psychiatry and Behavioral Sciences, Vanderbilt University Medical Center, Nashville, TN, USA
e-mail: melissa.cyperski@vumc.org

L. N. Niec, C. E. Schoonover (eds.), *Telemental Health Care for Children and Families*,
https://doi.org/10.1007/978-3-031-69264-2_9

For instance, when compared to their non-SGM peers, LGBTQ+ youth experience significantly higher rates of mental health problems, including depression, anxiety, and suicidal ideation (Fish, 2020; Seager van Dyk et al., 2024). In a recent national survey on the mental health of approximately 28,000 LGBTQ+ young people in the USA, the Trevor Project (2023) discovered that 81% of LGBTQ+ young people wanted mental healthcare; however, 56% of youth who wanted to participate in mental health services in the past year were not able to access it. When questioned further, youth stated they were unable to access care for a variety of reasons, such as an inability to afford services (38%), not wanting to ask their parent/caregiver for permission (41%), and a lack of parental support or consent (20%). Additionally, youth expressed LGBTQ+ identity-specific concerns or barriers to services including fear of being outed (27%) and worries that clinicians may not understand or respond affirmatively to their sexual orientation or gender identity (The Trevor Project, 2023).

Effective mental health services are desired and are critical to improving psychosocial functioning, but access to general child-focused mental health services is limited (American Academy of Child & Adolescent Psychiatry [AACAP], 2022). Access is further constrained when seeking LGBTQ-affirmative care (Fish et al., 2023). Many mental health clinicians recognize the importance of affirmative, competent care for LGBTQ+ youth; however, clinicians also report they lack training, skill, and confidence in providing LGBTQ-affirmative care (Fish et al., 2023). According to the 2019 GLSEN School Climate Survey, 87% of school mental health professionals (e.g., school counselors, social workers, and psychologists) believed it was their duty and responsibility to provide supportive counseling to LGBTQ+ youth, but 37% indicated they received no formal preparation regarding working with LGBTQ+ students, and 76% reported having little to no prior training (GLSEN et al., 2019).

LGBTQ+ individuals also report that it is challenging to find mental health services that are sensitive to the unique needs and experiences of holding a marginalized sexual orientation, gender identity, and/or gender expression (SOGIE). Barriers to accessing care include a lack of providers or agencies offering LGBTQ-specific services and experiences of inappropriate, poor-quality care with microaggressions and stigma exhibited by mental health providers (Fish et al., 2023). Alternatively, when LGBTQ+ clients have the opportunity to engage in culturally appropriate services, they are less likely to drop out of treatment and tend to be more satisfied with their experiences, including improved therapeutic relationships (Whaibeh et al., 2020) and enhanced outcomes, such as reductions in symptoms of anxiety and depression (Fish et al., 2023).

The need for affirmative mental healthcare is clear, especially amid an ever-increasing number of young people who identify as LGBTQ+. However, there is an alarming disparity in the field with a lack of competent mental health providers trained and prepared to meet the demand. This discrepancy emphasizes the urgent need to develop affirmative mental health professionals and disseminate evidence-based best practices for LGBTQ+ clients (Fish et al., 2023; Pachankis et al., 2022).

To support this aim, telehealth may play an essential role in increasing access to specialty care for remote, marginalized, or otherwise underserved populations (Castro et al., 2023). The need for accessible, affirmative telehealth interventions became even more prominent following COVID-19 social distancing protocols. The pandemic furthered isolation among the LGBTQ+ community and worsened mental health for many SGM youth by requiring them to remain in unaffirming or unsupportive environments for extended periods following stay-at-home orders (Fish et al., 2020). Therefore, in hopes of increasing access and improving outcomes for LGBTQ+ youth, the purpose of this chapter is to support mental health professionals who wish to provide affirmative care to LGBTQ+ youth and their families via telehealth. We will define affirmative care, summarize the available research, and offer initial recommendations for conducting services via telehealth. Finally, we will integrate and synthesize information through an illustrative case presentation.

LGBTQ+ Affirmative Care

Participating in affirmative, culturally competent care can improve patient engagement, strengthen the therapeutic alliance, and enhance psychosocial outcomes—all while reducing exposure to negative experiences, like bias and stigma from unaffirming providers (Whaibeh et al., 2020). Affirmative care is "an approach to healthcare delivery in which organizations, programs, and providers recognize, validate, and support the identity stated or expressed by the individuals served" (Mendoza et al., 2020, p. 31). LGBTQ-affirmative providers are encouraged to create safe spaces for SGM clients, as well as to be "serious students" of the LGBTQ+ community which includes engaging in continued education and establishing a foundation of knowledge about language, cultural experiences, and within-group differences (Mendoza et al., 2020, p. 37).

Other experts have suggested that knowledge and validation are insufficient for providing affirmative care. Affirmative care is not simply about offering support within the healthcare setting but is also recognized as a practice of activism and advocacy (Mendoza et al., 2020). Affirming providers are thus called to recognize and respond to the oppression and stigma experienced by LGBTQ+ individuals who exist within a society full of cisgender, heterosexual norms (Austin & Craig, 2015b). In the therapeutic context, this may include but is not limited to practices such as assessing experiences of trauma and discrimination, including within the healthcare setting, which may impact the client's engagement or trust in the provider, and considering interpersonal power dynamics or systems of oppression that may be recreated in the therapeutic relationship (Mendoza et al., 2020). Providers are also expected to be self-aware of the assumptions, biases, and values they express directly or indirectly to clients (Whaibeh et al., 2020). In particular, as clinicians strive to contextualize and celebrate a patient's identity, they must remember that LGBTQ+ clients may or may not identify strongly with their SOGIE; pushing the provider's agenda and treating a client as if they wish or need to discuss their SOGIE in the therapeutic setting when they do not can have unintended, invalidating consequences (Mendoza et al., 2020).

Minority Stress

LGBTQ+ youth represent a highly stigmatized and disadvantaged population. Compared to their non-SGM peers, LGBTQ+ youth are at greater risk for adversity, such as social isolation, family rejection, homelessness, and a lack of educational and employment opportunities (Craig et al., 2021c). Minority stress theory (Meyer, 2003) is vital to understanding these and other disparities faced by LGBTQ+ youth and is a critical component of any mental health assessment or intervention. Underscoring the critical need for a minority stress theory lens, Clark et al. (2024) examined self-report measures from 286 adolescents in a psychiatric hospital. They discovered the SGM adolescents had greater clinical symptom severity than their non-SGM peers on the unit and that symptoms were associated with recent (i.e., past 30 days) and lifetime exposure to minority stress (Clark et al., 2024).

Minority stress theory describes the identity-specific distal and proximal stressors faced by LGBTQ+ people. External to the individual, distal stressors include experiences such as harassment, discrimination, victimization (Hatzenbuehler, 2009), or misgendering (Puckett et al., 2023a; Testa et al., 2015). Proximal stressors include internal psychological responses such as internalized stigma, expectations of rejection, and concealment of identity, which may stem from exposure to distal stressors or other lived experiences within the sociopolitical climate (Puckett et al., 2023b).

Distal stressors are routine, everyday experiences in the lives of LGBTQ+ youth. In a sample of 94 racially diverse sexual minority adolescents, Mereish et al. (2021) discovered that participants experienced an average of 16.96 minority stressors during a 21-day monitoring period. Daily minority stressors were associated with more negative affect, particularly on days when youth experienced sexual identity-specific stressors (e.g., "I was harassed because I am bisexual"; Mereish et al., 2021). Similarly, transgender/gender diverse (TGD) individuals reported experiencing marginalization at least once every 4 days, on average (Puckett et al., 2023b). In the 2021 GLSEN School Climate Survey, a representative sample of more than 22,000 LGBTQ+ youth ages 13 to 21 from across the USA were asked about their experiences in education. Nearly all LGBTQ+ youth (97%) reported hearing homophobic remarks at school, with the large majority (93.7%) indicating they felt uncomfortable or distressed because of the comments. Additionally, in the past year, 76.1% of LGBTQ+ youth experienced verbal harassment (e.g., threatened, called names); 53.7% were sexually harassed (e.g., unwanted touching, sexual remarks); 31.2% were physically harassed (e.g., pushed, shoved); and 12.5% were physically assaulted (e.g., punched, kicked, injured with a weapon) because of their SOGIE (Kosciw et al., 2022).

Notably, experiences of minority stress are likely to intensify during periods of sociopolitical conflict (Gonzalez et al., 2018). In the USA and around the world, anti-LGBTQ+ rhetoric and legislation are rampant. Given the current hostility toward the LGBTQ+ community, the Human Rights Campaign (HRC) declared a state of emergency for LGBTQ+ Americans in 2023 (HRC Staff, 2023). Each year, more bills are proposed in US state legislatures and passed into law—the majority of which target LGBTQ+ youth and TGD young people, in particular. LGBTQ+ youth across the USA have been subjected to harmful legislation that may restrict their right to display pride in their identity at school, play sports, use the bathroom, or receive healthcare (American Civil Liberties Union [ACLU], 2024). Therefore, there is a clear need to offer support and affirmation to as many LGBTQ+ youth as possible.

Telehealth

The principles and practice guidelines set forth by affirmative care are applicable regardless of the type of intervention or location of service, including telehealth, but more information is needed to optimize and nuance service delivery. In a racially diverse sample of youth receiving psychotherapy for anxiety in a community mental health center, telehealth was perceived to be convenient and practical; however, youth also believed that potential barriers (e.g., technical difficulties, lack of privacy) could hinder uptake and utilization. The authors noted that more research is needed regarding telemental health services among marginalized and under-resourced communities to gain an enhanced understanding of access, acceptability, and effectiveness (Castro et al., 2023).

Addressing Barriers to Care

Telehealth is particularly promising for increasing access among LGBTQ+ patients who do not live in urban areas where many LGBTQ-affirming providers practice (Waad, 2019). However, more research is needed to understand the service needs and unique perspectives of LGBTQ+ youth. The bulk of available research to date has been conducted with TGD youth specifically and the acceptability or feasibility of participating in gender-affirming care via telehealth. Findings reveal that few pediatric healthcare providers have the specialty knowledge and training to offer gender-affirming care and those who do typically practice in urban academic medical centers with the capacity to accommodate surrounding rural areas but may present significant geographic barriers to care. Estimates revealed that over 30% of patients traveled more than 1 h to access pediatric gender-affirming care (Sequeira et al., 2021). Thus, telemedicine may reduce geographic or other structural barriers to care (e.g., cost, travel, time off from work or school) and increase access to specialty care, such as affirmative care for TGD youth.

In a sample of 57 TGD youth, participants reported broad acceptability of telehealth and firmly believed that telehealth should remain an option for care, even though many individuals preferred in-person visits. Among youth surveyed for the study, 79% preferred meeting in person for initial visits, while fewer preferred in person follow-up visits (47%). In addition to considering initial vs. follow-up visits, support for telehealth varied depending on the anticipated service or visit type; specifically, youth preferred in-person visits for services such as establishing care (79%), sexual health (86%), and surgical consultation (90%). Behavioral health visits with a social worker (52%) and discussing fertility preservation (52%) were equally acceptable for telehealth vs. in-person visits (Sequeira et al., 2022). Findings were consistent with other studies (e.g., Apple et al., 2022) which indicated a high degree of patient and caregiver satisfaction with gender-affirming behavioral health services delivered via telehealth. In sum, the majority of TGD youth believed that all gender-related services, including mental healthcare, should be available via telehealth. To further increase utilization and satisfaction, pediatric gender care providers were advised to continue offering telemedicine services while implementing protocols for enhanced comfort and to address patient concerns related to privacy or hesitation regarding camera use, especially for dysphoric youth who may be uncomfortable with seeing themselves on the screen (Sequeira et al., 2022).

Additional Benefits of Virtual Programming

Given the extent to which youth exist in an increasingly digital world, children and adolescents likely feel comfortable navigating the necessary technology for telehealth services. Indeed, most youth in the USA routinely use the Internet for educational and personal reasons. There is conflicting research on whether LGBTQ+ youth spend more time engaging in online activities (e.g., social media, messaging) than their non-SGM peers. Some studies indicate no differences (e.g., Ceglarek & Ward, 2016), while others suggest that some LGBTQ+ youth spend more time online than their heterosexual counterparts (e.g., Luk et al., 2019), particularly in seeking identity-related support, resources, and information (McInroy & Craig, 2018).

In a large, national sample of LGBTQ+ youth, over 13,000 adolescents 13–18 years old in the USA reported about their daily life experiences (Goldberg et al., 2023), including Internet usage. Most LGBTQ+ youth reported using the Internet to find information that helped them understand their SGM identity (95.3%) and sexual or reproductive health (82.5%). LGBTQ+ youth also shared that they use the Internet as a tool for social connection, with 50% reporting they have at least one close friend online, and 68.3% had participated in online social communities specific to LGBTQ+ peers (Flohr et al., 2023). Findings suggest that the Internet can serve as a place of acceptance, connection, and belonging, which is particularly important for LGBTQ+ youth who may not be out in real life or who live in unaffirming contexts.

Indeed, recent studies have shown that engaging in online activities can be beneficial to the mental health and resilience of LGBTQ+ youth. For example, results from an online survey of over 6,000 diverse LGBTQ+ youth aged 14–29 years in the USA and Canada revealed that the benefits of social media usage can be multifaceted (i.e., emotional support and development, general education, entertainment, and identity-specific information) (Craig et al., 2021a). In their sample, younger participants were more likely to use social media to their benefit than older LGBTQ+ teens and young adults, suggesting there may exist subgroups or developmental stages for which virtual engagement is particularly helpful. Results are consistent with recommendations from Fish et al. (2020) to consider a developmental framework when working with LGBTQ+ youth.

While there are many potential benefits, LGBTQ+ youth are also subjected to stigma and discrimination online as well, at rates comparable to their experiences with stigma and discrimination "in real life." The majority (96%) of SGM youth reported viewing online content that was offensive and hurtful toward LGBTQ+ people, and approximately 50% of youth experienced identity-based cyberbullying in the past year (Flohr et al., 2023). Supervision and care should be taken whenever youth are interacting online, particularly for younger cohorts, to ensure that Internet and social media use remains safe and that SGM youth are not subjected to cyberbullying or placed at risk for other forms of victimization (Flohr et al., 2023; McConnell et al., 2017).

Evidence-Based Digital Interventions

Given their expressed desire and need for mental health services, as well as their comfort and ease with navigating technology and the Internet, LGBTQ+ youth appear to be primed to respond favorably to technology-based mental health interventions (Craig et al., 2021c). However, limited research is available to guide telehealth practice specific to the experiences and needs of LGBTQ+ individuals, and this is an essential area of future study.

In one study, Lucassen et al. (2018) conducted focus groups to learn more about Internet use and LGBTQ+ youth mental health; participants shared that they were interested and open to participating in digital mental health services. Focus group participants also offered constructive criticism to improve acceptability, suggesting that virtual therapies should be visually appealing and modern, as well as accurate, up-to-date, and inclusive of LGBTQ-specific needs (Lucassen et al., 2018).

The majority of extant telehealth research to date has focused on SGM adults. Gilbey et al. (2020) identified over 24 interventions designed to address mental, physical, and sexual health concerns among LGBTQ+ individuals. However, most published studies at the time were conducted with gay or bisexual men, and interventions primarily focused on specific health-promoting behaviors (e.g., HIV prevention, substance use prevention) (Gilbey et al., 2020; Hall et al., 2019; Schwinn et al., 2015).

Among LGBTQ+ youth specifically, emerging evidence identified the potential benefit of digital interventions to reduce mental health symptoms like depression, anxiety, and stress. To better understand current findings, Liu et al. (2023) compiled a systematic review of digital interventions and their effect on LGBTQ+ mental health, including people ages 12–29 from several developed countries worldwide. Fifteen empirical studies were identified for inclusion in the review. Digital interventions were examined and characterized into four categories: structured formal (e.g., telehealth, interactive video modules), structured informal (e.g., "serious games" that teach coping skills through gameplay), unstructured formal (e.g., facilitated chat, mobile applications), and unstructured informal (e.g., social media). Structured and unstructured formal interventions demonstrated preliminary evidence for mental health symptom reduction (Liu et al., 2023). However, several important limitations were noted among the available studies, including a lack of participant diversity and questionable generalizability across cultures or sociopolitical contexts. Additionally, 3 of the 15 studies utilized randomized controlled trials (RCTs), while only 2 identified studies involved direct interaction with a mental health professional—as opposed to self-guided modules or activities (Liu et al., 2023)—which is typically associated with improved outcomes (Grist et al., 2019).

Of the available digital interventions, Rainbow SPARX (Lucassen et al., 2015) and AFFIRM Online (Craig et al., 2021d) have the most robust program descriptions and findings relevant to LGBTQ+ youth. Rainbow SPARX was developed for sexual minority youth and intended to deliver cognitive behavioral therapy (CBT) skills training (e.g., relaxation training, behavioral activation, cognitive restructuring) through a videogame platform. Among 21 sexual minority youth from New Zealand aged 13–19 years old, completion of Rainbow SPARX produced a significant decrease in depressive symptoms with improvements maintained at a 3-month follow-up (Lucassen et al., 2015).

SGM youth have since suggested additional ways the Rainbow SPARX program can be enhanced, such as making more inclusive avatars (e.g., gender expression, pronouns) and offering the opportunity to repeat modules for additional practice with a specific skill (Lucassen et al., 2023). Studies of telehealth-based CBT with LGBTQ+ populations have primarily utilized structured module-based programs such as Rainbow SPARX. Although this may be an accessible and easy-to-use format, the content is predetermined. It does not allow for the tailoring, flexibility, or nuance that comes from interacting with a mental health provider in real time (Craig et al., 2021c), leaving room for considerable innovation and improvement.

Developed in Canada, AFFIRM (Craig et al., 2014, 2019; Craig & Austin, 2016) is a manualized CBT group intervention. It is considered the first empirically supported treatment for LGBTQ+ youth. In response to the COVID-19 pandemic, Craig and colleagues (2021d) adapted the eight-session offline intervention for synchronous online delivery via Zoom. Throughout the course, mental health professionals aim to affirm LGBTQ+ youths' identities and acknowledge their experiences of identity-specific stigma or discrimination. Youth are also supported in developing coping skills through CBT strategies such as psychoeducation, reflection, and practice (Craig et al., 2021c). Additional details about the AFFIRM modules and methods are described by the developers (Craig et al., 2019; Craig & Austin, 2016), including their community stakeholder approach (Austin & Craig, 2015a), training program for professional facilitators (Craig et al., 2021b), and adaptations for virtual delivery (Craig et al., 2021c, d).

Consistent with in-person delivery (Austin et al., 2018; Craig & Austin, 2016), AFFIRM Online demonstrated promising results among 46 SGM participants from North America aged 14–29 years. Upon completing the program, participants experienced a significant reduction in depression and improved coping when compared to waitlist controls (Craig et al., 2021d).

Developers of AFFIRM were pleased to find comparable results online and offline, highlighting the potential for telehealth to improve access or engagement in services and promote mental health recovery among LGBTQ+ youth (Craig et al., 2021d). However, more research is needed to confirm the applicability, feasibility, and generalizability of AFFIRM or other CBT-based telehealth interventions with individual patients. More research is also needed to understand efficacy and effectiveness with participants from various cultural backgrounds and sociopolitical climates, including unaffirming environments (Hall et al., 2019).

Treatment Recommendations

CBT Adaptations

Several effective CBT-based interventions for LGBTQ+ youth have been identified previously (Bochicchio et al., 2022), but there is a considerable gap in research regarding telemental health interventions (Craig et al., 2021c). Professional organizations and governing licensure bodies have outlined guidelines and considerations for mental health practice via telehealth (e.g., Joint Task Force, 2013). However, while tools and techniques from evidence-based practices such as CBT can be utilized to address core mental health symptoms (e.g., mood, anxiety, traumatic stress) and support improvements in psychosocial functioning, more information is needed about specific clinical strategies to use in the virtual office to meet the needs of LGBTQ+ young people.

Craig and colleagues (2021c) described several adaptations they made to AFFIRM Online when transitioning from in-person to telehealth delivery during the COVID-19 pandemic. For example, they extended the treatment orientation phase to enhance participants' comfort, competency, and sense of safety in the virtual world. Therapeutic engagement was promoted with increased check-ins and frequent opportunities for feedback, as well as normalizing any potential challenges or discomfort with the online platform. With regard to CBT skills training adaptations, AFFIRM facilitators modified activities for online content presentation and task completion, such as through electronic form completion, use of a digital whiteboard, screen sharing, and use of a chat feature. Program facilitators and participants also spent increased time collaborating on how to complete therapy homework assignments feasibly at home asynchronously (Craig et al., 2021c). Additional themes and considerations for telehealth practice with SGM youth are provided below.

Confidentiality

Regardless of the patient population, the best practice guidelines for telehealth consistently highlight the importance of providing informed consent, including limits of confidentiality and mandated reporting. Confidentiality and safety are especially important when working with LGBTQ+ youth, given the increased likelihood of encountering a serious or adverse event, such as suicidal ideation or trauma (Johns et al., 2020). Additionally, prior studies have revealed that many adolescents feel worried and fearful about discussing their mental health or other sensitive topics within the family home (Castro et al., 2023), including SGM youth. According to the Trevor Project (2023), approximately 21% of LGBTQ+ youth did not participate in mental health services because they did not want to receive mental healthcare virtually at home, despite wanting and needing support. Safety concerns must be assessed and addressed in context to prevent unintentionally exposing SGM identities or otherwise endangering LGBTQ+ youth by subjecting them to possible discrimination or abuse, such as experiencing caregiver rejection when joining telehealth sessions from an unaccepting family member's home or being harassed by unaffirming teachers and peers when visits are conducted in the school setting (Craig et al., 2021c; McInroy, 2016).

Therefore, it is imperative that providers assess the youth's comfort before proceeding with the telehealth session or discussion of sensitive content. For instance, assessment may include verifying who is nearby and able to hear the conversation. Providers should also be prepared to take any steps needed to remedy the situation or enhance the youth's comfort and perceived sense of safety. Confidentiality and sensitivity must also be applied to written communications, as well, to avoid an unsanctioned, possibly harmful disclosure of identity. Providers should consider what may be disclosed through clinical documentation (e.g., name, pronouns, topics of conversation); such information may be well received and affirming of an individual client's experiences, or it may result in information that is shared unintentionally with legal guardians, insurance companies, or interdisciplinary colleagues. Some youth may also have concerns about information being transmitted and stored electronically or a general lack of privacy in the digital realm, which should be addressed accurately and accordingly as needed.

Caregiver and Family Functioning

With appropriate protocols and assurances in place, telemedicine could reduce barriers related to parental lack of acceptance or affirmation for SGM identities. Indeed, previous research has demonstrated that TGD adolescents with lower levels of perceived parental support were significantly more interested in receiving care via telehealth (Sequeira et al., 2021). Local laws governing parental consent for mental health services still apply, but youth participation in telehealth services may reduce cost, burden, transportation needs, or other barriers to service participation that require parental involvement and dependence on unsafe or unaffirming caregivers (Fish, 2020).

Too many LGBTQ+ youth experience adversity, hostility, or rejection within their family. Recent data from a nationally representative sample revealed that over 57% of LGBTQ+ youth have experienced some form of rejection from their caregivers (Goldberg et al., 2023). Higher rates of family rejection are associated with worse physical and mental health outcomes, including increased likelihood of substance use, depression, and attempting suicide (Ryan et al., 2009). However, there is hope. If caregivers shift from highly rejecting to slightly rejecting behaviors, they can reduce risk and improve psychosocial outcomes for their SGM child (Ryan et al., 2009). For example, if caregivers begin to use a TGD young person's chosen name and pronouns, they can significantly reduce depressive symptoms and suicidal behavior (Russell et al., 2018).

Clinicians should remain vigilant about the experiences of LGBTQ+ youth and their caregivers, particularly for youth who connect with their provider over telehealth while they remain within an unaffirming home environment. As indicated, clinicians can offer supportive services directly and/or refer for additional parent- or family-focused mental healthcare. With increased access and decreased attendance burden, telehealth may provide unique opportunities for clinicians to engage caregivers in therapy when deemed appropriate and help shift toward affirmative parenting practices. Ryan (2009) offers additional information and suggestions about ways caregivers and families can support LGBTQ+ youth.

Affirmative Care and LGBTQ-Specific Needs

Providers are recommended to maintain their affirmative behaviors and approaches to treatment when meeting with patients over telehealth, including ensuring that their virtual presence and online office space maintains a safe and welcoming atmosphere. This could include, but is certainly not limited to, using context-specific cues that send messages of safety and affirmation, such as using pronouns in digital signature or adjusting Pride flag to be visible in frame. For further study about affirmative care practices on- or offline, refer to texts (e.g., Keo-Meier & Ehrensaft, 2018; Pachankis & Safren, 2019) and discipline-specific practice guidelines, such as the American Psychological Association (2015; Nakamura et al., 2022) or the American Academy of Child and Adolescent Psychiatry (Adelson, 2012).

For gender-affirming care specifically, providers are advised to consider TGD youth's comfort with virtual platforms and any hesitation pertaining to camera use or hearing their voice, especially for dysphoric youth (Sequeira et al., 2022). Therefore, providers may wish to collaborate with youth to determine clinically appropriate strategies to promote engagement and comfort in the virtual platform and titrating use over time. For example, youth may use chat feature exclusively at first and gradually increase their use of speaking voice; alternatively, youth may wish to turn off their camera, pin their provider's video for view instead of their own, or adjust their camera to focus on a feature they are more comfortable with (e.g., eyes and hair). Additionally, behavioral healthcare providers may be called upon to support a patient who is considering a social transition or seeking gender-affirming medical care. Details about gender-affirming care and the role of mental health providers are beyond the scope of this chapter; however, providers are encouraged to study and seek further training (e.g., Coleman et al., 2022) in order to serve TGD youth best. It will be essential for mental health providers to remain aware of the local laws and any resources for TGD youth available in their area, particularly in regions with gender-affirming care bans.

Minority Stress

According to Puckett and colleagues (2023b), to be effective, behavioral health providers must recognize the adverse experiences of LGBTQ+ youth, including the frequency and nature of minority stressors. Additionally, clinicians are encouraged to explore how distal stressors lead to distress or mental health impairment (Hatzenbuehler, 2009) and intervene accordingly. For example, research has demonstrated that experiences of stigma are associated with deficits in emotion regulation, such as increased rumination among sexual minority youth (Hatzenbuehler et al., 2008) and increased negative or anxious affect among TGD adults (Puckett et al., 2023b). Therefore, to address and respond to minority stress, LGBTQ+ youth may benefit from direct clinical interventions such as psychoeducation about the cycle of distress and skill-building to enhance positive coping, such as through cognitive strategies to decrease rumination (Hatzenbuehler & Pachankis, 2016). Psychotherapy may also wish to promote protective factors, such as suggested by Testa et al. (2015) who highlighted that a sense of belonging or connection to the community and pride in one's SOGIE enhance resilience in the face of minority stress.

In virtual adaptions of affirmative care for LGBTQ+ youth, Rainbow SPRARX modules included content encouraging youth to recognize identity-specific bias or stressors, to identify positive aspects of their identity, and to maintain hope (Lucassen et al., 2015). Similarly, AFFIRM Online included content devoted specifically to recognizing the impact of minority stress and information about cultivating social support (Craig et al., 2021d).

For further consideration, Pachankis et al. (2023) proposed a model and framework by which clinicians can adapt treatment and better understand the impact of minority stress on SGM clients.

Case Study

The following case study is based on outpatient telehealth sessions and focuses on an LGBTQ+ youth named "Maria." A pseudonym has been used to promote safety and confidentiality.

Maria (she/her) is 15 years old and Latina. At the onset of treatment, she reported her SOGIE identity as cisgender and straight. She was seeking psychotherapy and psychiatric medication management due to experiences of depression, anxiety, and stress, particularly at school. Maria worried she did not fit in and felt as though she did not have friends; her concerns were punctuated by a recent move to a new, predominately white high school and separation from her middle school friends. Even though she had all As and was engaged in various extracurricular activities, she worried about her grades and whether her teachers liked her. She also had a positive relationship with her parents but worried about disappointing them; having immigrated to the USA prior to when Maria was born, sometimes she and her parents disagreed over cultural values, such as gender norms and how a "good girl" should dress or behave. They also expressed doubts about her mental health diagnoses and the need for treatment, often relying on their Christian faith and prayer as a solution to life's challenges.

Initial therapy sessions were conducted in person, but the family expressed a desire to transition to telehealth services to avoid a lengthy commute to the office and time off work to transport Maria. Without caregivers transporting her to sessions, Maria primarily participated in telehealth visits independently from her bedroom. During one session, Maria's engagement was noticeably different; she spoke in clipped, short sentences and hushed tones. The clinician observed this change in behavior, and, upon inquiry, Maria stated her dad was working from home, sitting at the dining room table which was directly below her room. Sensing her discomfort, the clinician asked if she would prefer to terminate the session and reschedule for another day. Maria shared that she had something she was eager to talk about but did not want her dad to hear. Maria and the clinician collaboratively explored ways to help her feel more comfortable. She turned on some music to create background noise, continued speaking at a low volume, and intermittently used the chat messaging feature on the telehealth platform instead of speaking aloud.

In the chat, she shared with the clinician for the first time that she had a crush on a female peer at school and wanted to ask her on a date. Maria also revealed that she had identified as bisexual for several years, but never told anyone. The therapist thanked Maria for trusting her and for sharing her truth.

The therapist asked how to help at this time, and Maria expressed she would need one of her parents to transport her to the date and did not know whether to tell them about her crush or the nature of their relationship. She worried about how her parents would respond if they found out about her sexual identity since she had heard them make disparaging remarks about LGBTQ+ people in the past. Her concerns were worsened by fears they would accuse her of being burdensome, "disrespectful," or a "bad daughter."

Maria and her therapist carefully considered how to proceed, exploring factors including but not limited to her intersectional identities (e.g., race/ethnicity, religion, sexuality), her relationship(s) with her parent(s), and her romantic interest. With careful consideration and discussion during sessions, Maria decided now was not the time to tell her parents. She hoped to tell them one day and was encouraged by the clinician to listen to her intuition, collect observations about how they might respond, and continue to discuss together in sessions in the future. In light of her worries, the clinician assured Maria that telehealth sessions remained confidential and no information about her identity would be discussed or documented for her parents to see.

As for Maria's mental health, CBT skills were taught, with assistance of a digital whiteboard and the chat feature, such as when practicing identifying and restructuring unhelpful thoughts. Maria practiced various coping skills to use when urges to self-harm arose or when her worry became overwhelming. Suicide risk assessment and safety planning interventions were utilized as needed, including identifying affirmative, safe people in her life who could provide additional support in times of need. The therapist also provided psychoeducation about minority stress theory and helped Maria understand that some of her worries were in response to minority stressors and possible internalized stigma. Additionally, Maria and her therapist considered the potential psychological impact of concealment of her identity from important people in her life and identified the people, places, or spaces where she could connect with others in an authentic, meaningful way. For example, she expressed interest in attending a virtual support group with other SGM teens which was facilitated by a local LGBTQ+ community organization.

Throughout the course of treatment, Maria was engaged and reflective. With time, she was able to engage in distress tolerance and emotion regulation skills with increased mastery. She learned cognitive coping skills to interrupt patterns of rumination and to challenge maladaptive cognitions (e.g., "I will never be good enough," "Everyone only pretends to like me"). Maria was also connected with protective factors through behavioral activation, social connection, and a sense of pride in her bisexual identity. The therapist remained available to support Maria with her remaining treatment goals including managing her mental health symptoms. The therapist also routinely assessed Maria's perceived sense of comfort and safety in the home by asking Maria about her experiences and her relationship with her parents. Maria was reminded periodically that conjoint family therapy was available if/when desired and appropriate.

Several months later, Maria's mother called the therapist and expressed concerns that Maria appeared to be withdrawing from family activities and isolating more than a typical teenager. The clinician thanked the mother for her observations and agreed to assess Maria's mental health functioning at the next session, but did not share information without Maria's assent. At that time, Maria shared that she was doing well overall but was still uncertain about how her parents would respond and did not want to disclose her identity; she agreed this might contribute to staying in her room or sharing less with her parents, but mostly believed she was a "normal" teenager. Maria collaborated with the clinician to determine what information could be shared with her parents to address their concerns about her mental health, including a recognition of strengths and her commitment to remaining engaged in therapy. She remained eager to go on more dates with her girlfriend and was connected with an affirming group of peers at school, many of whom also identified as SGM.

Conclusions

A growing number of LGBTQ+ youth want and need mental healthcare to improve their psychosocial functioning and to help them explore their identities or manage SGM identity-specific stressors; however, access to child-focused mental health services is limited and further constrained when seeking LGBTQ-affirmative care, specifically. It is imperative that we increase the number of affirming, trained mental health professionals in the field. Additionally, telehealth has been identified as a promising advancement in healthcare with the potential to reduce barriers and improve access to culturally sensitive care. LGBTQ+ youth have reported openness to engage in telehealth services but, understandably, want to ensure providers are competent and affirming and that treatment can adequately meet their needs.

Affirmative CBT interventions have demonstrated effectiveness with LGBTQ+ youth, but limited research has examined adaptions and applications for telehealth interventions. Rainbow SPARX (Lucassen et al., 2015) and AFFIRM Online (Craig et al., 2021d) are two structured, digital CBT interventions designed for LGBTQ+ youth that have been well-documented and shown to reduce symptoms of depression or anxiety. More research is needed to better understand how telehealth and other technology-based interventions can be implemented successfully to support LGBTQ+ youth, particularly with youth who are unaffirmed in their identities or live in hostile sociopolitical climates.

Finally, as Waad (2019) highlighted, increasing access to affirmative, evidence-based telehealth services is important to improving LGBTQ+ youth mental health, but it is not sufficient. Additional solutions and comprehensive changes will be needed to combat stigma and structural inequalities that perpetuate health disparities for LGBTQ+ individuals across the USA and around the world.

References

Adelson, S. L. (2012). Practice parameter on gay, lesbian, or bisexual sexual orientation, gender nonconformity, and gender discordance in children and adolescents. *Journal of the American Academy of Child & Adolescent Psychiatry, 51*(9), 957–974. https://doi.org/10.1016/j.jaac.2012.07.004

American Academy of Child & Adolescent Psychiatry (AACAP). (2022, May 4). *Severe shortage of child and adolescent psychiatrists illustrated in AACAP workforce maps.* https://www.aacap.org/aacap/zLatest_News/Severe_Shortage_Child_Adolescent_Psychiatrists_Illustrated_AACAP_Workforce_Maps.aspx

American Civil Liberties Union (ACLU). (2024, March 15). *Mapping attacks on LGBTQ rights in U.S. state legislatures in 2024.* https://www.aclu.org/legislative-attacks-on-lgbtq-rights-2024

American Psychological Association. (2015). Guidelines for psychological practice with transgender and gender nonconforming people. *The American Psychologist, 70*(9), 832–864. https://doi.org/10.1037/a0039906

Apple, D. E., Lett, E., Wood, S., Freeman Baber, K., Chuo, J., Schwartz, L. A., Petsis, D., Faust, H., & Dowshen, N. (2022). Acceptability of telehealth for gender-affirming care in transgender and gender diverse youth and their caregivers. *Transgender Health, 7*(2), 159–164. https://doi.org/10.1089/trgh.2020.0166

Austin, A., & Craig, S. L. (2015a). Empirically supported interventions for sexual and gender minority youth. *Journal of Evidence-Informed Social Work, 12*(6), 567–578. https://doi.org/10.1080/15433714.2014.884958

Austin, A., & Craig, S. L. (2015b). Transgender affirmative cognitive behavioral therapy: Clinical considerations and applications. *Professional Psychology: Research and Practice, 46*(1), 21–29. https://doi.org/10.1037/a0038642

Austin, A., Craig, S. L., & D'Souza, S. A. (2018). An AFFIRMative cognitive behavioral intervention for transgender youth: Preliminary effectiveness. *Professional Psychology: Research and Practice, 49*(1), 1–8. https://doi.org/10.1037/pro0000154

Bochicchio, L., Reeder, K., Ivanoff, A., Pope, H., & Stefancic, A. (2022). Psychotherapeutic interventions for LGBTQ youth: A systematic review. *Journal of LGBT Youth, 19*(2), 152–179. https://doi.org/10.1080/19361653.2020.1766393

Castro, M. J., Rodriguez, R. J., Hudson, B., Weersing, V. R., Kipke, M., Peterson, B. S., & West, A. E. (2023). Delivery of cognitive behavioral therapy with diverse, underresourced youth using telehealth: Advancing equity through consumer perspectives. *Evidence-Based Practice in Child and Adolescent Mental Health, 8*(2), 206–220. https://doi.org/10.1080/23794925.2022.2062687

Ceglarek, P. J. D., & Ward, L. M. (2016). A tool for help or harm? How associations between social networking use, social support, and mental health differ for sexual minority and heterosexual youth. *Computers in Human Behavior, 65*, 201–209. https://doi.org/10.1016/j.chb.2016.07.051

Clark, K. A., Schwartzman, J. M., & Bettis, A. H. (2024). Sexual and gender minority stress and clinical symptom severity in psychiatrically hospitalized adolescents. *Psychiatry Research, 334*, 115838. https://doi.org/10.1016/j.psychres.2024.115838

Coleman, E., Radix, A. E., Bouman, W. P., Brown, G. R., De Vries, A. L. C., Deutsch, M. B., Ettner, R., Fraser, L., Goodman, M., Green, J., Hancock, A. B., Johnson, T. W., Karasic, D. H., Knudson, G. A., Leibowitz, S. F., Meyer-Bahlburg, H. F. L., Monstrey, S. J., Motmans, J., Nahata, L., et al. (2022). Standards of care for the health of transgender and gender diverse people, version 8. *International Journal of Transgender Health, 23*(sup1), S1–S259. https://doi.org/10.1080/26895269.2022.2100644

Craig, S. L., & Austin, A. (2016). The AFFIRM open pilot feasibility study: A brief affirmative cognitive behavioral coping skills group intervention for sexual and gender minority youth. *Children and Youth Services Review, 64*, 136–144. https://doi.org/10.1016/j.childyouth.2016.02.022

Craig, S. L., Austin, A., & McInroy, L. B. (2014). School-based groups to support multiethnic sexual minority youth resiliency: Preliminary effectiveness. *Child and Adolescent Social Work Journal, 31*(1), 87–106. https://doi.org/10.1007/s10560-013-0311-7

Craig, S. L., McInroy, L. B., Eaton, A. D., Iacono, G., Leung, V. W., Austin, A., & Dobinson, C. (2019). An affirmative coping skills intervention to improve the mental and sexual health of sexual and gender minority youth (project youth AFFIRM): Protocol for an implementation study. *JMIR Research Protocols, 8*(6), e13462. https://doi.org/10.2196/13462

Craig, S. L., Eaton, A. D., McInroy, L. B., Leung, V. W. Y., & Krishnan, S. (2021a). Can social media participation enhance LGBTQ+ youth Well-being? Development of the social media benefits scale. *Social Media + Society, 7*(1), 2056305121988931. https://doi.org/10.1177/2056305121988931

Craig, S. L., Iacono, G., Austin, A., Eaton, A. D., Pang, N., Leung, V. W. Y., & Frey, C. J. (2021b). The role of facilitator training in intervention delivery: Preparing clinicians to deliver AFFIRMative group cognitive behavioral therapy to sexual and gender minority youth. *Journal of Gay & Lesbian Social Services, 33*(1), 56–77. https://doi.org/10.1080/10538720.2020.1836704

Craig, S. L., Iacono, G., Pascoe, R., & Austin, A. (2021c). Adapting clinical skills to telehealth: Applications of affirmative cognitive-behavioral therapy with LGBTQ+ youth. *Clinical Social Work Journal, 49*(4), 471–483. https://doi.org/10.1007/s10615-021-00796-x

Craig, S. L., Leung, V. W. Y., Pascoe, R., Pang, N., Iacono, G., Austin, A., & Dillon, F. (2021d). AFFIRM online: Utilising an affirmative cognitive–behavioural digital intervention to improve mental health, access, and engagement among LGBTQA+ youth and young adults. *International Journal of Environmental Research and Public Health, 18*(4), 1541. https://doi.org/10.3390/ijerph18041541

Filice, E., & Meyer, S. B. (2018). Patterns, predictors, and outcomes of mental health service utilization among lesbians, gay men, and bisexuals: A scoping review. *Journal of Gay & Lesbian Mental Health, 22*(2), 162–195. https://doi.org/10.1080/19359705.2017.1418468

Fish, J. N. (2020). Future directions in understanding and addressing mental health among LGBTQ youth. *Journal of Clinical Child & Adolescent Psychology, 49*(6), 943–956. https://doi.org/10.1080/15374416.2020.1815207

Fish, J. N., McInroy, L. B., Paceley, M. S., Williams, N. D., Henderson, S., Levine, D. S., & Edsall, R. N. (2020). "I'm kinda stuck at home with unsupportive parents right now": LGBTQ youths' experiences with COVID-19 and the importance of online support. *Journal of Adolescent Health, 67*(3), 450–452. https://doi.org/10.1016/j.jadohealth.2020.06.002

Fish, J. N., King-Marshall, E. C., Turpin, R. E., Aparicio, E. M., & Boekeloo, B. O. (2023). Assessing the implementation of an LGBTQ+ mental health services training program to determine feasibility and acceptability during the COVID-19 pandemic. *Prevention Science, 25*, 109–123. https://doi.org/10.1007/s11121-023-01505-5

Flohr, C. J., Goldberg, S. K., Lewis, T., & Jones, R. (2023). *LGBTQ+ youth and the internet*. Human Rights Campaign Foundation. https://hrc-prod-requests.s3-us-west-2.amazonaws.com/LGBTQ-Youth-and-the-Internet-11.cleaned.pdf

Gilbey, D., Morgan, H., Lin, A., & Perry, Y. (2020). Effectiveness, acceptability, and feasibility of digital health interventions for LGBTQ+ young people: Systematic review. *Journal of Medical Internet Research, 22*(12), e20158. https://doi.org/10.2196/20158

GLSEN, ASCA, ACCSW, & SSWAA. (2019). *Supporting safe & healthy schools for lesbian, gay, bisexual, transgender, and queer students: A national survey of school counselors, social workers, and psychologists*. https://www.glsen.org/schoolmentalhealth

Goldberg, S. K., Lewis, T., Kahn, E., & Watson, R. (2023). *2023 LGBTQ+ youth report*. Human Rights Campaign Foundation. https://reports.hrc.org/2023-lgbtq-youth-report

Gonzalez, K. A., Ramirez, J. L., & Galupo, M. P. (2018). Increase in GLBTQ minority stress following the 2016 US presidential election. *Journal of GLBT Family Studies, 14*(1–2), 130–151. https://doi.org/10.1080/1550428X.2017.1420849

Grist, R., Croker, A., Denne, M., & Stallard, P. (2019). Technology delivered interventions for depression and anxiety in children and adolescents: A systematic review and meta-analysis.

Clinical Child and Family Psychology Review, 22(2), 147–171. https://doi.org/10.1007/s10567-018-0271-8

Hall, W. J., Ruiz Rosado, B., & Chapman, M. V. (2019). Findings from a feasibility study of an adapted cognitive behavioral therapy group intervention to reduce depression among LGBTQ (lesbian, gay, bisexual, transgender, or queer) young people. *Journal of Clinical Medicine, 8*(7), 949. https://doi.org/10.3390/jcm8070949

Hatzenbuehler, M. L. (2009). How does sexual minority stigma "get under the skin"? A psychological mediation framework. *Psychological Bulletin, 135*(5), 707–730. https://doi.org/10.1037/a0016441

Hatzenbuehler, M. L., & Pachankis, J. E. (2016). Stigma and minority stress as social determinants of health among lesbian, gay, bisexual, and transgender youth: Research evidence and clinical implications. *Pediatric Clinics of North America, 63*(6), 985–997. https://doi.org/10.1016/j.pcl.2016.07.003

Hatzenbuehler, M. L., McLaughlin, K. A., & Nolen-Hoeksema, S. (2008). Emotion regulation and internalizing symptoms in a longitudinal study of sexual minority and heterosexual adolescents. *Journal of Child Psychology and Psychiatry, and Allied Disciplines, 49*(12), 1270–1278. https://doi.org/10.1111/j.1469-7610.2008.01924.x

HRC Staff. (2023, June 6). For the first time ever, human rights campaign officially declares 'state of emergency' for LGBTQ Americans; issues national warning and guidebook to ensure safety for LGBTQ+ residents and travelers. Human Rights Campaign. https://www.hrc.org/press-releases/for-the-first-time-ever-human-rights-campaign-officially-declares-state-of-emergency-for-lgbtq-americans-issues-national-warning-and-guidebook-to-ensure-safety-for-lgbtq-residents-and-travelers

Johns, M. M., Lowry, R., Haderxhanaj, L. T., Rasberry, C. N., Robin, L., Scales, L., Stone, D., & Suarez, N. A. (2020). Trends in violence victimization and suicide risk by sexual identity among high school students—Youth risk behavior survey, United States, 2015–2019. *MMWR Supplements, 69*(1), 19–27. https://doi.org/10.15585/mmwr.su6901a3

Joint Task Force for the Development of Telepsychology Guidelines for Psychologists. (2013). Guidelines for the practice of telepsychology. *American Psychologist, 68*(9), 791–800. https://doi.org/10.1037/a0035001

Jones, J. M. (2024, March 13). *LGBTQ+ identification in U.S. now at 7.6%*. Gallup. https://news.gallup.com/poll/611864/lgbtq-identification.aspx

Keo-Meier, C., & Ehrensaft, D. (Eds.). (2018). *The gender affirmative model: An interdisciplinary approach to supporting transgender and gender expansive children*. American Psychological Association.

Kosciw, J. G., Clark, C. M., & Menard, L. (2022). *The 2021 National School Climate Survey: The experiences of LGBTQ+ youth in our nation's schools*. GLSEN. https://www.glsen.org/research/2021-national-school-climate-survey

Liu, Y., Wu, Y. C., Fu, H., Guo, W. Y., & Wang, X. (2023). Digital intervention in improving the outcomes of mental health among LGBTQ+ youth: A systematic review. *Frontiers in Psychology, 14*, 1242928. https://doi.org/10.3389/fpsyg.2023.1242928

Lucassen, M. F., Merry, S. N., Hatcher, S., & Frampton, C. M. A. (2015). Rainbow SPARX: A novel approach to addressing depression in sexual minority youth. *Cognitive and Behavioral Practice, 22*(2), 203–216. https://doi.org/10.1016/j.cbpra.2013.12.008

Lucassen, M., Samra, R., Iacovides, I., Fleming, T., Shepherd, M., Stasiak, K., & Wallace, L. (2018). How LGBT+ young people use the internet in relation to their mental health and envisage the use of e-therapy: Exploratory study. *JMIR Serious Games, 6*(4), e11249. https://doi.org/10.2196/11249

Lucassen, M. F., Stasiak, K., Fleming, T., Shepherd, M., & Merry, S. N. (2023). Enhancing an online cognitive behavioural therapy intervention for depression: Harnessing the feedback of sexual and gender minority youth to help improve SPARX. *Australasian Psychiatry, 31*(3), 247–254. https://doi.org/10.1177/10398562231153061

Luk, J. W., Gilman, S. E., Sita, K. R., Cheng, C., Haynie, D. L., & Simons-Morton, B. G. (2019). Cyber behaviors among heterosexual and sexual minority youth: Subgroup differences and associations with health indicators. *Cyberpsychology, Behavior, and Social Networking, 22*(5), 315–324. https://doi.org/10.1089/cyber.2018.0408

McConnell, E. A., Clifford, A., Korpak, A. K., Phillips, G., & Birkett, M. (2017). Identity, victimization, and support: Facebook experiences and mental health among LGBTQ youth. *Computers in Human Behavior, 76*, 237–244. https://doi.org/10.1016/j.chb.2017.07.026

McInroy, L. B. (2016). Pitfalls, potentials, and ethics of online survey research: LGBTQ and other marginalized and hard-to-access youths. *Social Work Research, 40*(2), 83–94. https://doi.org/10.1093/swr/svw005

McInroy, L. B., & Craig, S. L. (2018). Online fandom, identity milestones, and self-identification of sexual/gender minority youth. *Journal of LGBT Youth, 15*(3), 179–196. https://doi.org/10.1080/19361653.2018.1459220

Mendoza, N. S., Moreno, F. A., Hishaw, G. A., Gaw, A. C., Fortuna, L. R., Skubel, A., Porche, M. V., Roessel, M. H., Shore, J., & Gallegos, A. (2020). Affirmative care across cultures: Broadening application. *Focus, 18*(1), 31–39. https://doi.org/10.1176/appi.focus.20190030

Mereish, E. H., Miranda, R., Liu, Y., & Hawthorne, D. J. (2021). A daily diary study of minority stress and negative and positive affect among racially diverse sexual minority adolescents. *Journal of Counseling Psychology, 68*(6), 670–681. https://doi.org/10.1037/cou0000556

Meyer, I. H. (2003). Prejudice, social stress, and mental health in lesbian, gay, and bisexual populations: Conceptual issues and research evidence. *Psychological Bulletin, 129*(5), 674–697. https://doi.org/10.1037/0033-2909.129.5.674

Nakamura, N., Dispenza, F., Abreu, R. L., Ollen, E. W., Pantalone, D. W., Canillas, G., Gormley, B., & Vencill, J. A. (2022). The APA guidelines for psychological practice with sexual minority persons: An executive summary of the 2021 revision. *The American Psychologist, 77*(8), 953–962. https://doi.org/10.1037/amp0000939

Pachankis, J. E., & Safren, S. A. (Eds.). (2019). *Handbook of evidence-based mental health practice with sexual and gender minorities*. Oxford University Press.

Pachankis, J. E., Soulliard, Z. A., Seager van Dyk, I., Layland, E. K., Clark, K. A., Levine, D. S., & Jackson, S. D. (2022). Training in LGBTQ-affirmative cognitive behavioral therapy: A randomized controlled trial across LGBTQ community centers. *Journal of Consulting and Clinical Psychology, 90*(7), 582–599. https://doi.org/10.1037/ccp0000745

Pachankis, J. E., Soulliard, Z. A., Morris, F., & Seager Van Dyk, I. (2023). A model for adapting evidence-based interventions to be LGBQ-affirmative: Putting minority stress principles and case conceptualization into clinical research and practice. *Cognitive and Behavioral Practice, 30*(1), 1–17. https://doi.org/10.1016/j.cbpra.2021.11.005

Platt, L. F., Wolf, J. K., & Scheitle, C. P. (2018). Patterns of mental health care utilization among sexual orientation minority groups. *Journal of Homosexuality, 65*(2), 135–153. https://doi.org/10.1080/00918369.2017.1311552

Puckett, J. A., Aboussouan, A. B., Ralston, A. L., Mustanski, B., & Newcomb, M. E. (2023a). Systems of cissexism and the daily production of stress for transgender and gender diverse people. *International Journal of Transgender Health, 24*(1), 113–126. https://doi.org/10.1080/26895269.2021.1937437

Puckett, J. A., Dyar, C., Maroney, M. R., Mustanski, B., & Newcomb, M. E. (2023b). Daily experiences of minority stress and mental health in transgender and gender-diverse individuals. *Journal of Psychopathology and Clinical Science, 132*(3), 340–350. https://doi.org/10.1037/abn0000814

Russell, S. T., Pollitt, A. M., Li, G., & Grossman, A. H. (2018). Chosen name use is linked to reduced depressive symptoms, suicidal ideation, and suicidal behavior among transgender youth. *The Journal of Adolescent Health, 63*(4), 503–505. https://doi.org/10.1016/j.jadohealth.2018.02.003

Ryan, C. (2009). *Supportive families, healthy children: Helping families with lesbian, gay, bisexual & transgender children*. Family Acceptance Project, Marian Wright Edelman Institute, San Francisco State University.

Ryan, C., Huebner, D., Diaz, R. M., & Sanchez, J. (2009). Family rejection as a predictor of negative health outcomes in white and Latino lesbian, gay, and bisexual young adults. *Pediatrics, 123*(1), 346–352. https://doi.org/10.1542/peds.2007-3524

Schwinn, T. M., Thom, B., Schinke, S. P., & Hopkins, J. (2015). Preventing drug use among sexual-minority youths: Findings from a tailored, web-based intervention. *The Journal of Adolescent Health, 56*(5), 571–573. https://doi.org/10.1016/j.jadohealth.2014.12.015

Seager van Dyk, I., Sena, R., McCord, C., Kodish, T., & DeAntonio, M. (2024). Affirming LGBTQIA+ youth in inpatient psychiatric settings. *Journal of the American Academy of Child & Adolescent Psychiatry, 63*(3), 296–300. https://doi.org/10.1016/j.jaac.2023.04.020

Sequeira, G. M., Kidd, K. M., Coulter, R. W. S., Miller, E., Fortenberry, D., Garofalo, R., Richardson, L. P., & Ray, K. N. (2021). Transgender youths' perspectives on telehealth for delivery of gender-affirming care. *Journal of Adolescent Health, 68*(6), 1207–1210. https://doi.org/10.1016/j.jadohealth.2020.08.028

Sequeira, G. M., Kidd, K. M., Rankine, J., Miller, E., Ray, K. N., Fortenberry, J. D., & Richardson, L. P. (2022). Gender-diverse youth's experiences and satisfaction with telemedicine for gender-affirming care during the COVID-19 pandemic. *Transgender Health, 7*(2), 127–134. https://doi.org/10.1089/trgh.2020.0148

Testa, R. J., Habarth, J., Peta, J., Balsam, K., & Bockting, W. (2015). Development of the gender minority stress and resilience measure. *Psychology of Sexual Orientation and Gender Diversity, 2*(1), 65–77. https://doi.org/10.1037/sgd0000081

The Trevor Project. (2023). *2023 U.S. national survey on the mental health of LGBTQ young people*. The Trevor Project. https://www.thetrevorproject.org/

Waad, A. (2019). Caring for our community: Telehealth interventions as a promising practice for addressing population health disparities of LGBTQ+ communities in health care settings. *Delaware Journal of Public Health, 5*(3), 12–15. https://doi.org/10.32481/djph.2019.06.005

Whaibeh, E., Mahmoud, H., & Vogt, E. L. (2020). Reducing the treatment gap for LGBT mental health needs: The potential of telepsychiatry. *The Journal of Behavioral Health Services & Research, 47*(3), 424–431. https://doi.org/10.1007/s11414-019-09677-1

Part VI
Future Directions

Chapter 10
Future Directions in Telemental Health Care: Science Fiction or Grand Solution?

Larissa N. Niec

The idea that communication technology could be used to increase access to quality mental health care for children and families has existed for more than 100 years. However, over the century, telemental health programs have come and gone in fits and starts. Significant barriers long prevented telemental health from being implemented at scale. Only when the COVID-19 pandemic forced the majority of mental health providers to offer services remotely and reimbursement policies opened to remote health care did we see the possibility that telemental health services might truly increase access to care for a significant number of children.

The assessment and intervention practices included in this book address some of the most severe or frequently occurring child psychological issues, e.g., conduct disorder, trauma and anxiety disorders, and autism spectrum disorder. In each case, the interventions were originally developed to be implemented in person and had an evidence base for in-person implementation prior to being adapted to a telemental health modality. Although the evidence base for telemental health has grown more rapidly since 2020, rigorously controlled studies of telemental health implementation remain the exception rather than the rule. Thus, starting with interventions that have a solid theoretical basis and empirical support for in-person administration is sound practice. The question now is, "Where is technology taking mental health care next?"

Telemental health has come a long way in a relatively short time, forced to advance by the pandemic shutdowns of 2020 and 2021. In some ways, the field was more than ready to advance. The existing telecommunication technology permitted

L. N. Niec (✉)
Center for Children, Families, and Communities, Central Michigan University, Mount Pleasant, MI, USA
e-mail: niec1l@cmich.edu

L. N. Niec, C. E. Schoonover (eds.), *Telemental Health Care for Children and Families*,
https://doi.org/10.1007/978-3-031-69264-2_10

users to easily and economically communicate via video-conferencing platforms, and most households included the devices necessary for video-conferencing. In a recent survey, 80% of Americans reported that they have high-speed Internet at home, 90% said they had a smartphone, and 95% reported they use the Internet (Pew Research Center, 2024). Prior to the pandemic, it was largely our skepticism and discomfort as providers and the failure of insurance companies to include remote care as a reimbursable service that held back the dissemination of telemental health.

We have now been pushed over some of the biggest hurdles blocking wide-reaching implementation. Providers' comfort with the modality has changed dramatically. A survey of mental health treatment facilities found that as of 2023, 80% (n = 980) of facilities that were accepting new patients offered telehealth services (Cantor et al., 2024), and 67% of psychologists surveyed reported they offered hybrid telehealth/in-person services (American Psychological Association, 2023). State mental health licensure policies that facilitated telehealth, such as PSYPACT and the Social Work Interstate Licensure Compact, have changed the mental health-care landscape by allowing therapists to provide services in many states with health provider shortages. While it is unclear whether all of these policies—such as insurance reimbursement schedules—will be maintained, others are here to stay.

As previously noted, more rigorous research on telemental health implementation is still urgently needed. Prior to the COVID-19 pandemic, very few evidence-based, child-focused interventions had any empirical support for remote implementation. During the pandemic, most published studies were descriptive or single group designs. Although this book itself demonstrates that the research in the field is expanding, it is telling that only six interventions met the criteria to be included.

Finally, problems with telemental health care remain that have not yet been solved. For instance, a significant number of families live in areas where poor Internet connectivity inhibits the use of video-conferencing platforms or low-resourced communities cannot afford the necessary equipment to receive remote health care. Although recent Health Resources and Services Administration (HRSA) funds specifically focused on increasing the infrastructure in rural communities necessary for telemental health to be successful, it is unlikely that such funds will begin to reach the numbers of communities in need of support. This issue is directly linked to gaping mental health disparities across socioeconomic levels, as private mental health facilities are more likely to be able to offer telemental health care than publicly run facilities (Cantor et al., 2024). Striving for health equity means continuing to work to make empirically supported telemental health interventions available to underserved communities.

Although this book focuses on the implementation of telemental health interventions via synchronous interactions between therapists and families, the next technology-influenced mental healthcare modalities, already far into development, are robotic- and artificial intelligence (AI)-based services. As these technologies move forward, providers must consider a number of important questions. For instance, should robots replace humans in the psychological interview and diagnostic process? A small-scale study in Japan evaluated whether robotic interviewers might have benefits over human interviewers for people experiencing depressive symptoms (Matsushima et al., 2024). Individuals with and without depression were interviewed by a humanoid robot, which could simulate emotional expression, and a human mental health provider. After an interview with the robot, individuals with depression rated the robot as significantly more "easy to talk to" and easier to talk to than people they knew. On difficult topics, such as sexual concerns, participants reported less shame in speaking with the robot than the human. There were no differences in the validity of the interview across robotic and human interviewers. Although this was not an AI intervention—the robot was controlled by a human operator in another location—participants were unaware that the robot was not spontaneously interacting with them. This study, while preliminary, considers the use of robotics in mental health services from a positive angle and provides some intriguing initial findings. Much more research is necessary in this area.

In the integration of AI with mental health care, we are at an exciting crossroads and a risky one. It is important for providers not to make quick judgments about new and augmented services just because they are different from the modalities to which we are accustomed. We need to only look at the positive changes in telemental health use from pre- to post-pandemic to see the limitations inherent in becoming entrenched against a new technology. However, it is essential that mental health providers and patient advocates remain up to date with the science—what AI is capable of and what the empirical evidence suggests about its use in mental health care—in order to contribute to decisions about how it is used. It is our obligation to consider issues such as the efficacy of the intervention modality, its ability to promote equity in health care, the cultural responsiveness of the service, and our patients' freedom to choose their care (e.g., whether their provider is human, robotic, or AI-driven; Alhuwaydi, 2024; Thakkar et al., 2024). It is essential for mental health providers and our patients to play a role in setting the direction for the integration of AI in mental health care. As with telemental health care, the new technologies may offer promising benefits, but it takes the collaboration of multiple systems for those promises to be realized.

References

Alhuwaydi, A. M. (2024). Exploring the role of artificial intelligence in mental healthcare: Current trends and future directions – A narrative review for a comprehensive insight. *Risk Management and Healthcare Policy, 17*, 1339–1348. https://doi.org/10.2147/RMHP.S461562

American Psychological Association. (2023). *Infographic: Percentage of psychologists offering remote or in-person treatment, 2020–2023*. https://www.apa.org/pubs/reports/practitioner/2023-infographics/telehealth-location

Cantor, J., Schuler, M. S., Matthews, S., Kofner, A., Breslau, J., & McBain, R. K. (2024). Availability of mental telehealth services in the US. *JAMA health forum, 5*(2), e235142. https://doi.org/10.1001/jamahealthforum.2023.5142

Matsushima, T., Yoshikawa, Y., Matsuo, K., Kurahara, K., Uehara, Y., Nakao, T., Ishiguro, H., Kumazaki, H., & Kato, T. A. (2024). Development of depression assessment tools using humanoid robots -Can tele-operated robots talk with depressive persons like humans? *Journal of Psychiatric Research, 170*, 187–194. https://doi.org/10.1016/j.jpsychires.2023.12.014

Pew Research Center. (2024, January). *Americans' use of mobile technology and home broadband.* Retrieved June 9, 2024 from https://www.pewresearch.org/internet/2024/01/31/americans-use-of-mobile-technology-and-home-broadband

Thakkar, A., Gupta, A., & De Sousa, A. (2024). Artificial intelligence in positive mental health: a narrative review. *Frontiers in Digital Health, 6*, 1280235. https://doi.org/10.3389/fdgth.2024.1280235

Index

A
Access to treatment, 130
Adolescents, 3–12, 41, 51–54, 58, 59, 63, 70, 71, 75, 76, 79, 86, 94, 95, 97, 145, 179, 180, 182, 184, 188–190
Affirmative care, 181, 183, 184, 189–191
Anxiety disorders, 51–64, 174, 201
Applied behavior analysis (ABA), 91–105, 125
Artificial intelligence (AI), 175, 202
Assessment, 4, 19, 60, 77, 92, 125, 146, 182, 201
Attachment, 136–140, 142, 144, 149, 153, 159
Attitudes to telehealth care, 5–7, 12
Autism spectrum disorder (ASD), 91, 94–97, 99, 101, 113–130, 159, 169, 174, 201

B
Barriers to telehealth care, 4–7, 9, 39, 52, 64, 70, 76, 85, 98, 113, 114, 146
Behavioral therapy, 102

C
Challenging behaviors, 91–95, 97–101, 103, 104, 150
Cognitive-behavioral therapy (CBT), 51–64, 69–86, 144, 152, 186–188, 192, 193
Cognitive functioning, 19–44, 136

E
Ethical practice of telemental health care, 8, 43, 124
Evaluations, 5, 19, 20, 22–25, 35–43, 93

F
Future directions, 201–203

H
History of telehealth, 4–7

I
Infant and early childhood mental health, 153

L
LGBTQ, 179–193

M
Mental health care access, 3
Mothers, 42, 58, 76, 101, 127, 136, 170, 192

N
Neurodevelopmental disabilities, 32, 91, 104

P
Parent-child interaction therapy (PCIT), 52, 56, 159–175
Parenting, 12, 57, 70, 71, 78–79, 113, 118, 125, 126, 128, 129, 136–138, 141, 142, 144–146, 148–153, 160, 161, 163, 164, 166, 173, 174, 189
Parent intervention, 113, 114, 116, 117, 153
Parent training, 60, 113–130, 161

L. N. Niec, C. E. Schoonover (eds.), *Telemental Health Care for Children and Families*, https://doi.org/10.1007/978-3-031-69264-2

Posttraumatic stress disorder (PTSD), 69, 70, 72, 77, 78, 85, 145, 153

S

Sexual and gender minority (SGM), 179, 181, 182, 184–189, 191–193

T

Telemental health, 3–12, 70, 113–130, 135–154, 183, 187, 201–203
Teletesting, 19, 27–41, 44
Trauma-informed, 136, 137, 144, 149, 150, 152, 153

V

Virtual, 39, 55–60, 63, 77, 124, 139–144, 146–153, 172, 184–185, 187, 189, 190, 192

The manufacturer's authorised representative in the EU is Springer Nature Customer Service Centre GmbH, Europaplatz 3, 69115 Heidelberg, Germany. If you have any concerns regarding our products, please contact ProductSafety@springernature.com

Printed and bound by CPI Group (UK) Ltd, Croydon, CR0 4YY

01/10/2026

02225966-0004